The Fields That I Once Walked

The Rise and Fall of the American Middle Class

FOREWORD

First off, I would like to thank everyone who purchased and read my first book, "All our Hands are Stained." Without your support and encouragement, I would not have decided to venture into writing again.

Before we start our contemplation throughout this book, I want you to give you this date in labor history, May 5, 1981. Why is this date so important, you may ask? Because that day signaled a significant shift in how employers and employees could interact in the workplace. This is the day the President Ronald Reagan fired the striking members of the Professional Air Traffic Controllers union or as it was known, PATCO. He did so under the premise that, according to Federal law, federal employees could not strike. However, the corporate oligarchy, saw this as a green light to hammer the workers for their most basic right, the right to collectively bargain.

Since that time, workers in American companies demanded concessions from their employees, either in the form of wage kickbacks or benefit concessions. Pensions, the gold standard, as well as the unwritten social contract in which an employee would give 30 years or more of sweat, muscle and dedicated service in exchange for a gold watch, possibly a dinner with the bosses and co-workers, and a monthly check they could count on to supplement their old-age pension they got from Social Security. That way they could enjoy their golden years doing things they always wanted to do instead of spending time at the company.

Consider for just one moment you sitting at home, watching your favorite television show, or driving along the many miles of crumbling roads and bridges in this nation of ours. What is the one thing we are all exposed to? Besides, air pollution, of course. Advertising. From the time we are old enough to understand the concept, we are exposed in the form of print, video or audio advertising in an effort to consume, consume, consume.

We are no longer a nation of savers. In fact, statistics show that most families have little to no savings in the bank. This pales in comparison to their grandparents, otherwise known as the Greatest Generation, you know, the generation which lived through the Great

Depression, and fought World War II, and laid the ground work for the most spoiled generation in the history of the United States, the Baby Boomers.

The Baby Boomers introduced two very dangerous concepts which are not threatening our nation's economic existence. First, is the ideal our economy can survive without a strong manufacturing base. Second, that the driving force of our economy be nothing more than conspicuous consumption.

I am going to expand on both these points throughout this book and discuss how we, as the American people have been pretty much, the instrument of our own economic demise.

America used to be number one in Manufacturing, researched & development, as well as education. Now we are Number one in three (and only three categories,) number of adults incarcerated adults per capita, the number of adults who believe in Angels, and number of handgun deaths per capita. I find it almost disgraceful that the only country that put a man on the moon is now better known for their reality television stars.

What we used to be was a great Republic, a thing beacon of freedom and democracy to the rest of the world. However, 180 of the 190 some odd countries on planet Earth can also claim that they have freedom and liberty. We, in the United States in the second decade of the twenty first century is more akin to a crumbling empire. And my voice is not alone. Voices such as economist Paul Krugman and former Secretary of Labor Robert Reich have both pointed out the quite clearly the if we, as a nation, continue on our current course, we are setting ourselves up for an economic disaster that will make The Great Depression look mild by comparison.

The major difference between now and then is people

CHAPTER I

A LITTLE ABOUT ME AND HOW I GOT TO WHERE I AM TODAY

I have many memories of both my grandfather and father working. My grandfather worked in the Baltimore Ship Yards from 1941 until 1944, then he moved his wife, my Uncle Clyde (age 9,) and my dad (age 3,) back home to Eastern Kentucky to work at the American Rolling Mill Company (ARMCO) Ashland Works, eventually he became a Millwright, and retired in 1974 after 30 years of service. My grandfather could and would fix anything. Having grown up during the Great Depression, his generation learned the value of frugality and fixing things instead of throwing them away. He passed those same values on to my father, a man worked for the railroad for 41 years, first as a hostler, then as a fireman, and then as a Railroad Engineer. But they wanted a better life for their son and grandson, so I went to college, namely, the University of Kentucky, and proceeded to fail miserably my first go round. A lack of maturity and preparation for college accounted for my failures.

So I had an opportunity to go to work at the same steel mill as my grandfather. I hired in as summer help. My first shift was mowing grass and weed eating at the old Norton Foundry. I immediately fell in love the job. I was making $10.10 an hour (in 1987 the minimum wage was $3.35/hour,) so I thought I was rich! Eventually, Labor Reserve placed me in the Transportation & Labor Department, pretty much it was a department for folks who started off at the bottom and liked it there. But I wanted more, I wanted to get hired on as a permanent employee, and move into a position where I could make more money. I wanted to move into a position in operations. So I hung around guys who had been around awhile. Me and green hat, showing off I was a new employee, but I also showed a was a workhorse. The foreman had a job, I was the first to jump in. They had a grease pit you needed cleaned, I was the first in and last out. In fact, I recall one instance where the foreman, a fellow by the nickname of "Codface" Scott, left me and a group of about 6 New hires who had hired in after me (therefore I was the one with the most Seniority,) to clean up grease pits at the Tandem Cold Mill. All of the sudden a Maintenance Foreman was asking them, "Who was the pusher on this job?" Suddenly they were all pointing to me. He came over to me and was asking questions regarding the status of our work and was asking permission for his men to move in to take an overhead crane to remove pieces of the mill out for maintenance. Naturally, I agreed because it would give my crew a break and allow us access to other parts which needed cleaning. My uncle was also a Millwright in this Department, that helped. Pretty soon, the word spread.

When my time was up, I sat at the house for a month anxiously waiting for a phone call while applying for other jobs. Finally, on October 11, 1987, I received the phone call which would change my life forever, literally. I was offered and accepted a position at ARMCO STEEL. As with any new hire, I started out in labor reserve, and that damn green hat again. But this time I learned that the first thing you want to do was ditch the green hat. As soon as you got assigned to a department, you traded in your green hat for their hat. Well, I got assign right out the gate to Transportation and Labor, and immediately traded my green hat for a white one!

As a said previously, T&L, as it was known, was a place for folks who started off at the bottom and liked it there. But not me, after working in T&L for nine months, I bid on and prevailed on a bid (based on seniority,) to move into operations. My new department was the Hot Strip Mill, my unit was the Soaking Pits. Being low man on the totem pole, I started listening to the old timers and realized that all of them were fucking insane. No literally, these guys were crazy. First off, the majority were obsessed with golf, not that it was a bad thing, they even got me hooked years later. Second, you didn't know people by their given names, but by nicknames (mine was "The Slug," not for a bullet but for the garden pest, because I once took too long to complete a job because I wanted to do it right, but the leader wanted to do it fast so he could take a nap, which cause a huge argument between he and I. Instead of bitching, I embraced my new found nickname, even adding to my own notoriety by joking saying that I worked in two speeds, slow and stop. Others joined in, naming the Old open-hearth building, building 80,"Slug's place," in which someone had spray painted in huge twenty-foot letters, S L U G on the side of the building. If I had my druthers, I would have stayed there until retirement. In fact, I would have enough time in as of 2014 to retire and spend quality time with my grandson.

But this was not to be. Because in 1989, some dumb asses in Middletown, Ohio (where the higher management of the Eastern Steel Division resided,) decided the they were going to convert the abandoned bloom caster at Ashland into a slab caster and send them to

Middletown for final processing. No more nights, no more Hot Strip Mill at Ashland. And they wanted the workers to pay for the conversion. If the vote did not go the company's way, they would shut Ashland down and go exclusively with Middletown. Needless to say, there was lot of soul searching and hand wringing. There was a lot of good jobs on the line. Ashland had an almost unlimited supply of water. But Ashland did have the Steelworkers union, while Middletown had the Armco Employees Independent Federation, pretty much a company union. So the attitude towards Ashland by management was less than friendly. But the vote was approved by a razor thin margin, probably due to a lot of arm twisting by the churches, community, and wives of the men. Because of the talk in all the lunchrooms not a damn person voted for the concessions. But the concessions were not that bad, it wasn't a giveaway, it was a loan. Once the caster hit certain production levels, we started getting our money back in payments. This was all well and good, the union leadership told us, we could trust the company this time. The old timers said that the company had one interest in mind, to bust the union. The layoffs regardless of which way the vote went. Luckily, I listened. Right after the caster vote, I decided to take an independent study course from the University of Kentucky about the Civil War, every lesson the professor and I would have this diatribe over a different topic surrounding the Civil War. While he was a full PhD, I was neither intimidated nor deterred by the subject matter. I got a "B" after the final. I was hungry and wanted more and ARMCO had a tuition assistance program so I signed up. I took every independent study course I could get my hands on while simultaneously applying for admission to Morehead State University for the Management program. At one point, I was taking three classes by independent study as well as three classes in the classroom and working 40+ hours at ARMCO. Oh, did I mention that I had a wife, daughter, and a son on the way while all this was going on? Yeah, just thought I'd throw that in there as well.

The ball dropped on July 31, 1992. That day, 1500 of my fellow ARMCO workers and myself hit the bricks. Our good jobs were gone, forever. Luckily, I had one semester to go until I was a college graduate, or so I thought. What followed was six years of school, work, more school, clinical depression, Prozac, two additional years of unemployment, two years of playing Mr. Mom (which was cool since I got to help my son walk and daily tea parties with my daughter.) But after all was said and done and six years, I went from steelmaker to social worker. I had an understanding of the workings of the human mind as well as human behavior and motivation.

So why am I sharing probably the most hurtful time in my life, in book form, with you. Quite frankly, this is therapy. Not for me, for anyone who has lost their job in this ever shrinking job market. And the sad part about it, in this era of corporate oligarchy and austerity, things do not look like they are going to get any better. That is the purpose of this book, to examine America after May 5, 1981 and view the social, political and economic landscape as it pertains to the middle and working classes since that day and try to explain how in the hell could the American people be so blind as to vote against their own self interests.

Rick Manning, Vice-president of Americans for Limited Government, a Right Wing think tank fund by David and Charles Koch, whom, I'll talk about a bit later, published this opinion piece I recently read:

"Labor Day is the traditional last day of summer, often celebrated by final trips to the shore and followed by public pool closings and other signs that the world is battening down the hatches for colder weather.

However, what most don't realize is that the day itself was originally created by organized labor to call attention to the contributions of workers. A public relations stunt designed to provide labor unions a focal point in their never ending battle with management.

A lot has changed for organized labor since Labor Day was federally recognized 120 years ago.

The then burgeoning movement has gained massive political power and influence across the century, only to see it decline precipitously to a point where today only 6.7 percent of the private sector workforce belong to labor unions. In fact, there are currently more union members who are public employees than in the private sector.

This transition of labor union membership from private sector to public employee dominated has massive implications for the future.

A public sector oriented union's focus will naturally be on supporting politicians who support expanding the size and scope of government, even at the expense of the private sector workforce.

This conversion can be seen in Big Labor's political fealty to the Democratic Party and their bigger and bigger government mantra. Today's Big Labor supports politicians who are committed to destroying unionized mining jobs through the EPA, scoff at the value of more than ten thousand union jobs created by building the Keystone XL pipeline, and actively push for amnesty for illegal aliens who can only drive down the cost of labor hurting wages.

The days of a Jimmy Hoffa's Teamsters Union endorsing Richard Nixon seem far away as labor leaders are more interested today in creating the low hanging fruit public employee union jobs rather than confronting far left politicians who are killing private sector unions through their policies.

While the United Mine Workers of America may have balked at endorsing President Obama in 2012 after his disastrous policies targeted much of their workforce for extinction, their former president, Richard Trumka, in his new role as head of the AFL-CIO continues to play the role of presidential cheerleader.

Construction unions like the International Brotherhood of Electrical Workers give lip service to supporting private sector jobs through projects like building the Keystone XL pipeline, yet in the lead up to the 2012 election for president, the union wrote a scathing attack on Republican nominee Mitt Romney based upon Republican Governors pushing measures that reined in public employee union power in their states.

While the piece claimed to not tell their members how to vote, it left no doubt about who the union supported, the very same guy whose administration has thrown its collective weight against the very kind of mass construction project that gives their membership work.

And that tells the whole story. On Labor Day 2014, Big Labor no longer represents the private sector workers interests, instead they have become nothing more than big government shills who put hard hats on to capture a public relations illusion from decades past.

A fitting picture for a holiday whose origins were nothing more than PR puffery in the first place.

If today's Big Labor were caught in a fit of honesty, they would likely suggest that the day's name be changed to Public Employee Appreciation Day. Of course, with 93 percent of the private sector workforce eschewing labor unions altogether, rather than maintaining the Big Labor fiction, it would be fitting for Congress to change the holiday's name to "final back to school sale Monday" and call the day what it is for most Americans – nothing more or less than a practical demarcation of what it truly is the unofficial day of summer. "

While Mr. Manning is correct that 93% no longer can or will enjoy the benefits of belonging to a union, he glosses over all the current worker rights that was the direct result of union lobbying. We still enjoy some of those benefits, although I feel we could do much, much better in regard to worker rights and occupational health and safety oversight. Too many times in the past, workers fought, struck, and in some instances died to secure these rights for the working men and women in this country. Something that over the past three decades has been sorely lacking. As I continue to preach, Americans have the attention span of gnat. They have been conditioned to have a very short attention span. And our educational system has failed in that we have not taught our population to critically think. But sadly, most Americans do view Labor day as just another three- day weekend.

I'd like to throw out some interesting statistics regarding labor before we go any farther in our discussion:

More than 156 million people make up the U.S. labor force, including people who are working and those who are unemployed.

More than 146 million workers aged 16 and up are currently employed. In 2013, the labor force was 53 percent men, and 47 percent women.

One in five workers is 55 or older.

Americans made a median hourly wage of $16.87 as of May 2013.

Seventy-two percent of workers had access to employer-provided healthcare, 65 percent had paid sick leave, and 12 percent had paid family leave in 2013.

There are nearly 28 million minimum wage workers in the U.S., 88 percent of whom are over the age of 20 and more than a quarter of whom are working parents.

The federal minimum wage is $7.25. Raising the minimum wage to $10.10 would increase these 28 million workers' wages by $35 billion over the next two years.

Minimum wage is not a living wage: fast food industry workers alone receive about $7 billion per year in government assistance just to get by.

Employers pay into the unemployment insurance program for nearly all workers, which then provides benefits should you become unemployed through no fault of your own.

The share of long-term unemployed workers (those unemployed for six months or more) peaked at nearly 45 percent of all unemployed workers in 2010, the highest rate it has ever been. Today, more than 3.1 million workers – about a third of all the unemployed – have been unemployed for six months or more.

Studies show that spending on UI benefits provides one of the greatest returns on investment among policies designed to boost the economy and create jobs. For every $1 spent on UI, nearly $2 is put back in local economies.

Interesting statistics? I thought this would lay the foundation for our discussions going forth.

CHAPTER 2

There was a time in this country where a young man (and sometimes young lady,) could graduate from high school (or college if one was so inclined,) and almost immediately go to work for an employer on the condition that after thirty or forty years of service, the employee is rewarded with a gold watch, possibly a retirement party or dinner, and a nice pension. Not any longer, today there are three applicants for every job opening. Since the start of the Great Recession, 8.8 million jobs were lost. Of the jobs lost, those which paid between $14 to $21 an hour made up 60% of those jobs lost. For those of you keeping score, those wages equal between $29,120 and $43,680, solidly middle class jobs. While lower paying jobs made up 58% of the jobs created during the recovery. So let's be brutally honest, workers today are used until they either become too expensive or too old to be profitable. Yes, I said old, for the simple fact that once an employee reaches a certain age his wages and benefits become, according to HR and accounting too much to keep them around. Now, of course, the media and business community attempt to soften the blow by reframing the topic by calling it re-engineering, reorganization, or just good old downsizing.

Whatever it is called, it is meant to lessen the brutality of the act itself, but it invades a very basic reality. That those people whose jobs are eliminated or are being eliminated are real people who real families, real expenses, and real mortgages to pay as well as sometimes real medical problems that they or their children suffer. These are not bad, lazy or unproductive people as the current Republican leadership would have you believe. These were hard working people, who played by the rules and played by the rules. They played by the rules and sent their children to school in hopes of making life a bit easier for the next generation, all for a piece of the " American dream" of the middle-class. But employers had something entirely different in mind. While their employees wanted to be left alone and live their lives, the corporate oligarchy wanted nothing less than to turn us into mindless drones, working only to work for the corporate good for as little wages and benefits as possible, but be expected to be obedient consumers.

When it comes to putting employees first, employers, especially small businessmen (or as the Republicans love to call them, "job creators," corporate management as well as executives talk the talk, but rarely, if ever, walk the walk. They are be holding to the shareholders and the bottom line. Let me give you a brief management lesson here. There are three things which every business needs to function. LAND, LABOR, AND CAPITAL. LAND is where you place your business. CAPITAL is the material used in a business, not only stuff to make, but office supplies, computers, etc. LABOR is the folks that actually make stuff or make sure your business runs and makes a profit.

In the past, like in the 19th century, financially troubled businesses would cut wages and hours, but when the business would pick back up, the wages would be kept low, but the hours would be increased to insane levels. Also, women and child labor would be exploited to the highest possible amount due to them working for the lowest possible wages.

Compared to the horrid poverty in such large eastern cities as New York and Boston, was to vulgar displays of wealth by the nouveaux riche. They built mansions of stone and marble, employed servants, and lived in a level of luxury never before seen in this country. Some made their profits from Civil War profiteering. Others made their fortunes from oil, steel and railroads or the manipulation of stocks and bonds. Not only did their mansions far outpace those of European royalty, they exercised enormous political and economic power on the local, state and national levels. Their fancy carriages were drawn by the finest horses money could buy, their yachts were sometimes equipped with lavish pipe organs, and they entertained with lavish parties, during a time when their fellow men, women and children were dying of starvation or in terrible need, showing a complete lack of concern and social responsibility. Sounds familiar, doesn't it? Remember, I was talking about the late 19th and early 20th century, not the early 21st century.

Now, we do the exact same bullshit, except of course, we do not use child labor. That was outlawed in the 1930s, at least for now, but Mark my words, there is already a move by some conservatives to have poor children do janitorial work at school in order to earn their school lunches. They say it is to teach them the "value of work." Bullshit, it is a way, they can exploit children into providing free labor.

Before I go any further, I want to state for the record I am not anti-capitalism nor am I anti-business. But I am anti predatory capitalism. That being said, let us continue our discussion. Of three items necessary for a business, only labor is a cost which a company can control. By doing so, a company can greatly increase their bottom line. Combine that with slashing benefits and pensions, and you have the potential to make yourself a superstar in the business world. During the 1980's, names like T. Boone Pickens and Carl Icahn, were in the news on an almost daily basis regarding a company they had set in their sights. If they were successful in their attempt, usually by accumulating large amounts of debt, otherwise known as a leveraged buyout, and the selloff pieces of the acquired companies to pay off the debt. This method was called *asset stripping.* Interesting, how it is so cold and calculated. *Asset* stripping, not to mention job stripping. I recall in the early 1980s, in the transition between the Carter and Reagan administrations, how the kids whose parents worked at Ashland Oil were so damn excited when Reagan was elected. How they bought into his "Morning in American.", mainly because they had heard from their parents how bad a President Carter was. Granted, American self-esteem was pretty low in the late 1970s. We had just got of Vietnam, gas prices were going up and up, leisure suits were in fashion (Yikes!!), Disco was everywhere (double yikes,) but probably the most grievous thing in the eyes of most Americans was the fact that 52 Americans were being held hostage in Iran, and President Carter did little, except try to negotiate for their return, but Reagan told Iran they should release the hostages, "or else." But during the 1980 election cycle, something strange occupied. The religious right, led by the Reverend Jerry Falwell and the Moral Majority, mobilized voters, particularly in the Midwest and in the South, to vote Republican. It should be interesting to note that the South has some of the poorest counties and states in the country, so how could they be convinced to vote against their own self-interest.

But now, it appears that corporations are even trying to cut back not only labor expenses, but also capital expenditures. The equipment used by many U.S. manufacturers is getting creaky. Even as economic indicators rise, domestic capital spending has remained anemic by historical standards, especially in manufacturing.

In contrast, companies have spent heavily on acquisitions and stock buybacks. That choice could hobble efforts by U.S. firms to compete more effectively with foreign rivals in the years ahead.

The average age of industrial equipment in the U.S. has risen above 10 years, the highest since 1938, economists at Morgan Stanley said in a recent report.

The growth of all types of capital spending by U.S. firms grew just 3% last year, far below the long-term average of more than 8%, Morgan Stanley says. The firm sees only modest improvement ahead: 3.8% growth this year and 5.3% in 2015.

When it comes to acquisitions, U.S. firms are eager to write big checks. U.S.-based industrial firms spent $80.7 billion in the first half, up from $69.5 billion in 2013's first half and the highest level since the giddy days of 1999, according to researcher Dealogic.

Factory equipment can be less exciting than acquisitions. The Association for Manufacturing Technology reported that U.S. orders for machine tools and other equipment used to shape metals and other raw materials into products in the first half were down 2.7% from a year earlier. Pat McGibbon, a vice president at the association, cites uncertainty over interest rates, the economy and taxes.

One big unknown is whether Congress will restore so-called bonus depreciation, which allows companies to write off new equipment faster, cutting their tax bills and making capital spending more tempting.

Another factor may be that global companies in recent years have concentrated much of their investment in fast-growing parts of Asia and Latin America rather than in the U.S. and Europe.

Some big manufacturers are reducing capital spending this year. For instance, Caterpillar Inc.'s capital spending fell to $710 million in this year's first half from $1.39 billion a year earlier. The company's chief executive, Doug Oberhelman, told analysts in July that Caterpillar had invested heavily in recent years and "so we're in pretty good shape with all that." Meanwhile, the company is ramping up share buybacks.

Turmoil in the Middle East, Ukraine and elsewhere may make some firms even more hesitant to invest in equipment. David Farr, chief executive of Emerson Electric Co., told analysts in early August that jitters were hurting sales of his company's products, which include factory automation equipment. "The geopolitical situations are probably some of the worst I've ever seen," said Mr. Farr. "The world's talking about negative things."

Despite the negatives, Daniel Meckstroth, chief economist at the Manufacturers Alliance for Productivity and Innovation, a research organization, expects an upswing in capital spending. For one thing, he says, old equipment can be nursed only so long before it has to be replaced: "We've postponed investment for so long that it almost has to occur." For another, many of the CEOs making acquisitions will find that they need to make capital investments that previous owners deferred.

In a recent article entitled *What Makes People vote Republican,* psychologist Johnathon Haidt made several observations regarding voting conservative (against one's own self-interest and self-preservation, which could constitute a mental illness,) and attitudes towards conservatism. In the introduction he wrote,

"What makes people vote Republican? Why in particular do working class and rural Americans usually vote for pro-business Republicans when their economic interests would seem better served by Democratic policies? We psychologists have been have been examining the origins of ideology ever since Hitler sent us Germany's best psychologists, and we reported long ago the strict parenting and a variety of personal insecurities work together to turn people against liberalism, diversity, and progress. But now we can map the brains, genes, and unconscious activities of conservatives, we have defined our diagnosis: conservatism is a partially inheritable personality trait that predisposes some people to be cognitively inflexible, fond of hierarchy, and inordinately afraid of uncertainty, change, and death. People vote Republican because Republicans offer "moral clarity" - that is a simple vision of good and evil that activates deep seated fears in much of the electorate. Democrats, in contrast, appeal to reason with their long-term explorations of policy options for a complex world."

So now, as of the writing of this book, it is an election year, and once again, both political parties are doing their typical mudslinging when it comes to the economy. The Republican party is once again advocating their typical argument of aggressively adhering to the supply-side economic policies of the past thirty years. The Democratic party are advocating and investment more in people, not corporations. But I am of the opinion, and it is strictly my opinion, that many Americans are slowly starting to realize that the American Dream is leaving them behind. Let's face it, Americans are scared now. They are confused and lost.

People are looking for answers and they realize they are rapidly running out of time. They have no pensions to fall back on, every time they turn on the news or pick up a newspaper, they see a factory or company shutting down and reducing their workforce. Naturally, the jobs are usually are being sent overseas, where the workers are paid far cheaper than American workers.

Such is the story in a town not too far away from me, Huntington, West Virginia. Forty years ago, Huntington was an industrial city, with steel mills, railroad and glass factories as their major employers. Now, the major employers are Amazon.com, InfoCision, GC Services, and DirectTV. All of which are call centers. Now they do have a major University as well as two Medical Centers, but the education required to work at those employers make them prohibitive for them to be considered as "major" employers, even though they pump literally millions of dollars into the local economy.

The end result? Huntington now has a major substance (namely Opioid and Methamphetamine) abuse problem among the lower socio-economic classes. Naturally, this has placed a burden on police, EMS, Medical, as well as already strained social service agencies. This has left elected and social service agencies scrambling to address this issue to lessen the impact upon that city. But Huntington is not alone. Town after small town throughout America is coming to grips with is new scourge brought about by a lack of economic opportunity.

So there you have it from a mental health professional. Liberals are cerebral, and conservatives are more emotional. Conservatism is running very close akin to a mental illness. There are two types of conservatives. Social conservatives, those who believe that abortion is wrong under any circumstance, the death penalty, as well as health care should only be ran in a capitalist system, where the insurance companies, not doctors, determine the level of care. There should be no rights extended to gays, women, minority groups or anyone who doesn't fit their narrow view of the world. They believe in the unregulated support of gun rights and gun ownership. Then there are the economic conservatives, who believe that under no circumstance should the government impose any tax, rule, regulation or impediment to business from making and aching the maximization of profit. That includes wages, environmental regulations, taxation, workplace rules, and Social Security,

Worker's Compensation, and other protections which have been enacted over the years. So basically, what the religious right did tapped into the fears of both the social conservatives as well as the laisse-faire aspects of the economic conservatives to wind up electing Reagan as President. Problem was Reagan's personal belief system ran contrary to those political philosophies he espoused and his proteges carried forth. He actually believed that workers should have the right to organize and form unions. He also believed in American greatness as well as competitiveness. But as we all have seen in the past thirty years, this has not been the case.

CHAPTER 3

The crux of Reagan was that taxes were way too high. When Reagan came into office in 1981, the top tax rate was 70%, when he left office in 1989, the top tax rate was 28%. By contrast, during the New Deal era until the 1960's, the top tax rate was a whopping 90%. During that time, we managed to successfully pay for a World War, build a network of interstate highways (which was sent up for national defense, not commerce,) and was the last Republican administration (Eisenhower) to generate a budget surplus. So much for preaching fiscal responsibility. You see the exact social programs the GOP are complaining so much about make up only approximately 4 or 5 per cent of the total federal budget. And Social Security and Medicare are not even programs which they should be a matter of discussion, since they are insurance program which Americans pay into their entire working lives in order to be take advantage of during their retirement years. Naturally, they wish to privatize those programs in order to give both Wall Street investment firms more money to gamble with and insurance companies more profits for themselves. However, what they fail to point out, or even reveal to the American people, is our defense budget gobbles up 54% of our annual spending. This is greater than any other nation on Earth, including Russia or China. After the Soviet Union fell in 1989, there was a lot of discussion about a "peace dividend," because we would not have to have to be spending money to keep up "with those damn commies." Guess the peace dividend works about as well as trickle-down economics.

Trickle-down economics" and the "trickle-down theory" are terms in United States politics to refer to the idea that tax breaks or other economic benefits provided to businesses and upper income levels will benefit poorer members of society by improving the economy as a whole. The term has been attributed to humorist Will Rogers, who said during the Great Depression that "money was all appropriated for the top in hopes that it would trickle down to the needy."

Proponents of tax cuts often claim that savings and investment are essential to the economy, and thus fewer taxes (for any and all income brackets) need not harm any other income bracket. Economist George Reisman, a proponent of tax cuts, said the following:

"Of course, many people will characterize the line of argument I have just given as the 'trickle-down' theory. There is nothing trickle-down about it. There is only the fact that capital accumulation and economic progress depend on saving and innovation and that these in turn depend on the freedom to make high profits and accumulate great wealth. The only alternative to improvement for all, through economic progress, achieved in this way, is the futile attempt of some men to gain at the expense of others by means of looting and plundering. This, the loot-and-plunder theory, is the alternative advocated by the critics of the misnamed trickle-down theory."

Today, "trickle-down economics" is most closely identified with the economic policies known as "Reaganomics" or laissez-faire. David Stockman, who as Reagan's budget director championed these cuts at first but then became skeptical of them, told journalist William Greider that the "supply-side economics" is the trickle-down idea: "It's kind of hard to sell 'trickle down,' so the supply-side formula was the only way to get a tax policy that was really 'trickle down.' Supply-side is 'trickle-down' theory."

Economist Thomas Sowell has written that the actual path of money in a private enterprise economy is quite the opposite of that claimed by people who refer to the trickle-down theory. He noted that money invested in new business ventures is first paid out to employees, suppliers, and contractors. Only some time later, if the business is profitable, does money return to the business owners—but in the absence of a profit motive, which is reduced in the aggregate by a raise in marginal tax rates in the upper tiers, this activity does not occur. Sowell further has made the case[6] that no economist has ever advocated a "trickle-down" theory of economics, which is rather a misnomer attributed to certain economic ideas by political critics who either willfully distort or misunderstand the actual stated goals of their political opponents.

Although the term "trickle down" is mainly political and does not denote a specific economic theory, some economic theories reflect the meaning of this pejorative. Some macro-economic models assume that a certain proportion of each dollar of income will be saved. This is called the marginal propensity to save. Many studies have found that the marginal propensity to save is considerably higher among wealthier people. Policies, including tax cuts, that seek to increase saving are often aimed at the wealthy for this reason. Saving usually means some form of investment, as even money placed in savings accounts is ultimately invested by the banks.

But how many of us in the middle-class actually have any money left over after the bills are paid actually have any money to save? If most folks are like my family, not many. Most of us are too busy paying for food, housing, maybe some new clothes, and utilities. All of which has increased over the years, but wages (or at least purchasing power) have remained stagnant or declined over the years. So why does the conservative movement insist on keep beating the drums of what has proven to be, for most Americans, really bad for them. Two reasons, first off, economic conservatives don't care about us little guys. They expect us to be obedient employees, servants, wage slaves, what have you. They want us to think that if we continue to go on the endless hamster wheel in hopes of eventually of becoming rich, we will continue to keep doing what we are doing and pay no attention to the man behind the curtain.

Second, again boils down to the distraction effect. If the social conservatives keep the populace distracted by social issues, then they will be ill advised (as well as ill informed) as the folks on the upper crust picks their pockets. But their message is clear: Taxes bad, big government bad, low taxes good, smaller government good, and family values very good. All of these messages resonates with middle America who desire to return to a simpler, easier time.

Problem is the times they are referring to no longer exists. Conservatives want the family values of the 1950s, with the economic policies of the 1920s combined with the workplace policies of the 19th century. The America that the conservatives and middle America is as extinct as the passenger pigeon. Being nostalgic is nothing wrong, just wrong especially when it comes to the economic survival of our society. Now why do at least 50% of Americans keep buying into it? Again, humans reacted to fear, especially fear of the unknown. That is not to say that we never had economic downturns before. Looking back at American history, we average a downturn about once a decade. But the one that hit in 2001 was particularly nasty. Due to the predatory nature of loans which led to the bursting of the housing bubble. As a result, over one million homes were foreclosed, pushing many families for the first time into homelessness.

The fundamental law of capitalism is: When workers have more money, businesses have more customers. Which makes middle-class consumers — not rich businesspeople — the true job creators. A thriving middle class isn't a consequence of growth — which is what the trickle-down advocates would tell you. A thriving middle class is the source of growth and prosperity in capitalist economies.

Our economy has changed, lest you think that the minimum wage is for teenagers. The average age of a fast-food worker is 28. And minimum wage jobs aren't confined to a small corner of the economy. By 2040, it is estimated that 48 percent of all American jobs will be low-wage service jobs. We need to reckon with this. What will our economy be like when it's dominated by low paying service jobs? What proportion of the population do we want to live on food stamps? 50 percent? Does this matter? Should we care?

Business people tell me they cannot afford higher wages. Not true. They can adjust to all sorts of higher costs. The minimum wage is much higher here in Seattle than in Alabama, and McDonald's thrives in both places. Businesses adjust to higher costs, even when they say they can't.

Our economy can be safe and effective only if it is governed by rules. Some capitalists actually don't care about other people, their communities or the future. Their behavior, if left unchecked, has a massive effect on everyone else. When Wal-Mart or McDonald's or any other guy like me pays workers the minimum wage, that's our way of saying, "I would pay you less, except then I'd go to prison."

Which brings us to the civic dimension of what the campaign to raise the minimum wage to $15 is really about. We're undeniably becoming a more unequal society—in incomes and in opportunity. The danger is that economic inequality always begets political inequality, which always begets more economic inequality. Low-wage workers stuck on a path to poverty are not only weak customers; they're also anemic taxpayers, absent citizens and inattentive neighbors.

Economic prosperity doesn't trickle down, and neither does civic prosperity. Both are middle-out phenomena. When workers earn enough from one job to live on, they are far more likely to be contributors to civic prosperity — in your community. Parents who need only one job, not two or three to get by, can be available to help their kids with homework and keep them out of trouble — in your school. They can look out for you and your neighbors, volunteer, and contribute — in your school and church. Our prosperity does not all come home in our paycheck. Living in a community of people who are paid enough to contribute to your community, rather than require its help, may be more important than your salary. Prosperity and poverty are like viruses. They infect us all — for good or ill.

An economic arrangement that pays a Wall Street worker tens of millions of dollars per year to do high-frequency trading and pays just tens of thousands to workers who grow or serve our food, build our homes, educate our children, or risk their lives to protect us isn't an expression of the true value or economic necessity of these jobs. It simply reflects a difference in bargaining power and status.

Inclusive economies always outperform and outlast plutocracies. That's why investments in the middle class work, and tax breaks for the rich don't. The oldest and most important conflict in human societies is the battle over the concentration of wealth and power. Those at the top will forever tell those at the bottom that our respective positions are righteous and good for all. Historically we called that divine right. Today we have trickle-down economics.

The trickle-down explanation for economic growth holds that the richer the rich get, the better our economy does. But it also clearly implies that if the poor get poorer, that must be good for our economy. Nonsense.

Some of the people who benefit most from that explanation are desperate for you to believe this is the only way a capitalist economy can work. At the end of the day, raising the minimum wage to $15 isn't about just rejecting their version of capitalism. It's about replacing it with one that works for every American.

Americans loathe taxes. I loathe taxes. I cringe when I go to H & R Block and sit down with my nice tax preparer named Dale (yes, she is an awesome lady, and just wanted to give a shout out to her,) and we go through the W2s, recipients, and other tax related documents and wait for her to analyze what we made versus what we owed the government. Always set aside more out of our checks to cover the taxes. But the is nothing wrong with tax avoidance, but I do have a problem with out and out evasion of paying taxes. I remember Jesus saying in the Bible, "Render unto Caesar the things that are Caesar's, and render unto God the things that are God's." Ever since the 1980's, the Republicans, and the religious right have not only wanted what are God's but also what is Caesar's.

This message has resonated with both the working and middle classes in this country. They feel that their money is being wasted by the government on such frivolous things as food stamps, welfare, unemployment, Social Security, school lunch programs and other government things which we really do not need. At least that was what Reagan said during the 1980 campaign when asked about an African-American lady driving a Cadillac around her neighborhood and she just so happen to be collecting government assistance. Reagan cleverly coined the term, "welfare queen," and the press took and ran with it. Only problem is, she doesn't exist, and never existed. Reagan made her up, to score political points. Now everyone, especially a woman, who collects public assistance is a welfare queen and is demonized. Does not matter her circumstance. And if it is a family with a male head of household who has been disabled, the suspicion is ten times worse. It goes back to the Elizabethan Poor Laws which were passed by the British Parliament in the 1500s. It divided the poor into two classes, worthy and unworthy poor. The only problem with the message of the Republican party, ALL poor are unworthy, they just need to work a bit harder, be more frugal, get off drugs, quit smoking, quit drinking, go to church, yadda, yadda, yadda. Back in 1996, Congress passed the Personal Responsibility and Work Opportunity Reconciliation Act. Otherwise known as welfare reform, it was a promise made by Bill Clinton to "fundamentally change welfare as we know it." Backed up a GOP controlled House of Representatives and its Speaker, Newt Gingrich, they completely decimated just part of the social safety net, little did we know the fun was just beginning. But it was the 1990s, people were making money hand over fist in both the .com industry as well as the housing industry with giving sub-prime mortgages. Times were good. But Clinton did do one thing, he raised the top rate on income taxes from its Reagan era low of 27% to 35%. Naturally, the GOP went fucking ape shit. The Republican adherence to supply side economic theory overrides any other considerations when it comes to logical discussion regarding the economy. But do not think I am going to give my liberal brethren a free pass.

Later on in this book, I am going to blast them for a couple of brilliant moves which cost Americans literally hundreds of thousands of good paying manufacturing sector jobs.

Let talk for a few minutes about supply side economic theory. Reagan embraced it, the 80s loved it. Supply side economic theory, simply put if you cut taxes, businesses and individuals on the top end will have more money to spent thus "trickling down" to the middle and lower incomes. Does anyone see anything wrong with this picture? Does one not take into account the fact that there is the matter of greed? No one took into account the fact that the very wealthy in this country would move their wealth to banks in the Grand Caymans, Jamaica, or other off shore Locations to avoid federal tax. As of the writing of this book, several corporations are now attempting to take advantage of an IRS regulation which allows them to merge with a foreign company or just relocate to a former country outright to avoid paying taxes. This process is called inversion. An example of this was Walgreens, an extremely large pharmaceutical chain, was recently toying with the ideal of relocating their headquarters to Switzerland, solely for the purpose of avoiding American corporate taxes. The day that they decided not to relocate, Wall Street responded accordingly. Walgreen's stock price plummeted. So much for King, and country as well as your employees. Recently, the American restaurant chain, Burger King, announced that it was purchasing Canadian restaurant chain Tim Horton's and will soon move their corporate headquarters to Canada, all to avoid paying U.S. Corporate taxes. As a reward, Burger King's stock shot up by 20%. Wall Street knows no loyalty to counties or boundaries, only profits. They only respect the almighty dollar, not people who have hopes or dreams or aspirations. Profits over people, such is Capitalism. But there is another view of economics, one that believes the governmental spending can actually be beneficial to an economy.

This practice, called tax inversion, is just the largest ploy in which the American corporations are attempting to avoid paying the U.S. Corporate Tax Rate. This goes back to the question of corporate personhood. They want the privileges of personhood, with none of the responsibilities. Tax inversion, or corporate inversion, is the relocation of a corporation's headquarters to a lower-tax nation, or corporate haven, usually while retaining its material operations in its higher-tax country of origin. The term is most frequently used in relation to US corporations. Corporate inversions are a relatively recent phenomenon. Although it is difficult to be definitive, the practice first became prevalent in the 1990s, with US corporations seeking to relocate to tax havens such as Bermuda;[3] more recently, because of changes in US law, publicity has focused upon corporate inversions conducted by way of merger with companies in lower-tax foreign countries. The issue was first subjected to a great deal of publicity in April 2014 by the proposed merger between Pfizer and AstraZeneca

Tax inversions are a form of tax avoidance. They are driven by a combination of factors, but the most prevalent factor is that the US tax code (uniquely among developed nations) seeks to impose income tax on profits earned abroad by American corporations. This creates a strong incentive for American companies with large overseas markets to seek to recharacterize themselves as a foreign corporation if they want to return foreign earnings to stockholders without double taxation.

Tax inversions as a tax reduction maneuver have become a public policy issue, as substantial tax revenues are lost. American politicians and government officials, including President Barack Obama and Treasury Secretary Jack Lew .have issued statements calling tax inversions "unpatriotic", and various proposals have been discussed to prevent tax inversions where the relevant corporation is less than 50% foreign owned. The Economist has called recent calls in America to restrict companies from relocating abroad by way of merger "misguided" and called for wider tax reform to address what it describes as more fundamental flaws in the American corporate tax system instead.

One the opposing end of the scale, is Keynesian economics. Names after John Maynard Keynes, a British economist. In the 1930s, Keynes spearheaded a revolution in economic thinking, overturning the older ideas of neoclassical economics that held that free markets would, in the short to medium term, automatically provide full employment, as long as workers were flexible in their wage demands. Keynes instead argued that aggregate demand determined the overall level of economic activity, and that inadequate aggregate demand could lead to prolonged periods of high unemployment. According to Keynesian economics, state intervention was necessary to moderate "boom and bust" cycles of economic activity. He advocated the use of fiscal and monetary measures to mitigate the adverse effects of economic recessions and depressions. Following the outbreak of World

War II, Keynes's ideas concerning economic policy were adopted by leading Western economies. In 1942, Keynes was awarded a hereditary peerage as Baron Keynes of Tilton in the County of Sussex. Keynes died in 1946, but during the 1950s and 1960s the success of Keynesian economics resulted in almost all capitalist governments adopting its policy recommendations.

Keynes's influence waned in the 1970s, partly as a result of problems that began to afflict the Anglo-American economies from the start of the decade, and partly because of critiques from Milton Friedman and other economists who were pessimistic about the ability of governments to regulate the business cycle with fiscal policy. However, the advent of the global financial crisis of 2007–08 caused a resurgence in Keynesian thought. Keynesian economics provided the theoretical underpinning for economic policies undertaken in response to the crisis by President George W. Bush of the United States, Prime Minister Gordon Brown of the United Kingdom, and other heads of governments.

I was brought up to be considerate of others, both of their feelings and of their well-being. Every time I hear of a downsizing, layoff, of other mass termination, my stomach turns. I was also raised with compassion, compassion for my fellow man, regardless of race, creed, or sexual orientation. I have decided that most corporate leaders are soulless, not heartless, just soulless. They have to be in order to make some of the decisions they make. It's nothing personal, it's just business. But then again, there should be a human element to business.

In his book, *The Wealth of Nations,* Adam Smith talked about "the invisible hand," which was supposed to govern businesses to do the right things and behave in a manner consistently which was good and proper for the benefit for society. But and I wish to make this absolutely clear, he failed to take into account the human element of greed. During the 2012 presidential election, Republican candidate Mitt Romney's former company, Bain Capital, a massive company founded for the sole purpose of buying companies, selling off unproductive, unprofitable business units. This made Mr. Romney more of a fortune than what he had inherited from his father, the former governor of Michigan as well as President of American Motors Company. Ol' Mitt became the real life version of Gordon Gecko, the antagonist in the movie "Wall Street." A candidate every working person loved to hate. Needless to say, Romney was defeated by the good sense of the American people, despite the efforts of the elites who pumped millions of dollars in an effort to influence the election in their favor.

During the campaign, candidate Romney, during a campaign fundraiser, talked about how 47% where unable or unwilling to strive to better themselves by hard work. This was a direct slap in the face of every child, elderly, homeless and disabled American. Basically, Mr. Romney labeled anyone of the "takers" in society as "unworthy poor." This goes against the American value of caring of those less fortunate, despite the constant bombardment of the right wing media stating that welfare and other social safety net programs are a drain on the economy. When economic studies have proven the exact opposite is true. The problem in this country is the myth of rugged individualism. The attitude of that anyone can be successful if they just work hard enough and pull themselves up by their bootstraps. I am reminded of a saying by John Steinbeck, *"Socialism never got a foothold in America because the population thinks they are embarrassed millionaires."* Which is true, everybody has been conditioned to believe that they could strike it rich at any time, and we definitely refuse to pay one dime more in taxes, just in case. Therefore, we continue to support tax cuts for the rich. Again, while the Republicans advocate tax cuts, they only advocate them for corporations and the wealthy. Once again, the Republicans have conned the American people into voting against their own best interests. Most of the American people have not received a sufficient education in Civics, Political Science or History to understand the political process or what causes the political parties have historically supported.

Another issue I fault the American people with is a simple failure to understand the basics of economics. But that is alright since economics is considered a social science, and lately America has expressed a disdain for anything that remotely resembles a science, no wonder conservatives are literally able to get away with some of their tricks over the past few years. A word I have constantly heard being thrown about is the word, "socialism," which most folks equate with the word communism. This is a favorite word amongst conservatives when describing any progressive idea or program, including anything which might benefit working men or women. They argue that it would be detrimental to the economy or to business. Of course, this strikes a chord with most people as we have been living in economically insecure times, folks just don't want to upset the apple cart or do anything which might endanger their jobs.

On the opposite end of the scale is my old employer, Amazon.com. Founded on July 5, 1994 by Jeff Bezos, what started as an online book seller has now evolved into the world's largest online retailer. Not only does it continue to sell books, both in paper and electronic form, but also almost every retail product known to man, from candy bars to literally, the kitchen sink. Amazon attempts to treat both its external customers and internal customers well. They are always looking to improve the experience for both. They have high expectations for their employees and promote those in their culture.

But it appears the many American workers have gotten a belly full of the corporate oligarchy's behaviors. Recently in multiple cities in our country, fast food workers walked off their jobs (yes, you could call it a strike,) in order to call attention to not only their working conditions, but their pay. They struck calling for a $15 per hour wage and the ability to form a union. Now, this author, being a fan of both organized labor and a decent living wage for *all* workers, regardless of where they work. Let's face it, working at McDonald's is not the most glamorous job in the world, but it is a job. And it is the only job the some can folks can find. I can hear some conservatives screaming now. Work harder. Apply yourself. Get an education. Blah. Blah. Blah. What some don't realize is that some fast food workers have college degrees. ***SURPRISE!*** I worked at an employer that has all types of college degrees, including engineering degrees. Are you shocked? Amazed? People who are highly educated working in a call center? Yeah, because the job market in the area is so damn tight.

Recently, the regional grocery store chain, Market Basket, whose board fired its CEO because he was too compassion towards his employees. As a result, the employees struck, and customers boycotted the store. As a result of these combined efforts of both employees and consumers, they sent a clear message to the company's board that they fucked up. As a result, the board caved and restored the CEO to his position. See what can be done when workers stand up for their rights or what they believe in? Strength in numbers. It has always worked in the past, and it continues to work in the present day. You see, nothing gets a Capitalist's attention than when his bottom line is impacted. The only major problem is that you sometimes have to be willing to lose in the short-term when you go on strike. And I am a pragmatist when it comes to striking, because I have always felt it should be used as a last resort. But lately management has felt they controlled not only the deck, but the game as well as the players in the game.

Now, in 2020, most things have not improved on this front. The minimum wage is stagnant at $7.25 an hour. Yet, the wages and bonuses for the 1% of American's has gone up significantly. Also, in March 2020, we started having our 100-year pandemic of a virus called COVID-19 or the Coronavirus. As of the writing of this, some 116,000 Americans have died from this pandemic. After six weeks of staying indoors, people started getting restless and demanded that the economy reopen. However, they personally wanted to continue to work from home. But the people demanded that the **SERVICE** workers to return to their jobs, all because they wanted haircuts and eat lunch at Applebee's.

CHAPTER 4

To understand the impact of how the economy has changed since the 1980s allow me to throw a couple of numbers out to you. In the 1980s, 40% of our economy was based on manufacturing. Today, it is only 12%. Do I have your attention, yet? In a little over thirty years, we have moved from a strong manufacturing base in our country to an almost non-existent base? Why? First off, our country gave them Carte Blanche to do so. In the 1990s, the Clinton administration (see, I told you that I would take a swipe at the liberals as well,) negotiated two trade agreements which proved to be a boon to corporations and a punch to the gut to American labor. The first was the North American Free Trade Agreement, otherwise known as NAFTA. This created a tariff free zone with the United States, Canada, and Mexico. Since both the United States and Canada had a large union presence, especially in the automobile industry, saw their jobs more south of the border to maquiladoras, factories located close to the Mexican border in which their employees, mostly young women, where worked 12 to 14 hours per day, six day a week in various industries from the automotive to pharmaceutical industries. The worst part about this is those employees where paid a few dollars a day, compared to American workers who made up to $20 an hour. This was a boon to American corporations which made a rush to Mexico in order to make more profits. But since 2002, due the advent of even cheaper labor in locations such as Vietnam, China, and India, several Maquiladoras have shut down and relocated to those countries. These countries pay less than a few dollars a month, along with little or no worker protections available in this country. From 2000 to 2011, an average of 17 manufacturers shut down plants in the United States.

The other trade agreement was called the General Agreement on Tariffs and Trade, otherwise known as GATT. The 1986 Uruguay round was the ambitious round since the inception of GATT in 1947, given the fact that 123 countries, including the United States, which covers things such as textiles, agriculture, intellectual property, services as well as capital. Wow, when you look at this and think about it, there is no aspect of American life these trade agreements have not touched. Some people will ask what is the big deal? The problem is that our politicians, economists, and others told us that these agreements would be beneficial to both Americans and their economy. Jobs would be created and we all would benefit. Sadly, neither has occupied. Our good paying manufacturing jobs have disappeared and been replaced by lower paying service sector jobs.

After the election of Donald Trump to the Presidency, one of his major campaign promises were to renegotiate NAFTA under the guise of American First philosophy. What replaced it was The United States-Mexico-Canada Agreement, also known as the USMCA, is a trade deal between the three nations which was signed on November 30, 2018. The USMCA replaces the North American Free Trade Agreement (NAFTA), which had been in effect since January of 1994. Under the terms of NAFTA, tariffs on many goods passing between North America's three major economic powers were gradually phased out. By 2008, tariffs on various agricultural and textiles products, automobiles, and other goods were reduced or eliminated. USMCA came about as a result of U.S. President Donald Trump's efforts to replace NAFTA based on an argument that the terms of NAFTA were unfair to the United States. USMCA began as the U.S.-Mexico Trade Agreement, announced in late August of 2018. A few weeks later, on September 30, 2018, the United States and Canada formally agreed to replace NAFTA with the new agreement, and the USMCA was finalized a few weeks later.

It is clear that American families have been struggling in recent decades. Less obvious are the forces that are responsible for this reversal of fortune. However, a significant body of research now points to a confluence of economic and social trends that many scholars agree have played a crucial role in the rise of financial insecurity.

Corporate boards lavish them with massive pay packages and politicians venerate them as "job creators." But it turns out that America's business chieftains would rather not create full-time jobs to do what needs doing if they can possibly avoid it, according to the latest annual survey from the Harvard Business School (HBS).

About 46 percent of HBS alumni say their firms would rather invest in technology to fill their labor needs than hire humans, compared to just 26 percent who disagree with that sentiment. A full 49 percent say their company "prefers to rely on vendors that can be outsourced rather than hire additional employees," and "firms that increased their reliance on part-time workers during the past three years outnumbered those that relied less on part-timers by a ratio of two to one," the school's survey report says.

The survey report also remarks on "the recent divergence of outcomes, with firms…thriving and workers struggling" in the U.S. economy. It calls business leaders who do not measure their success partly through their company's contributions to the standard of living for Americans "shortsighted" because the business world "has a profound stake in the prosperity of the average American" and "cannot succeed for long while their communities languish." As with a recent Standard & Poor's investment analysis that made news for summarizing the longstanding economist consensus that economic inequality hurts outcomes for everyone, these passages of the Harvard Business School report do not contain new information. They are notable instead because they illustrate that America's economic elites may be taking a healthier view of how their well-being is interlocked with that of middle- and low-income Americans.

Whatever growth there may be in elite awareness that middle-class economic outcomes matter, though, the finding that employers would rather outsource or robotify than hire Americans indicates that labor costs are still one of the business world's favorite places to cut corners. From the sweatshop-like warehouses that help Amazon undercut other retailers on price to wage theft and misclassification at fast food chains and American ports, the modern U.S. economy is rife with examples of that tendency to trim labor costs in service of profits. The elite attitudes on display in the Harvard survey contrast sharply with the working-class outrage that is driving strikes and other low-wage worker activism in the fast food, shipping, commercial logistics, and retail sectors.

One potential model for bridging that gap comes from Seattle. After more than a year of pressure from workers and far-left activists and politicians, a minimum wage of $15 became a political inevitability. The business community got on board with the idea in order to avoid being left out of the process of determining what that $15 wage law would contain. The resulting coalition of union power, business owners, and on-the-ground service providers and activists produced a compromise bill that will help link business success to working-class gains in Seattle for decades to come.

Since the 1970s, work in the United States has undergone a dramatic transformation—a regression from the New Deal quest for stability and from shared prosperity to insecurity security to a state in which work is precarious. In the words of sociologist Arne L. Kalleberg, work has become more "uncertain, unpredictable, and risky from the point of view of the worker."

One reason for the rise of precarious work is the wholesale restructuring of the American economy from one based on manufacturing to one based on services. After World War II the manufacturing sector comprised 40 percent of the labor force; by 2005, that share had fallen to only 12 percent. The service sector now makes up about 80 percent of the jobs in the United States. Durable manufacturing jobs (autoworker, machinist, chemical engineer) offering higher wages and good benefits have been replaced by service sector jobs (store clerk, cashier, home health-care aide) that pay less, offer few or no benefits, and are more insecure.

Moreover, while the manufacturing sector tends to create good jobs at every employment level, the service sector tends to create a relatively small number of high-skill, high-paying jobs (in fields like finance, consulting, and medicine) along with a large number of low-skill, low-paid jobs (in retailing, child care, and hospitality). The result is that secure, semiskilled middle-income jobs like those that once fueled the rapid expansion of the American middle class are increasingly hard to find.

Now, service sector jobs can be divided into two categories. First, the well-paying category which includes doctors, nurses and attorneys. The second doesn't pay so well. Those include, janitors, certified nursing assistants, and bank tellers, all of which pay at or close to the minimum wage. As of the writing of the book, the minimum wage stands at $7.25 per hour. Meaning that a person who works 2,080 per year (the standard work hours in a year,) earns $15,080 per year. Now this means that a family of four falls below the federal poverty guidelines of $23,550 as well as the guidelines for a family of two of $15,510. Currently there is no state in the union in which a person can work full time making minimum wage and pay rent. But the majority of employees do not work their minimum wage employees 40 hours per week or even 36. Why you may ask? Simple, they do not want to pay benefits, particularly health insurance, which would cause their labor costs to skyrocket.

Of course, you are thinking to yourself, yes but the majority of minimum wage earners are pimply faced teenagers working to have a little spending money. And you would be wrong in that assumption. Labor department figures show that the majority of minimum wage earners are female, usually single parents, between the ages of 30 and 40, and is usually drawing some form of public assistance. You know welfare, Medicaid, and of course, that drain on every taxpayer's money, FOOD STAMPS.

What? Public assistance? Yes, they qualify for public assistance. The two biggest culprits in this game of Wal-Mart and McDonald's. In fact, McDonald's as part of their employee training gives its trainees lessons on how to seek out and access public assistance programs. And Wal-Mart goes so far as to have holiday food drives for their employees, not for the needy in their own communities, BUT FOR THEIR OWN DAMN EMPLOYEES. C'mon just do the math. Just multiply $7.25 (the current minimum wage) by and where from 30 to 35 hours a week and see what numbers you generate. Then deduct taxes, and then attempt to generate living expenses from the remaining amount. Bet you can't do it. And with Wal-Mart employees drawing SNAP benefits, where do you think they do all their food shopping?

Of course, there are those in the corporate oligarchy which will staunchly argue that what is called "the social safety net," costs too much and needs to be eliminated. But here is the counter argument to that. All social programs meaning SNAP benefits, TANF, and Medicaid take up only 1% of the Federal Budget. By comparison, the military's budget is a mind boggling 56%. Just a 3% cut to our military budget would end world hunger. Food for thought, no pun intended

 A fundamental misconception about America's welfare state misleads millions of voters to reflexively support ever bigger and more generous government. William Voegeli fingers the attitude in his book, Never Enough: America's Limitless Welfare State: "no matter how large the welfare state, liberal politicians and writers have accused it of being shamefully small" and "contemptibly austere."

 Barbara Ehrenreich expresses the attitude in her book, Nickeled and Dimed: "guilt doesn't go anywhere near far enough; the appropriate emotion is shame" regarding the stingy miserliness of America's welfare state. In light of the current budget debate, with Former House Budget Committee Chairman and Speaker of the House Paul Ryan putting fundamental entitlement reform on the table, this misconception especially needs to be corrected.

America's welfare state is not a principality. It is a vast empire bigger than the entire budgets of almost every other country in the world. Just one program, Medicaid, cost the federal government $275 billion in 2010, which is slated to rise to $451 billion by 2018. Counting state Medicaid expenditures, this one program cost taxpayers $425 billion in 2010, soaring to $800 billion by 2018. Under Obamacare, 85 million Americans will soon be on Medicaid, growing to nearly 100 million by 2021, according to the CBO.

But there are 184 additional federal, means-tested welfare programs, most jointly financed and administered with the states. In addition to Medicaid is the Children's Health Insurance Program (CHIP). Also included is Food Stamps, now officially called the Supplemental Nutrition Assistance Program (SNAP). Nearly 42 million Americans were receiving food stamps in 2010, up by a third since November, 2008. That is why President Obama's budget projects spending $75 billion on Food Stamps in 2011, double the $36 billion spent in 2008.

But that is not the only federal nutrition program for the needy. There is the Special Supplemental Nutrition Program for Women, Infants and Children (WIC), which targets assistance to pregnant women and mothers with small children. There is the means tested School Breakfast Program and School Lunch Program. There is the Summer Food Service Program for Children. There are the lower income components of the Child and Adult Care Food Program, the Emergency Food Assistance Program, and the Commodity Supplemental Food Program (CSFP). Then there is the Nutrition Program for the Elderly. All in all, literally cradle to grave service. By 2010, Federal spending for Food and Nutrition Assistance overall had climbed to roughly $100 billion a year.

Then there is federal housing assistance, totaling $77 billion in 2010. This includes expenditures for over 1 million public housing units owned by the government. It includes Section 8 rental assistance for nearly another 4 million private housing units. Then there is Rural Rental Assistance, Rural Housing Loans, and Rural Rental Housing Loans. Also included is Home Investment Partnerships (HOME), Community Development Block Grants (CDBG), Housing for Special Populations (Elderly and Disabled), Housing Opportunities for Persons with AIDS (HOPWA), Emergency Shelter Grants, the Supportive Housing program, the Single Room Occupancy program, the Shelter Plus Care program, and the Home Ownership and Opportunity for People Everywhere (HOPE) program, among others.

Besides medical care, food, and housing, the federal government also provides cash. The old New Deal era Aid to Families with Dependent Children (AFDC) is now Temporary Assistance for Needy Families (TANF), which pays cash mostly to single mothers with children. There is the Earned Income Tax Credit (EITC), which sends low income workers checks even though they usually owe no taxes to be credited against. The Child Tax Credit similarly provides cash to families with children. Supplemental Security Income (SSI) provides cash for the low income aged, blind and disabled. In 2010 such income security programs accounted for nearly another $200 billion in federal spending.

The federal government also provides means tested assistance through multiple programs for child care, education, job training, and the Low Income Energy Assistance Program (LIHEAP), the Social Services Block Grant, the Community Services Block Grant, and the Legal Services Corporation, among other programs.

The best estimate of the cost of the 185 federal means tested welfare programs for 2010 for the federal government alone is nearly $700 billion, up a third since 2008, according to the Heritage Foundation. Counting state spending, total welfare spending for 2010 reached nearly $900 billion, up nearly one-fourth since 2008 (24.3%).

Yet, by 2008, Robert Rector of the Heritage Foundation reports that total welfare spending already amounted to $16,800 per person in poverty, 4 times as much as the Census Bureau estimated was necessary to bring all of the poor up to the poverty level, eliminating all poverty in America. That would be $50,400 per poor family of three. Indeed, Charles Murray wrote a whole book, In Our Hands, A Plan to Replace America's Welfare State explaining that we already spend far more than enough to completely eliminate all poverty in America.

The soaring welfare spending since 2008 is not a temporary increase reflecting the recession, as it is not projected to decline after the economy recovers. By 2013, total annual welfare spending will have grown still more, to nearly $1 trillion. Over the 10-year period from 2009 to 2018, federal and state welfare spending will total $10.3 trillion. This does not include Obamacare's massive expansion of Medicaid, or the massive new entitlement providing subsidies for families making close to $100,000 per year, and beyond. Together, this abusive entitlement spending will add trillions more.

Even in 2005, government spending on these means tested welfare programs was 25% more than was spent on national defense, and that was at the height of the wars in the Middle East. Government overall, federal, state and local, spends more only on the big entitlements for retirees, Social Security and Medicare, and on education, and total welfare spending may have even shot beyond education by now. Indeed, over the past 2 decades, total welfare spending has been growing faster than Social Security and Medicare, about twice as fast as education, and nearly 3 times as fast as national defense.

Of course, the big picture comprises the entire scope of entitlement programs, including Social Security and Medicare. Social Security spending for 2010 was $721.5 billion, with Medicare spending totaling $457 billion for the year, for a combined total of $1.179 trillion. Adding in federal welfare spending for the year leaves a combined total for entitlement spending of $1.879 trillion. The total federal budget for that year was 3.720 trillion. So entitlement/welfare state spending overall for that year was just over 50% of the entire budget. Not exactly stingy. Okay, stop right there. Medicare and Social Security are NOT entitlements. They are social insurance programs designed to help out the elderly and disabled.

The War on Poverty famously began in 1965. From 1965 to 2008, the total spent only on means tested welfare for the poor in 2008 dollars has been nearly $16 trillion, according to the Heritage Foundation. Rector reports that has been more than all spending on all military conflicts from the American Revolution to today, in 2008 dollars.

What have we gotten for all of that spending? Poverty fell sharply after the Depression, before the War on Poverty, declining from 32% in 1950 to 22.4% in 1959 to 12.1% in 1969, soon after the War on Poverty programs became effective. Progress against poverty as measured by the poverty rate then abruptly stopped.

Former Speaker Ryan's budget only slows the growth of this welfare/entitlement empire. All of those commentators weeping, wailing and gnashing their teeth over Ryan's budget are not living in the real world. Of course we are. We do not want to happen to our poor what has happened to Greece or other European countries in the name of "austerity." We have corporations, like Wal-Mart, McDonald's, and Burger King, who pay their employees poverty wages, and would love nothing more than to pay them less so that their franchisees and company management can rake in six and seven figure salaries. But they expect their employees to utilize government assistance, the same government assistance programs they are always advocating to be done away with in the name of "fiscal responsibility.")

So here we sit while we work and are being taxed, we are subsidizing these giant corporation's employee's benefits. And the rich keep getting richer, and the rest of us get to fend for ourselves. You see, back in the 1890's possibly earlier, there started a movement in this country, called eugenics, basically building a better human being by sterilization of the poor and what was called the "feeble-minded." Now that definition was very broad, and the use of those laws were not effectively applied, and they were usually applied to the poor, the mentally ill and retarded. If you don't think it can't happen again. History always has a funny way of relating itself. Of course, you probably think I am off my rocker, but stranger things have happened. Like in the 1920s, there was an unspoken agreement between government and corporations where government would not interfere with the regulation of business and they would be allowed to make untold profits beholding ONLY to their stockholders. Government would take a "hands off" approach and have no accountability to the public or workers. In the process, they were allowed to cut worker wages to the bone. They were also allowed to ignore any type of consumer protections. Pretty much the concept of "Caveat Empator" was in full force. The expectation was that the corporations were to do the right thing and allow profits to trickle down to the rest of society as well as its workers. Remember this did not occur during the 21st century, it occurred almost nine decades previously. But after President Roosevelt came into office, Congress and he enacted massive reforms to the stock market and banking industries to curb their wild west style ways of doing business and hold them accountable to not only workers but also to the public. Of course, the first thing businesses advocated for once the corporatist gained sufficient foothold in the Congress was to repeal or weaken the very laws meant to protect us. Not just employment laws, but also workplace and occupational safety laws but also laws which govern overtime, sick leave, vacation, and healthcare and a multitude of other benefits the middle and working classes takes for granted that were fought for in the past.

The American people have the attention and memory span of a gnat. And that is what current politicians and power brokers enjoy. But ask them who won the World Series, or the last Super Bowl and they recall with Crystal clarity, but ask them what bills their state legislature passed in the last session which direct impacted them, they have no fucking clue.

Remember a few pages back when I was referring to *trickle-down economics?* Well, here we are living in the results. The problem is that the Republican as well as the Libertarian (tea party) is they still adhere to the philosophy that if the rich and their taxes are cut to non-existent level then they will invest their money into their business, create jobs, and grow their businesses. Sounds great, right? Sure it does. But as I alluded to earlier, we do not take into account the human element of greed. Greed in the form of off-shoring their money to avoid paying taxes. Now, the conservatives would argue that I am unfair picking on them. Not so, they have the resources to pay for attorneys and accountants to find those tax loopholes which we as the "great unwashed" do not have access. They also contribute large amounts of money to political campaigns in order to get the tax laws and regulations written to their favor (such as a deduction for the purchase of private jets.) Now, this goes back to the 19th century, when John D. Rockefeller made the statement that, "God gave me my wealth." Which lends itself to my argument that America is the only country on the planet where religion, politics, and economics has combined into some ungodly hybrid of religious act of economic activity. Thus they view any person who are poor as not as strong moral character as they are. Naturally, the media further and reinforce this stereotype by showing almost daily some person of a lower socio-economic status being arrested for some low level street crime, which the elevate to the level, by exaggeration, to the level of a capital offense. In Europe, they do not have a problem with violence or high crime rates. You see, after World War II, particularly the year 1947, every industrialized country, save one, the United States, enacted protections for their citizenry such as universal health care, guaranteed old age pensions, early childhood education, free college education, all these shown and have been proven to benefit their society as a whole. Naturally, the citizenry is expected to pay high taxes, but the way European society is set up, no one really seems to mind. The Congress, which was controlled by Republicans at the time (see another issue,) voted against such ideas, calling them "too Socialistic." You see Republicans don't have any true ideals or proposals on helping the country's poor. Instead, they continue with the same rhetoric they have used since the 1980s. A platform of "God, Guns, and Gays" to define their message and fire up their base. A base of voters who see the America of their youth slowly slipping away, but they are blaming the wrong people for its decline. As soon as they lost the 2012 election, they immediately started looking for ways to reach out to minority groups and women. But no sooner than they started doing so, they immediately started to pass legislation to hinder their efforts. Since women make up the majority of the population (51%) and the majority of the working poor are women, it would stand to reason that if Republicans wanted to court votes from this important voting bloc, they would do everything in their power to remove stumbling blocks to women, not place more in their way.

Every time we loosen the reins on the wealthy and corporations to run amuck in the economy, a financial crisis issues. The most recent was "The Great Recession," which started shortly after George W. Bush took office in 2001, cutting the top tier of taxes to 27%, stating that it would be a boon to the economy, instead practically due to the two wars in Iraq and Afghanistan, the Bush era tax cuts ended up costing the economy a total of $6 trillion and over 8 million jobs lost. These were not just in the manufacturing sector. Due to the GATT agreement, service sector jobs such as engineering and call centers moved off shore to take advantage of lower wages in third world countries. This left many workers out of a job permanently. Now long term unemployed are viewed with much suspicion every time they attempt to look for employment. Gaps in employment are looked at with suspicion. Able-bodied persons are viewed with more so than the disabled, elderly, and children who might need financial help. We choose to handle unemployment with unemployment compensation, job retraining, or job placement. The best reflections of our view of unemployment in America is the fact that unemployment is very short, usually 26 weeks.

The Trans-Pacific Partnership (TPP) is a proposed regional free trade agreement that is currently being negotiated by twelve countries throughout the Asia-Pacific region (Australia, Brunei Darussalam, Canada, Chile, Japan, Malaysia, Mexico, New Zealand, Peru, Singapore, the United States, and Vietnam). The agreement began in 2005 as the Trans-Pacific Strategic Partnership Agreement (TPSEP or P4). Member countries set the goal of wrapping up negotiations in 2012, but contentious issues such as agriculture, intellectual property, and services and investments have caused negotiations to continue into the present, with the last round set to meet in Ottawa from July 3 to July 12, 2014.[8][9] Passage of the TPP is one of the primary goals of the Obama administration's trade agenda.

The TPP intends to enhance trade and investment among the TPP partner countries, promote innovation, economic growth and development, and support the creation and retention of jobs.[10] Global health professionals, internet freedom activists, environmentalists, organized labor, advocacy groups, and elected officials have criticized and protested the negotiations, in large part because of the proceedings' secrecy, the agreement's expansive scope, and controversial clauses in drafts leaked publicly.

The negotiations to set up the TPSEP initially included three countries (Chile, New Zealand and Singapore), and Brunei subsequently joined the agreement.[citation needed] The original TPSEP agreement contains an accession clause and affirms the members' "commitment to encourage the accession to this Agreement by other economies".

In January 2008, the US agreed to enter into talks with the Pacific 4 (P4) members regarding trade liberalization in financial services. On 22 September 2008, US Trade Representative Susan C. Schwab announced that the US would begin negotiations with the P4 countries to join the TPP, with the first round of talks in early 2009.

In November 2008, Australia, Vietnam, and Peru announced that they would join the P4 trade bloc. In October 2010, Malaysia announced that it had also joined the TPP negotiations.

In June 2012, Canada and Mexico announced that they were joining the TPP negotiations. Mexico's interest in joining was initially met with concern among TPP negotiators about its customs policies.

In 2010, Canada had become an observer in the TPP talks, and expressed interest in officially joining, but was not committed to join, purportedly because the US and New Zealand blocked it due to concerns over Canadian agricultural policy (i.e. supply management)—specifically dairy—and intellectual property-rights protection. Several pro-business and internationalist Canadian media outlets raised concerns about this as a missed opportunity. In a feature in the Financial Post, former Canadian trade-negotiator Peter Clark claimed that the US Obama Administration had strategically outmaneuvered the Canadian Harper Government. Wendy Dobson and Diana Kuzmanovic for The School of Public Policy, University of Calgary, argued for the economic necessity of the TPP to Canada. Embassy warned that Canada's position in APEC could be compromised by being excluded from both the US-oriented TPP and the proposed China-oriented ASEAN +3 trade agreement (or the broader Comprehensive Economic Partnership for East Asia).

Canada and Mexico formally became TPP negotiating participants in October 2012, following completion of the domestic consultation periods of the other nine members.

Japan officially joined the TPP negotiations on July 23, 2013. Prime Minister Abe's decision to commit Japan to joining the TPP should be understood as a necessary complement to his efforts to stimulate the Japanese economy with monetary easing and the related depreciation of the Yen. These efforts alone, without the type of economic reform the TPP will lead to, are unlikely to produce long-term improvements in Japan's growth prospects.

South Korea was interested in joining in November 2010, and was invited to the TPP negotiating rounds by the US after the successful conclusion of its Free trade agreement between the United States of America and the Republic of Korea in late December.[37] South Korea already has bilateral trade agreements with some TPP members, but areas such as vehicle manufacturing and agriculture still need to be agreed upon, making further multilateral TPP negotiations somewhat complicated.

Other countries interested in TPP membership include Taiwan, the Philippines, Laos, Colombia, and Indonesia. Cambodia, Bangladesh and India have also been mentioned as possible candidates. Despite initial opposition, China is interested in joining the TPP eventually.

On 20 November 2012 during a visit by President of the United States Barack Obama, Thailand's government announced its wish to join the TPP negotiations. Expecting Thailand to join after the process is finalized for Canada and Mexico, law professor Jane Kelsey said that it "will be in the extraordinary position of having to accept any existing agreed text, sight unseen."

The most notable country not involved in the negotiations is China. According to the Brookings Institute, the most fundamental challenge for the TPP project regarding China is that "it may not constitute a powerful enough enticement to propel China to sign on to these new standards on trade and investment. China so far has reacted by accelerating its own trade initiatives in Asia."

The TPSEP was previously known as the Pacific Three Closer Economic Partnership (P3-CEP), its negotiations launched on the sidelines of the 2002 APEC Leaders' Meeting in Los Cabos, Mexico, by Prime Ministers Helen Clark of New Zealand, Goh Chok Tong of Singapore and Chilean President Ricardo Lagos. Brunei first took part as a full negotiating party in the fifth round of talks in April 2005, after which the trade bloc became known as the Pacific-4 (P4). Although all original and negotiating parties are members of the Asia-Pacific Economic Cooperation (APEC), the TPSEP and TPP are not APEC initiatives. However, the TPP is considered to be a pathfinder for the proposed Free Trade Area of the Asia Pacific (FTAAP), an APEC initiative.

The original agreement was concluded by Brunei, Chile, New Zealand and Singapore on 3 June 2005,[2] and entered into force on 28 May 2006 for New Zealand and Singapore, 12 July 2006 for Brunei, and 8 November 2006 for Chile.[50] It is a comprehensive agreement, affecting trade in goods, rules of origin, trade remedies, sanitary and phytosanitary measures, technical barriers to trade, trade in services, intellectual property, government procurement and competition policy. Among other things, it called for reduction by 90 percent of all tariffs between member countries by 1 January 2006, and reduction of all trade tariffs to zero by the year 2015.

On the last day of the 2010 APEC summit, leaders of the nine negotiating countries endorsed the proposal advanced by US President Barack Obama that set a target for settlement of negotiations by the next APEC summit in November 2011.However, negotiations have continued through 2012, 2013 and 2014.

After the inauguration of Barack Obama in January 2009, the anticipated March 2009 negotiations were postponed. However, in his first trip to Asia in November 2009, president Obama reaffirmed the US's commitment to the TPP, and on 14 December 2009, new US Trade Representative Ron Kirk notified Congress that President Obama planned to enter TPP negotiations "with the objective of shaping a high-standard, broad-based regional pact".

Since that time, 19 formal rounds of TPP negotiations have been held:

1st round: 15–19 March 2010, Melbourne, Australia

The negotiating groups that met included industrial goods, agriculture, sanitary and phytosanitary standards, telecommunications, financial services, customs, rules of origin, government procurement, environment, and trade capacity building. Negotiators agreed to draft papers in preparation for the second round of negotiations.

2nd round: 14–18 June 2010, San Francisco, USA

This round included "determining the architecture for market access negotiations, deciding the relationship between the TPP and existing FTAs among the negotiating partners, addressing "horizontal" issues such as small business priorities, regulatory coherence, and other issues that reflect the way businesses operate and workers interact in the 21st century, and proceeding toward the tabling of text on all chapters of the agreement in the third negotiating round, scheduled for October in Brunei."

3rd round: 5–8 October 2010, Brunei

This round included "meetings on agriculture, services, investment, government procurement, competition, environment, and labor. The groups focused on the objectives that they had set for this round: preparation of consolidated text and proposals for cooperation. Negotiations will continue through Saturday, with groups on telecommunications, e-commerce, textiles, customs, technical barriers to trade, and trade capacity building beginning Friday."

4th round: 6–10 December 2010, Auckland, New Zealand

In the 4th round talks, the negotiating countries "began work on trade in goods, financial services, customs, labor, and intellectual property. They also discussed cross-cutting issues, including how to ensure that small- and medium-sized enterprises can take advantage of the TPP, promoting greater connectivity and the participation of U.S. firms in Asia-Pacific supply chains and enhancing the coherence of the regulatory systems of the TPP countries to make trade across the region more seamless."

5th round: 14–18 February 2011, Santiago, Chile

The Santiago, the negotiating countries "made further progress in developing the agreement's legal texts, which will spell out the rights and obligations each country will take on and that will cover all aspects of trade and investment relationships. The teams carefully reviewed the text proposals made by each country, ensuring understanding of each other's proposals so negotiations could advance. With consolidated negotiating texts in most areas, partners began seeking to narrow differences and to consider the interests and concerns of each country."

6th round: 24 March – 1 April 2011, Singapore

In Singapore, "the United States and TPP countries made substantial headway toward a key goal of developing the legal texts of the agreement, which include commitments covering all aspects of their trade and investment relationship. Recognizing the priority of this negotiation as well as the challenge of negotiating a regional agreement with nine countries, each country began showing the type of flexibility that will be needed to successfully conclude the negotiation. As a result, the teams were able to narrow the gaps in their positions on a wide range of issues across the more than 25 chapters of the agreement."

7th round: 15–24 June 2011, Ho Chi Minh City, Vietnam

In Vietnam, "among the issues on which the teams had particularly productive discussions were the new cross-cutting issues that will feature for the first time in the TPP. After consulting internally on the U.S. text tabled at the sixth round, they furthered their efforts to find common ground on the regulatory coherence text intended to make the regulatory systems of their countries operate in a more consistent and seamless manner and avoid the types of regulatory barriers that are increasingly among the key obstacles to trade. The teams also had constructive discussions on approaches to development in the TPP and the importance of ensuring that the agreement serves to close the development gap among TPP members."

8th round: 6–15 September 2011, Chicago, USA

"Negotiators from the nine TPP partner countries – Australia, Brunei Darussalam, Chile, Malaysia, New Zealand, Peru, Singapore, Vietnam, and the United States – are reporting good progress early in the eighth round of talks, expected to last through September 15. Negotiating groups that have already begun meetings include services, financial services, investment, customs, telecommunications, intellectual property rights (IPR), government procurement, sanitary and phytosanitary measures, and environment. Numerous negotiating teams are also holding bilateral meetings."

9th round: 22–29 October 2011, Lima, Peru

"During this round, negotiators built upon progress made in previous rounds and pressed forward toward the goal of reaching the broad outlines of an ambitious, jobs-focused agreement by the Asia-Pacific Economic Cooperation Leaders' meeting in Honolulu, HI next month. At APEC, President Obama and his counterparts from the other eight TPP countries will take stock of progress to date and discuss next steps."

10th round: 5–9 December 2011, Kuala Lumpur, Malaysia

11th round: 2–9 March 2012, Melbourne, Australia

12th round: 8–18 May 2012, Dallas, USA

13th round: 2–10 July 2012. San Diego, USA

14th round: 6–15 September 2012, Leesburg, Virginia, USA

15th round: 3–12 December 2012, Auckland, New Zealand

16th round: 4–13 March 2013 Singapore

17th round: 15–24 May 2013, Lima, Peru

18th round: 15–24 July 2013, Kota Kinabalu, Malaysia

19th round: 23–30 August 2013, Bandar Seri Begawan, Brunei

20th round: 3–13 July 2014 in Ottawa, Canada

The majority of United States free trade agreements are implemented as congressional-executive agreements. Unlike treaties, such agreements require a majority of the House and Senate to pass. Under "Trade Promotion Authority" (TPA), established by the Trade Act of 1974, Congress authorizes the President to negotiate "free trade agreements... if they are approved by both houses in a bill enacted into public law and other statutory conditions are met. "In early 2012, the Obama administration indicated that a requirement for the conclusion of TPP negotiations is the renewal of "fast track" Trade Promotion Authority. This would require the United States Congress to introduce and vote on an administration-authored bill for implementing the TPP with minimal debate and no amendments, with the entire process taking no more than 90 days. The Obama Administration and TPP proponents plan to introduce fast-track legislation and legislation on the TPP following the 2014 elections.

In April 2013 APEC members proposed, along with setting a possible target for settlement of the TPP by the 2013 APEC summit, that World Trade Organization (WTO) members set a target for settlement of the Doha Round mini-package by the ninth WTO ministerial conference (MC9), also to be held around the same time in Bali.

This call for inclusion and cooperation between the WTO and economic partnership agreements (also termed regional trade agreements) like the TPP comes after the statement by Pierre Lellouche who described the sentiment of the Doha round negotiations; "Although no one wants to say it, we must call a cat a cat...".

A leaked set of draft documents indicated that public concern had little impact on the negotiations. They also indicated there are strong disagreements between the US and negotiating parties regarding intellectual property, agricultural subsidies, and financial services.

Wikileaks' exposure of the Intellectual Property Rights and Environmental chapters of the TPP revealed "just how far apart the US is from the other nations involved in the treaty, with 19 points of disagreement in the area of intellectual property alone. One of the documents speaks of 'great pressure' being applied by the US." Australia in particular opposes the US's proposals for copyright protection and an element supported by all other nations involved to "limit the liability of ISPs for copyright infringement by their users." Another sticking point lies with Japan's reluctance to open up its agricultural markets.

 Political difficulties, particularly those related to the passage of a Trade Promotion Authority (TPA) by Congress, within the US present another cause of delay for the TPP negotiations. Receiving TPA from Congress is looking especially difficult for Obama since members of his own Democratic Party are against them, while Republicans generally support the trade talks. "The TPP and TPA pose a chicken-and-egg situation for Washington. Congress needs to pass TPA to bring the TPP negotiations to fruition, but the Obama administration must win favorable terms in the TPP to pull TPA legislation through Congress. Simply put, the administration cannot make Congress happy, unless it can report on the excellent terms that it has coaxed out of Japan."

Only certain sections of the drafts of the Trans-Pacific Partnership have been leaked to the public, and only summaries of other parts. Many of the provisions are modelled on previous trade and deregulation agreements. According to the website of the Office of the United States Trade Representative, TPP chapters include: competition, cooperation and capacity building, cross-border services, customs, e-commerce, environment, financial services, government procurement, intellectual property, investment, labor, legal issues, market access for goods, rules of origin, sanitary and phytosanitary standards, technical barriers to trade, telecommunications, temporary entry, textiles and apparel, trade remedies.

Also according to the USTR, the contents of the TPP seek to address issues that promote:

Comprehensive market access by eliminating tariffs and other barriers to goods and services trade and investment, so as to create new opportunities for our workers and businesses and immediate benefits for our consumers.

A fully regional agreement by facilitating the development of production and supply chains among TPP members, which will support the goals of job creation, improving living standards and welfare, and promoting sustainable growth among member countries.

Cross-cutting trade issues by building on work being done in APEC and other fora by incorporating four new cross-cutting issues in the TPP. These issues are:

Regulatory coherence: Commitments will promote trade between the countries by making trade among them more seamless and efficient.

Competitiveness and business facilitation: Commitments will enhance the domestic and regional competitiveness of each member country's economy and promote economic integration and jobs in the region, including through the development of regional production and supply chains.

Small- and Medium-Sized Enterprises: Commitments will address concerns small- and medium-sized businesses have raised about the difficulty in understanding and using trade agreements, encouraging these sized enterprises to trade internationally.

Development: Comprehensive and robust market liberalization, improvements in trade and investment enhancing disciplines, and other commitments will serve to strengthen institutions important for economic development and governance and thereby contribute significantly to advancing TPP countries' respective economic development priorities.

New trade challenges by promoting trade and investment in innovative products and services, including the digital economy and green technologies, and to ensure a competitive business environment across the TPP region.

Living agreement by enabling the updating of the agreement when needed to address trade issues that materialize in the future as well as new issues that arise with the expansion of the agreement to include new countries.

Some of the provisions relating to the enforcement of patents and copyrights alleged to be present in the US proposal for the agreement have been criticized as being excessively restrictive, providing intellectual property restraints beyond those in the Korea-US trade agreement and Anti-Counterfeiting Trade Agreement (ACTA).

 A number of United States Congresspeople, including Senator Bernard Sanders and Representatives Henry Waxman, Sander M. Levin, John Conyers, Jim McDermott, John Lewis, Pete Stark, Charles B. Rangel, Earl Blumenauer, and Lloyd Doggett, have expressed concerns about the effect the TPP requirements would have on access to medicine. In particular, they are concerned that the TPP focuses on protecting intellectual property to the detriment of efforts to provide access to affordable medicine in the developing world, particularly Vietnam, going against the foreign policy goals of the Obama administration and previous administrations. Additionally, they worry that the TPP would not be flexible enough to accommodate existing non-discriminatory drug reimbursement programs and the diverse health systems of member countries.

 Opponents of the Trans-Pacific Partnership say US corporations are hoping to weaken Pharmac's ability to get inexpensive, generic medicines by forcing New Zealand to pay for brand name drugs. Doctors and organizations like Medecins Sans Frontieres have also expressed concern. The New Zealand Government denies the claims, Trade Negotiations Minister Tim Groser saying opponents of the deal are "fools" who are "trying to wreck this agreement".

 Ken Akamatsu, creator of Japanese manga series Love Hina and Mahou Sensei Negima! expressed concern the agreement could decimate the derivative dōjinshi (self-published) works prevalent in Japan. Akamatsu argues that the TPP "would destroy derivative dōjinshi. And as a result, the power of the entire manga industry would also diminish." Kensaku Fukui, a lawyer and a Nihon University professor, expressed concerns that the TPP could allow companies to restrict or stop imports and exports of intellectual property, such as licensed merchandise. For example, IP holders could restrict or stop importers from shipping merchandise such as DVDs and other related goods related to an anime or manga property into one country to protect local distribution of licensed merchandise already in the country via local licensors.

At a Nico Nico live seminar called How Would TPP Change the Net and Copyrights? An In-Depth Examination: From Extending Copyright Terms to Changing the Law to Allow Unilateral Enforcement and Statutory Damages, artist Kazuhiko Hachiya warned that cosplay could also fall under the TPP, and such an agreement could give law enforcement officials broad interpretive authority in dictating how people could dress up. Critics also have derided the agreement could also harm Japanese culture, where some segments have developed through parody works.

On November 13, 2013, a complete draft of the treaty's Intellectual Property Rights chapter was published by WikiLeaks

According to The Nation's interpretation of leaked documents in 2012, countries would be obliged to conform all their domestic laws and regulations to the TPP's rules, even limiting how governments could spend their tax dollars. As of 2012, US negotiators were pursuing an investor-state dispute settlement mechanism, also known as corporate tribunals, which can be used to attack domestic public interest laws. This mechanism is a common provision in international trade and investment agreements, that grants an investor the right to initiate dispute settlement proceedings against a foreign government in their own right under international law. For example, if an investor invests in country "A", a member of a trade treaty, and country A breaches that treaty, then the investor may sue country A's government for the breach.

Critics of the investment protection regime argue that traditional investment treaty standards are incompatible with environmental law, human rights protection, and public welfare regulation, meaning that TPP will be used to force states to lower standards e.g., environmental and workers protection, or be sued for damages. The Australian government's position against investor state dispute settlement has been argued to support the rule of law and national energy security.

In 2012, critics such as consumer advocacy group Public Citizen's Global Trade Watch have called for more open negotiations for the agreement. U.S. Trade Representative Ron Kirk responded that he believes the Office of the United States Trade Representative (USTR) has conducted "the most engaged and transparent process as we possibly could," but that "some measure of discretion and confidentiality" are needed "to preserve negotiating strength and to encourage our partners to be willing to put issues on the table they may not otherwise." He dismissed the "tension" as natural and noted that when the Free Trade Area of the Americas drafts were released, negotiators were subsequently unable to reach a final agreement.

On 23 May 2012, United States Senator Ron Wyden (D-OR) introduced S. 3225, that would require the Office of the US Trade Representative to disclose its TPP documents to all members of Congress. Wyden said the bill clarifies the intent of 2002 legislation which was supposed to increase Congressional access to information about USTR activity, but which, according to Wyden, is being incorrectly interpreted by the USTR as justification to excessively limit such access. Wyden asserted:

The majority of Congress is being kept in the dark as to the substance of the TPP negotiations, while representatives of U.S. corporations—like Halliburton, Chevron, PHRMA, Comcast, and the Motion Picture Association of America—are being consulted and made privy to details of the agreement. More than two months after receiving the proper security credentials, my staff is still barred from viewing the details of the proposals that USTR is advancing. We hear that the process by which TPP is being negotiated has been a model of transparency. I disagree with that statement.

In 2013 Senator Elizabeth Warren (D-Mass), Rep. Alan Grayson (D-Fla.) and others have criticized the Obama administration's secrecy policies on the Trans-Pacific Pact.

The last round of negotiations was planned to take place in Vancouver, Canada, but two weeks before commencing, the meeting venue was moved across the country to Canada's capital, Ottawa. Inquiries from public interest groups about attending this round were ignored.

Before Japan entered TPP negotiations in July 2013, it was reported that it would allow the US to continue imposing tariffs on Japanese vehicles, despite a "major premise of the TPP [being] to eliminate all tariffs in principle." Japan is compromising on auto tariffs "because Tokyo wants to maintain tariffs on various agricultural products."

Another contentious issue in the TPP negotiations has been currency manipulation, wherein a country devalues its currency in order to boost exports and gain an advantage in trade. Politicians such as Senator Lindsey O. Graham and Representative Sander M. Levin "gathered a group of economists, manufacturing industry officials and labor leaders who agreed that the TPP should die unless it credibly prohibits countries from manipulating the value of their currency." Many economists claim that currency manipulation by Asian manufacturing countries have become pervasive, "allowing them to boost their exports at the expense of manufacturing companies in the United States and Europe." Furthermore, organizations such as the World Trade Organization or International Monetary Fund cannot control such currency manipulation, so some are claiming the United States should "use the free-trade talks to force an end to such actions."

The Australian Public Health Association (PHAA) stated in a media release, on 17 February 2014, in specific relation to the potential impact of the TPP on the health of Australia's population. A policy brief that emerged from a collaboration between academics and non-government organizations (NGOs) was the basis of the media release, as the group continued to undertake a Health Impact Assessment of the trade agreement at the time of the PHA's statement.

A poll conducted in December 2012 showed 64 percent of New Zealanders thought trade agreements, such as the TPP, that allow corporations to sue governments should be rejected.

2013, Economist Joseph Stiglitz warned that the TPP presented "grave risks" and it "serves the interests of the wealthiest." Organized labor in the United States argues that the trade deal would largely benefit big business at the expense of workers in the manufacturing and service industries.[101] The Economic Policy Institute and the Center for Economic and Policy Research have argued that the TPP could result in further job losses and declining wages. In December 2013, 151 House Democrats signed a letter written by Rosa DeLauro (D-Conn.) and George Miller (D-Calif.) opposing the fast track trade promotion authority for the TPP. Several House Republicans oppose the measure on the grounds that it empowers the executive branch. In January 2014, House Democrats refused to put forward a co-sponsor for the legislation, hampering the bill's prospects for passage.

In 2014, Noam Chomsky warned that the TPP is "designed to carry forward the neoliberal project to maximize profit and domination, and to set the working people in the world in competition with one another so as to lower wages to increase insecurity." Senator Bernie Sanders, who opposes fast track, has stated that trade agreements like the TPP "have ended up devastating working families and enriching large corporations. "Economist Paul Krugman reported "...I'll be undismayed and even a bit relieved if the T.P.P. just fades away." and "...there isn't a compelling case for this deal, from either a global or a national point of view. Nor does there seem to be anything like a political consensus in favor, abroad or at home."

Ilana Solomon, Sierra Club director of responsible trade, argued that the TPP "could directly threaten our climate and our environment [including] new rights that would be given to corporations, and new constraints on the fossil fuel industry all have a huge impact on our climate, water, and land." Upon the publication of a complete draft of the Environment Chapter and the corresponding Chairs' Report by Wikileaks in January 2014, the Natural Resources Defense Council and the World Wide Fund for Nature joined with the Sierra Club in criticizing the TPP. Julian Assange described the Environment Chapter as "a toothless public relations exercise with no enforcement mechanism."

In January 2014 The Washington Post's Editorial Board has opined that congressional sponsors of legislation to expedite approval of TPP in the U.S. have already included provisions to ensure that all TPP countries meet international labor and environmental standards, and that the U.S. "has been made more productive by broader international competition and more secure by broader international prosperity".

On 5 March 2012, a group of TPP protesters disrupted an outside broadcast of 7News Melbourne's 6pm bulletin in Melbourne, Australia's Federation Square venue. In New Zealand, a coalition of people concerned about the TPP formed an protest group called "It's Our Future "that aimed to raise public awareness prior to the Auckland round of negotiations, which occurred from 3 to 12 December 2012.During the Auckland round of negotiations, hundreds of protesters clashed with police outside the conference venue and lit a fire in the streets.

March 2013 four thousand Japanese farmers held a protest in Tokyo worried that cheap imports could severely damage the local agriculture industry.

Malaysian protesters dressed as zombies outside a shopping mall in Kuala Lumpur on 21 February 2014 to protest the impact of the TPP on the price of medicines, including treatment drugs for HIV. The protest group consisted of students, members of the Malaysian AIDS Council, as well as HIV-positive patients, with one patient explaining that, in Malaysian ringgit, he spent between RM500 and RM600 each month on treatment drugs, but this cost would increase to around RM3,000.

On 29 March 2014 fifteen protests took place across New Zealand against the TPP including a demonstration in Auckland of several thousand people. In a press release announcing the decision of the New Zealand Nurses Association's decision to join the protests, its policy analyst stated that the TPP could prevent government decisions beneficial to public health because "if private investors, such as tobacco companies, were affected they could sue the government."

But all is not lost with this trade agreement. Members of Congress are starting to pay attention to the upcoming, secretly-negotiated Trans-Pacific Partnership (TPP) "trade" agreement that isn't really about trade. And the public is also becoming aware that this runaway job-loss express train is coming straight at us.

The TPP agreement is being negotiated — in secret, even from Congress — between representatives of governments and giant, multinational corporations. (Government negotiators are not prevented from seeking lucrative corporate jobs if negotiations are completed in favor of those corporations.) Groups representing the interests of labor, environmental, consumer, human rights or other stakeholders in democracy are not at the negotiating table. And, not surprisingly, it appears that the agreement will promote the interests of giant, multinational corporations over the interests of labor, environmental, consumer, human rights or other stakeholders in democracy.

Negotiated in secret, what we know about the treaty comes from leaks. Only a few of the "chapters" of the agreement are actually about "trade" at all. The rest are about the "rights" of corporations and investors. Negotiated just as the worldwide democracy uprising threatens to reign in corporate interests, the agreement will limit governments' ability to write banking regulations, energy policy, food safety standards and even government purchasing decisions. It will allow corporations and investors to sue governments for lost profits if the governments try to make and enforce environmental, labor and other laws.

 The corporations are asking Congress to pass "Fast Track" Trade Promotion Authority. This would mean Congress yields its authority and duties under the Constitution, and just has a rushed up-or-down vote on whatever is presented to them. So this will be about which legislators the giant corporations own, and which they do not. (Of course this vote will occur during a major corporate-funded PR campaign that will rival the propaganda "run-up" to the Iraq war vote.)

Some members of Congress are circulating letters opposing "Fast Track" Trade Promotion Authority and are getting plenty of signatures from the "left" and the "right."

 Last week conservative House Republicans Michele Bachmann and Walter Jones joined Democratic Rep. Rosa DeLauro began gathering signatures of both Democratic and Republican members of Congress on letters opposing granting "Fast Track" Trade Promotion Authority. They complain that Congress has not played their Constitutionally-mandated part in shaping this deal, and Fast Track removes their Constitutional authority to review and amend any such agreement.

 In June 2/3 of newly-elected Democratic members of Congress warned against passing "Fast Track." Also in June 230 members of Congress signed a letter asking that TPP address currency manipulation.

 Last year many members of Congress signed letters objecting to the secrecy of the negotiations.

 Representative Alan Grayson has been all over this. he has penned posts, held meetings, sent emails, done radio show, and all kinds of other things to warn the public and rally opposition to TPP.

This public is slowly becoming aware of TPP and the threat it poses. (Corporate media is, of course, not covering this.) Last Saturday, for example, hundreds of people gathered at a rally in Madison Wisconsin to show their disapproval of TPP.

At the rally people chanted, "Secrets, secrets are no fun! TPP hurts everyone!"

Interestingly, those parts of the Tea Party that are not fronts for corporate interests are also trying to spread the news about this treaty. Got to give them credit, their radar is really catching this one.

Interestingly, those parts of the Tea Party that are not fronts for corporate interests are also trying to spread the news about this treaty. Got to give them credit, their radar is really catching this one.

Tea-Party concerns include the fact that the treaty would elevate a corporate-council above American sovereignty, and Fast-Track Trade Promotion Authority would strip Congress of its Constitutional role in shaping and approving the treaty.

One of the most interesting things about the TPP, NAFTA, GATT, and CAFTA is that if one of the signatory countries feels that they have been wronged by another signatory country, they can bring them before the WTO (World Trade Organization) for not playing by the rules of these agreements. One such incidents which recently happened was when the United States brought China before the WTO for illegally dumping tires on the U.S. market, undercutting U.S. tire manufacturers. Big deal. China paid a fine to the United States. Nothing more. Just a slap on the wrist. Isn't free trade fun?

However, upon the election of Donald Trump to the Presidency, he unilaterally withdrew the United States from The T.P.P., stating that this particular trade agreement was "bad for America," and he "was committed to bringing American jobs back home.

Few Americans are alive who can remember the last time that the fruits of both work and labor were distributed so unevenly, and when inequality was rising so quickly and so relentlessly. That time was the 1920s. And for those of us who are students of history know what happened and what will happen again if we continue this relentless pursuit of profits over people. I am reminded of what Ebenezer Scrooge said in the classic, *A Christmas* Carol,

"Have we no poorhouses," and "Let them die and decrease the surplus population." I feel that over the past 30 years, we have become more Dickensian in our thinking and more Orwellian in our treatment towards those who have found themselves on the short end of the economic stick. I wonder if we can continue to be so heartless.

Immediately after World War I, America was tired of the restrictions the war had placed upon American society. It also wanted nothing to do with Europe. It wanted to go back to the "good old days." So they elected a Republican, Warren G. Harding and a Republican Congress. They first thing they do, was to cut the taxes on the wealthiest Americans. This triggered a decade of speculation in the stock market, which continued through the Presidencies of both Calvin Coolidge and Herbert Hoover. It was Coolidge who made the statement that, "The business of America is business." Hoover had the infamous distinction of being President in October 1929, when the whole decade in which America was asleep finally got its wake-up call. The stock market crash which triggered The Great Depression. Of course, Hoover was either an ardent optimist, or completely oblivious to the fact that laissez faire Capitalism didn't self-correct. He constantly kept telling the American people that, "Prosperity was just around the corner." Unfortunately, prosperity never came, not without serious financial and social reforms, reforms these same Republicans are fighting to do away with. And we are relating the same behaviors today.

So what is there game plan now? You wish to destroy the middle-class? Breaking the unions. Once you break the unions, as it has been done in Right to Work States and during so many labor disputes where the companies locked out their employees and refused to bargain in good faith, unorganized labor would quickly fall into a passive place in their respective workplaces. A recent prime example of this was Hostess Bakeries. Everyone knows about Hostess, the makers of Twinkies. Hostess was a union shop, but it's executives during negotiations with its union workforce was given an ultimatum, either give us massive concessions in wages and benefits or they would shut the plants down. The unions refused to concede and Hostess declared bankruptcy. In doing so, the company's pension plans are raided to fund golden parachutes for the uppermost executives of the company.

Another way to destroy the middle-class is to destroy the American public education system. Recently, the American educational system has come under attack because students are not measuring up to standardized test scores. WHAT THE FUCK? Do the politicians neither realize nor understand that some students do not have stable enough home environments to carry on what is carried on in the classroom? Or do they not realize that some children are raised in single parent homes in which the parent has to work (and take time away from the child) in order to foster a learning environment? I consider myself lucky as I was raised in a two parent home, although my father mostly worked away from home with his job as a Railroad Engineer. But he had a dream and a goal that both his children get a college education so they never had to work physical labor as hard as he had to do. Both my sister and I are college graduates, and our children have either graduated college or are working on either trade or college degrees. My family, as my dad and mom instilled in us, a belief that education is a ticket to better jobs and upward mobility. Now, this absolutely drives the elites insane and frustrates their eventual plans to control the entire game. Now, before you dismiss me as a conspiracy theory crackpot, think about this, when it comes the budget cuts at the state level, where is usually want to cut education, but never corrections nor law enforcement. Of course, politicians want to get re-elected, and the quickest way to get re-elected is to play to the populace's fears. And crime pretty much hits home (think Maslow's Hierarchy of Needs base, Safety and Security.) To hell with fancy learnin', the gubment coming to take our guns and then they are goin' to send us to them thar FEMA Camps. Or at least that's what those pin headed bastards in the right wing media hate machine would have the American people believe. And a lot of them eat it up like a pig eating slop. We are now so focused upon the "God, Guns, and Gays" narrative, that we are sufficiently distracted from the economic issues which, in my humble opinion, is far more critical, than any moral issue which might be around in our society.

Union membership had been declining in the US since 1954, and since 1967, as union membership rates decreased, middle class incomes shrank correspondingly. In 2007, the labor department reported the first increase in union memberships in 25 years and the largest increase since 1979. Most of the recent gains in union membership have been in the service sector while the number of unionized employees in the manufacturing sector has declined. Most of the gains in the service sector have come in West Coast states like California where union membership is now at 16.7% compared with a national average of about 12.1%. Historically, the rapid growth of public employee unions since the 1960s has served to mask an even more dramatic decline in private-sector union membership.

At the apex of union density in the 1940s, only about 9.8% of public employees were represented by unions, while 33.9% of private, non-agricultural workers had such representation. In this decade, those proportions have essentially reversed, with 36% of public workers being represented by unions while private sector union density had plummeted to around 7%. The US Bureau of Labor Statistics most recent survey indicates that union membership in the US has risen to 12.4% of all workers, from 12.1% in 2007. For a short period, private sector union membership rebounded, increasing from 7.5% in 2007 to 7.6% in 2008.[37] However, that trend has since reversed. In 2013 there were 14.5 million members in the U.S., compared with 17.7 million in 1983. In 2013, the percentage of workers belonging to a union was 11.3%, compared to 20.1% in 1983. The rate for the private sector was 6.7%, and for the public sector 35.3%.

In this new environment, unions are struggling. Although manufacturing workers have a long history of labor organizing, service sector workers such as restaurant and retail employees do not, making it harder for service employee unions to grow. Moreover, globalization, technological changes, and the spread of flexible work arrangements have combined to enable employers to make an end run around unions by moving jobs to countries or parts of the United States where anti-union attitudes and laws predominate. As a consequence of these developments, union membership has steadily declined. In 1954, at the peak of union membership, 28 percent of employed workers were in unions. By 1983, only 20 percent of workers were union members. In 2012, union membership reached a historical low, with membership comprising only 11 percent of American workers. Among full-time workers, the median weekly earnings for union members is $943, while among nonunion workers the median weekly earnings are $742. The decline of unions has severely curtailed and diminished workers' ability to collectively bargain to maintain high wages and good benefits, indirectly fueling a steady decline in the value of the minimum wage. Moreover, the decline of unions has eroded a broader moral commitment to fair pay, which even nonunion workers previously benefited from.

Together, the rise of the service economy, globalization, the decline of unions, and the erosion of the old work contract between employers and employees have created a precarious work environment for more and more Americans. Between the 1980s and 2004, more than 30 million full-time workers lost their jobs involuntarily. And during the Great Recession of 2008–2009, another 8.9 million jobs were lost. In the past few years, long-term unemployment has reached levels not seen since the government began monitoring rates of joblessness after World War II.

Imagine, if you will, the downsized of America's workers posed shoulder to shoulder for an annual portrait, sort of a dysfunctional class portrait. Mostly young, male, blue-collar workers dominated the portraits in the late 1970s and 1980s. Today, more and more white collar people stare out from every row. Women have joined the ranks and there are more splashes of gray than before. Far more are dressed for office work than factory work.

Corporate downsizing is nothing new to the business world. Employment in the auto, steel and construction industries always rose and fell due to the cyclic nature of the economy. However, those individuals worked in those industries, learned to expect the "lean times" and plan for them accordingly. Of course, by in those days, one just had to wait by the phone and as soon as things picked back up, you went back to work. However, when the 1970s rolled around, America businesses found themselves competing for market share against companies from Japan and Germany, which had cheaper products and better quality than those made by domestic producers. This and combined with the fact that American manufacturing decided on a course of "planned obsolescence" for their products in an effort to get American consumers to purchase more of their products more often, hence the beginning of our "disposable society." Our businesses were forced to restructure. Since the end of World War II until the 1970s, the middle class in this country had been asleep in the American Dream, a nice home in the suburbs, a secure job, a raise every year, and a pension in which they could live out their golden years in exchange for 8 hours a day for 35 years. This, for almost 30 years, was an unwritten social contract between American workers and businesses, and the businesses hated being forced into this contract. This is something both corporate and the Republicans have dreamt of ever since the Social Security Act was passed. Since then, both parties have desired to shrink the size of government down, as it was becoming too large and it started to interfere with their version of Capitalism.

Most business attempted to adapt to the new world of global competition by applying one of more fundamental strategies. The first, was technology. Up until then there was a lot of fears concerning technology, then known as "automation." But with the advent of the silicon chip, computers shrunk from the size of a large room to a desk top to now most functions can be performed on our cell phones. However, during the 1970's, reality finally came to bear. In order to remain competitive, U.S. companies were going to have to use technology in some form. All of the sudden, jobs which were done by humans were now done either by computers or by robots. A prime example of this is General Motors, which in the early 1970s employed as many as 500,000 people. Today, GM, can manufacture just as many cars and trucks, with better quality, with less than 300,000 employees. Of course, heavy industry is not the only sector of the economy to downsized as a result of the use of technology. As computers entered the banking industry, every ATM installed did away with the jobs of three bank tellers.

The second strategy, which I have already touched on, was out-sourcing, both off-shoring for the cheaper labor and less restrictions on their business operations. At one point, businesses also contracted with specialists domestically who could do the job cheaper. Manpower, during the 1990's, surpassed General Motors as America's largest employer due to the fact that the temporary employment industry suddenly exploded as corporations attempted to mitigate the expense of full time employees. In the wonderful world of the "temp," benefits were rare and job security was practically non-existent. Not only were pay benefits rare in this new employment world, but high wages are GONE as well. When high wage manufacturing, technical or managerial jobs are eliminated, it is usually replaced by positions which pay fifty to seventy-five percent less. Oh, and America's largest employer at the time of this book's writing? Wal-Mart. Which is notorious for paying its employees low wages.

I recall a saying made by some who said you can tell a lot about a society by how it treats its most disadvantaged. If we apply that to Victorian England, they failed miserably. And if look at this country, we did pretty well up until the 1980s, then we started an all-out class warfare when the middle-class was pitted against the poor. And while the middle-class was so focused on how bad the poor was taking advantage of the system; the elites and corporations were given free rein to pillage the middle-class. Of course, you might think I am beating a dead horse here, but this message cannot be stressed enough. The American way of life is being threatened. Not only for our children, but for every future generation which follows. If things continue at the rate they are going, America is going to develop into a country much like the counties of South or Central America. A small group of rich and powerful elites who are well connected both economically as well as politically, and the balance of the population who lives day to day hanging on the edge of survival, with death from starvation and disease an ever present reality.

The importance of high paying wages cannot be overstated. When Henry Ford instituted the Five Dollar day in his automotive plants in 1914, it was not because of his concern for his fellow man nor his philanthropy. Ford recognized early on what would eventually become an accepted American economic principle; that the great industrialists could only profit from their investments in capital utilizing mass production only if the masses had enough money to buy Tin Lizzies and other goods. These wages would go onto form the basis for the American middle class whose purchasing power would fuel the engine of American economic growth.

Anyone earning a paycheck knows that raises are rare these days. But a paper released Wednesday shows that not only are wages flat from before the recession — they're falling.

Real hourly wages are down for workers at all education levels in the first half of this year compared to the first half of 2013, according to the Economic Policy Institute paper. Pay fell by 1.1 percent for people with high school diplomas, by 1 percent for people with some college, 1.6 percent for people with college degrees and by 2.7 percent for people with advanced degrees. "The last year has been a poor one for American workers' wages," writes Elise Gould, an economist with the institute, in the report.

Gould notes the pay decreases seen over the last year are part of a longer trend: Wages have pretty much been flat or on the decline since the start of the recession. In fact, the only group that hasn't seen a drop in real wages since 2007 is workers with advanced degrees, for which wages are basically flat.

Real hourly wages fell for almost all other workers — even for those with a college degree– between 2007 and 2014, according to the report. People with advanced degrees saw wages grow by 0.2 percent. Meanwhile, wages fell by 2.5 percent for people with college degrees and dropped by nearly 5 percent for people with high school diplomas.

The pay gap between workers at different education levels is widening, but Gould says the reason that's happening is problematic. It's not that the most skilled and most in-demand workers are being paid more, which would happen if companies were competing to hire highly skilled workers. Instead, everyone else is being paid less. (A paper released by the Federal Reserve Bank of St. Louis in July came to a similar conclusion.)

The same holds true when you look back over the past decade: People with college degrees and people with advanced degrees are making more than they did in 2000, while workers at all other levels of education are making less. Oddly enough, people with some college, meaning they started college but didn't graduate, are actually worse off than people who only have high school diplomas.

Gould says the bigger issue is that wages are not keeping up with increases in productivity. While workers have often been asked to do more after companies downsized during the recession, they still aren't getting paid much more for their labor.

The unemployment rate is down, but more people who want full-time work are settling for part-time jobs or giving up all together. "When there's a line of workers looking for a job, it's hard for workers to successfully negotiate for higher wages," Gould said. "Employers are really holding all the cards in terms of bargaining for wages."

Of course, that doesn't mean that individual workers have gone without a raise since 2007, only that on average, workers in those groups haven't made much progress in terms of pay. And even if real wages are down over the past several years, people with college degrees and graduate degrees still earn more, on average, than people without them.

There is a lobbyist in Washington right now, Grover Norquist, who through his group, Americans for Tax Reform, made the statement that he wanted nothing less than to shrink the size of government so small, "he could drown it in a bathtub." While his intentions may be well meaning, he ignores one of the basic tenets of government, that is to promoting the general welfare. In my opinion, the general welfare includes things like occupational and mine health and safety, environmental safety, clean air and water regulation, and transportation safety. It also should include money for the upkeep of our infrastructure, our schools, roads, bridges and rails as well as now the internet. Why, you might ask? Because the government can and does, even with all its faults and inefficiencies, does not have the incentive of the profit motive hanging over its head during the decision-making process. Again, I want to emphasize I am not non-profit nor anti-business. What I am is anti-Predatory business, and its practices.

And if you would like to add insult to injury, this past Labor Day, A conservative think tank is protesting the federal Labor Day holiday by staging a work-in on Monday in a gambit to celebrate "the freedom to keep your job when you choose not to join a union."

"We're calling it Right-to-Work Day," Tom McCabe, CEO of Washington state's Freedom Foundation, announced in a post on the organization's website. The name refers to an effort by conservative lawmakers across the country to advance so-called "right-to-work" legislation that would allow union members to opt out of paying union dues while still benefiting from union contracts.

"At the Freedom Foundation, we celebrate freedom of choice and transparency – ideals the labor movement has vowed to oppose. Consequently, we've chosen to spend our holiday honoring the right-to-work movement instead," the post says. McCabe goes on to argue that all problems in society can be "traced in some way back to the abuses of organized labor."

But according to research from the Economic Policy Institute, right-to-work laws — which have the impact of weakening unions and lowering union membership — have almost no impact on job growth and actually reduce wages for union and non-union workers by up to $1,500 a year. Workers are also less likely to receive "healthcare or pensions through their jobs" and are hurt on the job with greater frequency. "For instance, the occupational-fatality rate in the construction industry—one of the most hazardous in terms of workplace deaths—is 34 percent higher in right-to-work states than in states without such laws," David Madland, Director of the American Worker Project at the Center for American Progress Action Fund, notes.

Labor Day became a national holiday in 1894, after U.S. marshals killed two men in the ill-fated Pullman Strike, a railroad workers' boycott against high rent and low pay. Government violence against the labor movement became a major political issue and "in the immediate wake of the strike, legislation was rushed unanimously through both houses of Congress, and the bill arrived on President [Grover] Cleveland's desk just six days after his troops had broken the Pullman strike." In the succeeding years, labor unions built political momentum to pass the Fair Labor Standards Act, which helped create a federal framework for a shorter workweek, helped end child labor, and worked to negotiate for health coverage plans from employers.

Though unionization rates have been in decline for years, a recent analysis of Census data by the Center for American Progress, found that middle class Americans bring home a larger share of aggregate earnings in states that have high rates of union membership than in those where fewer workers are organized.

CHAPTER 5

So why is it the everyone suddenly deciding to look upon poor and long-term unemployed peoples with such disdain? It all goes back to the foundation of this country and the "Puritan work ethic." Americans in this country are notorious workaholics. Every bit of our society, from the moment we enter public education, through college, through graduate school, and as we enter and progress up the work ladder, we are literally pressured by teachers, professors, supervisors, and managers to sacrifice time, time with our loved ones, time with our parents, spouse, life partner, children, anyone who is significant in our lives to our employer. We've all done it at least once, some of us never learn the lesson. I learned mine the hard way. By getting injured on the job. Nothing gets you to go from rising star to *persona non grata* faster, especially when you work for a small business. But I digress. Employers also expect you to work long hours, weekends, even sacrifice your vacations all for the good of the company. An estimated 22 million Americans (20.5 per cent of the workforce) report working 49 hours a week. An additional 11.5 per cent report working 50 or more hours a week.

America is also the only industrialized country which does not have mandated vacations or sick leave. The average work week in the European Union is 32 hours. Of course, Americans are the first ones to call Europeans "lazy" and "shiftless." When in comparison Europeans are by in large, healthier, more productive, as well as happier. They also do not consult mental health treatment services as Americans do, nor are they prescribed anti-depressives or anti-anxiety medications as Americans are. To put it bluntly, Americans are as us clinicians put it, "a hot mess." And we pass that need to excel on to the next generation, not only do we expect our children to excel at school, but athletics, dance, piano, or whatever other extra-curricular activities their parents decide to drag them. They don't get to enjoy the one thing they have going for them: their childhood. Too soon our youth are expected to grown-up and become "miniature adults" way before their time.

I know right after my grandson was born, we automatically started planning his future. Especially what college he would attend. My God, the boy had not had his first shit yet and we already had him going to Harvard. But, being good grandparents, we bought him educational toys, age appropriate books and worked with him as soon as he started talking.

Naturally, hard work paid off, that and the fact was blessed with both his mother's and grandfather's genes, and was blessed with above average intelligence. But the little fellow is going to need much more than quick wit and a strong work ethic. He will also be competing with others in other countries for jobs in the "new" economy. Unfortunately, by the time my grandson reaches working age, unless something is done to stem the rising costs of both higher education as well as trade school, the aspects of training beyond high school will be beyond both him and most middle class families.

Unfortunately, he will also have to deal with something that we all currently have to deal with, the hard reality of income insecurity. It was Alan Greenspan, the former Chairman of the Federal Reserve who championed this ideal. He was quoted, "If workers are more insecure, that's very healthy for society, because if workers are insecure they won't ask for wages, they won't go on strikeouts won't call for benefits; they'll serve their masters gladly and passively. And that's optimal for corporations. What the fuck? Did he really get away with saying that? Why wasn't this reported? Simple. Because each of the major news outlets are owned by, you guessed it, major corporations. So they are not going to offend their corporate masters. And he was given the Presidential Medal of Freedom.

In 1913, both when the Federal Reserve was created and the income tax was instituted, J.P. Morgan, probably the most influential banker of the time, made the statement that with the passage of these two acts, "he now controlled the wealth of the country." Scary thought, isn't it? That a very few individuals control our money supply. To this day, Wall Street and Corporations have a major influence in the direction of American life and politics. One has to only look to recent Supreme Court decisions which equate money with free speech to understand that corporations and the very wealthy desire to spend enormous amounts of money in an effort to influence the political process. This is nothing new. However, we now have folks that the elite in this country and even the world is conspiring to make us all wage slaves. I do not believe that it is a conspiracy, but more of a consensus. A consensus that they are only are worthy of getting and keeping wealth. That we are the "great unwashed," unfit for anything other than assisting them in accumulating more wealth. I do not mean to sound so negative, but as it stands right now, twenty-four states have "right to work" laws, which prohibit agreements between labor unions and employers.

While labor statistics show that from 1980 to 2011, right to work states showed a 71% increase in employment compared to non-right to work States, they also have 3.2% lower wages, 2.6% lower employer sponsored health insurance plans as well as 4.8% lower employer sponsored pension plans. In other words, while people stand a better chance of getting a job in a right to work state, they WILL make less money, get less benefits, and receive a lower pension than their non RTW counterparts. But this RTW push has been the work of Republican state legislators. The most recent being the state of Michigan. Michigan, former home of the American automotive industry, and do NOT get me started about the city of Detroit, a city which was forced into bankruptcy because of the Wall Street bankers demands. One of the worst parts of this was the city was trying to shut off the water of the poor citizens while large businesses where allowed to use the water gratis.

Have you noticed a pattern yet? Economic inequality is becoming a very important issue in this country. And with every election, the issue becomes more apparent. But every time it is brought up for discussion, the business community as well as both conservative and libertarian forces in this country scream that it is "class warfare." How is it class warfare when we have children in this country going to bed hungry? Or we have such a clear racial divide between African-Americans and whites? Why do we talk about immigration reform one minute and then the next minute hire day workers or Latinos to work as housekeepers or lawn care workers? Tell me we don't have class differences in this country. Of course we do. The most endangered class in this country is, without question, the middle class, but the question is what is the middle-class? It is this ambiguity which makes a lot of people want to believe they are middle-class. By definition, middle-class, is anyone making between $25,000 to $100,000. It is then divided into three clear sub-divisions: The professional/managerial class, the lower middle-class, and the working class majority. Some studies have shown that 53% of Americans belong to the working middle-class. Now do you see why it is so very important to fight for the shrinking middle class? According to most modern theories of political economy, a large middle-class is a beneficial, stabilizing force in society as it doesn't have the explosive revolutionary tendencies of the lower classes nor the absolutist tendencies of the elites. In other words, the middle-class is the glue which holds our nation together, destroy it, and our country falls apart.

One aspect of the middle-class is conspicuous consumption. To this day, the upper middle-class in the United States holds the world record for having the largest homes, most appliances and most automobiles. Yet the same corporatist hell-bent on destroying the middle-class and definitely against raising the standard of living of millions of working poor in this country by raising the minimum wage still want these same people to continue consuming at the same rate(s despite lower wages or, in some cases, reduced purchasing power. This is the disconnect that the very wealthy have with the middle-class. They do not want them to achieve neither a comfortable standard of living nor have them attain their level of wealth. But such is the nature of Capitalism. It is highly competitive, almost cut throat. I have noticed over the years that people are increasingly angry. They are frustrated and upset. You can see it in their faces, their behaviors, how they act and interact with others. Are the angry at themselves? Or are they angry with their lives. Let's face it, going to work forty, fifty, sixty hours a week, sacrificing time away from home, family, and loved ones only to get a measly paycheck which is usually spent before we even get it home usually would piss off the most laid back of any of us. And our consumer driven culture does not help either. We are bombarded from the moment we wake up in the morning until the minute we go to bed how if we do not wear this brand of clothing or drive this particular brand of automobile we are not considered successful. We are a very vain culture. Our culture is one which worships both youth and beauty. In our culture, once a worker reaches a certain age, in the new economy, due to the costs associated with older workers are usually the first ones shown the door. But it is never told because of their age, naturally. Their jobs are usually bought out for pennies on the dollar or they are "let go" just prior for them to prior to them collecting their retirement. Just so the corporations can save a few measly bucks on the bottom line. Does this not piss anyone off as much as it does me? Or am I the only one here playing attention?

Therefore, the destruction of the American middle and working classes may eventually bring about the eventual collapse of American society.

But it is true that America has a deficit of workers. Willing workers. Capable workers. Skilled, or at least semi-skilled workers, who can do a job and do it well. There are at least one million jobs that go begging day after day if only employers could find workers to fill them.

This probably seems hard-to-believe. After all, how can America have a worker shortage when we have about 18 million Americans who are unemployed or underemployed? When the real unemployment rate is 12 percent?

What the fuck, Dwayne? You been preaching for the past twenty some pages as to how bad things are, and now you say we have a deficit of workers? I am right on both counts due to the fact that we for the past have been putting all our eggs in the college education basket. Parents, teachers, and guidance counselors have been selling every student who walked through their doors that they had to going to college or they would not amount to shit. And boy did we fall for it. Hook, line, and sinker. So off we went to college, studied hard and graduated with a degree and a mountain of student loan debt. I count myself as lucky. I was able to work 16 years in a very rewarding career helping people in a lot of different settings. But graduates now do not have the same opportunities, unless they get advanced degrees. We are now paying a huge price for not spending more money on vocational education in this country. Of course, nobody wanted to get their hands dirty for years except the uneducated. But now they have retired, and no one thought far enough ahead as to who was going to step into those jobs in the future. Well, the future is now.

But there are also millions of unemployed Americans who don't have the skill sets to match what employers are in need of. To make matters worse, a lot of these frustrated job searchers have college degrees that are about as marketable as the paper diploma they are written on.

So what kind of jobs are going unfilled?

* Manufacturing – We always hear we are losing good manufacturing jobs in America and those bedrock middle class jobs aren't coming back. Gregory Baise, the president of the Illinois Manufacturing Association, tells me that there are "some 500,000 jobs we can't fill. It's the biggest problem our industry faces.". The industry needs welders, pipefitters, electricians, engineers. It needs people skilled in robotics and basic engineering.

* Trucking – At any time over the last several years there have been about 30,000 too few truckers to run long haul routes. The American Trucking Association tells me the number could be closer to 50,000. This is admittedly a tough and high-stress job with lots of time away from friends and family. But they are jobs that pay $50,000 and up, and a lot more than that with overtime.

* Energy – Bloomberg reports that "Gulf Coast oil, gas and chemical companies will have to find 36,000 new qualified workers" by 2016. Many energy towns have unemployment rates of less than 3 percent – in other words, there's a worker shortage.

These aren't menial or "dead end" jobs. They typically pay between $50,000 and $90,000 a year and with benefits the compensation can climb to $100,000. That's rich in most nations.

Bob Funk, CEO of Express Employment Professionals, one of the nation's largest temporary employment agencies located in Oklahoma City, places more Americans into jobs than just about anyone. With nearly half-a million hires a year he tells me, he can find a job for "any American with a strong work ethic and can pass a drug test." He also estimates that the worker shortage – those with skills to fill available jobs – "is at least one million and probably higher than that."

Why is it so hard to fill these jobs?

One reason is the curse of the so-called "skills mismatch." American workers with high school or even college degrees just aren't technically qualified to do the jobs that are open. This is a stunning indictment of our school system at all levels considering that all in parents and taxpayers often invest as much as $200,000 or more in a child's education. We're not turning our kids into competent workers.

Some governors like Mike Pence of Indiana have moved to make vocational education more standard in the Hoosier State. It's a great idea and it's a start.

But this won't solve the whole problem because many companies are already willing to offer 3 to 6 months on the job training for trucking and manufacturing jobs. They will teach them men and women how to operate the machinery, the computers, and the scientific equipment. These aren't sweatshop jobs.

Mr. Funk cites figures that more than half of the applicants for these kinds of jobs in the temporary job market can't pass a drug test. "They are unemployable in that case," he says regretfully.

Then there is the issue that these jobs don't get filled because the work lacks glitz and glamour.

Too many Americans have come to view blue collar jobs or skilled artisan jobs as beneath them.

Contributing to this attitude is the wide availability of unemployment insurance, food stamps, mortgage bailout funds and other welfare. Taking these taxpayer handouts is somehow seen as normal and a first, not a last resort. One owner of a major trucking company told me last year, "drivers who get laid off don't come back until their unemployment benefits run out." This is documented by research from my colleagues at the Heritage Foundation who have found that "4 million Americans laid off in the recession faced effective marginal tax rates near or above 100 percent [because of welfare benefits], significantly reducing their attachment to the labor market."

There's no doubt America needs millions of more jobs. But we could put one million more people in jobs tomorrow if we get schools to train our kids with core competencies and if we could instill in Americans an old-fashioned work ethic. The only dead-end job is no job at all.

CHAPTER 6

Ok, before we proceed any further in this book, and to give you the reader some insight into why I feel that my belief that there is a direct correlation between the declaration of war on organized labor and the decline of the middle-class, I need to give you a little history lesson. Unions began forming in the mid-19th century in response to the social and economic impact of the industrial revolution. National labor unions began to form in the post-Civil War Era. The Knights of Labor emerged as a major force in the late 1880s, but it collapsed because of poor organization, lack of effective leadership, disagreement over goals, and strong opposition from employers and government forces.

The American Federation of Labor, founded in 1886 and led by Samuel Gompers until his death in 1924, proved much more durable. It arose as a loose coalition of various local unions. It helped coordinate and support strikes and eventually became a major player in national politics, usually on the side of the Democrats.

American labor unions benefitted greatly from the New Deal policies of Franklin Delano Roosevelt in the 1930s. The Wagner Act, in particular, legally protected the right of unions to organize. Unions from this point developed increasingly closer ties to the Democratic Party, and are considered a backbone element of the New Deal Coalition.

Pro-business conservatives gained control of Congress in 1946, and in 1947 passed the Taft-Hartley Act, drafted by Senator Robert A. Taft. President Truman vetoed it but the Conservative coalition overrode the veto. The new law (still in effect today) banned union contributions to political candidates, restricted the power of unions to call strikes that "threatened national security," and forced the expulsion of Communist union leaders. The unions campaigned vigorously for years to repeal the law but failed. During the late 1950s, the Landrum Griffith Act of 1959 passed in the wake of Congressional investigations of corruption and undemocratic internal politics in the Teamsters and other unions.

The percentage of workers belonging to a union (or "density") in the United States peaked in 1954 at almost 35% and the total number of union members peaked in 1979 at an estimated 21.0 million. Membership has declined since (currently 14.5 million and 11.3% of the labor force). Private sector union membership then began a steady decline that continues into the 2010s, but the membership of public sector unions grew steadily (now 37%).

 After 1960 public sector unions grew rapidly and secured good wages and high pensions for their members. While manufacturing and farming steadily declined, state- and local-government employment quadrupled from 4 million workers in 1950 to 12 million in 1976 and 16.6 million in 2009. Adding in the 3.7 million federal civilian employees, in 2010 8.4 million government workers were represented by unions including 31% of federal workers, 35% of state workers and 46% of local workers. As Daniel DiSalvo notes, "In today's public sector, good pay, generous benefits, and job security make possible a stable middle-class existence for nearly everyone from janitors to jailors."

By the 1970s, a rapidly increasing flow of imports (such as automobiles, steel and electronics from Germany and Japan, and clothing and shoes from Asia) undercut American producers. By the 1980s there was a large-scale shift in employment with fewer workers in high-wage sectors and more in the low-wage sectors. Many companies closed or moved factories to Southern states (where unions were weak), countered the threat of a strike by threatening to close or move a plant, or moved their factories offshore to low-wage countries. The number of major strikes and lockouts fell by 97% from 381 in 1970 to 187 in 1980 to only 11 in 2010. On the political front, the shrinking unions lost influence in the Democratic Party, and pro-Union liberal Republicans faded away. Union membership among workers in private industry shrank dramatically, though after 1970 there was growth in employees' unions of federal, state and local governments. The intellectual mood in the 1970s and 1980s favored deregulation and free competition. Numerous industries were deregulated, including airlines, trucking, railroads and telephones, over the objections of the unions involved. The climax came when President Ronald Reagan—a former union president—broke the Professional Air Traffic Controllers Organization (PATCO) strike in 1981, dealing a major blow to unions.

Although most industrialized countries have seen a drop in unionization rates, the drop in union density (the unionized proportion of the working population) has been more significant in the United States than elsewhere. Dropping unionization rates cannot be attributed entirely to changing market structures. In fact, scholars have shown the tremendous complexity inherent in explaining the decline of union density.

Public approval of unions climbed during the 1980s much as it did in other industrialized nations but declined to below 50% for the first time in 2009 during the Great Recession. It is not clear if this is a long term trend or a function of a high unemployment rate which historically correlates with lower public approval of labor unions. Another factor argued by both sides is business interests and supporters work together to undermine, challenge and campaign against unions and the benefits by "corporatizing" its leadership by calling union leadership "bosses". Drawing parallels between what a worker views an employer or "boss" being responsible for a less than satisfactory work life and the union being equal partnership in that dissatisfaction, may contribute to loss of faith in unions.

 One explanation for loss of public support is simply the lack of union power or critical mass. No longer do a sizable percentage of American workers belong to unions, or have family members who do. Unions no longer carry the "threat effect": the power of unions to raise wages of non-union shops by virtue of the threat of unions to organize those shops.

 Republicans, using conservative think tanks as idea farms, began to push through legislative blueprints to curb the power of public employee unions as well as eliminate business regulations. Now, I'm not saying that conservatives are evil, just greedy. They have truly bought into the Capitalist message of, "I got mine, fuck you." And it appears that they will go to almost any length to ensure that their agenda is fulfilled. One of the biggest players in this arena is ALEC.

 So what is ALEC? ALEC is not a lobby; it is not a front group. It is much more powerful than that. Through the secretive meetings of the American Legislative Exchange Council, corporate lobbyists and state legislators vote as equals on 'model bills' to change our rights that often benefit the corporations' bottom line at public expense. ALEC is a pay-to-play operation where corporations buy a seat and a vote on 'task forces' to advance their legislative wish lists and can get a tax break for donations, effectively passing these lobbying costs on to taxpayers.

Along with legislators, corporations have membership in ALEC. Corporations sit on ALEC task forces and vote with legislators to approve "model" bills. They have their own corporate governing board which meets jointly with the legislative board. (ALEC says that corporations do not vote on the board.) Corporations fund almost all of ALEC's operations.

Participating legislators, overwhelmingly conservative Republicans, then bring those proposals home and introduce them in statehouses across the land as their own brilliant ideas and important public policy innovations—without disclosing that corporations crafted and voted on the bills.

1. ALEC boasts that it has over 1,000 of these bills introduced by legislative members every year, with one in every five of them enacted into law. ALEC describes itself as a "unique," "unparalleled" and "unmatched" organization. We agree. It is as if a state legislature had been reconstituted, yet corporations had pushed the people out the door.

More than 98% of ALEC's revenues come from sources other than legislative dues, such as corporations, corporate trade groups, and corporate foundations. Each corporate member pays an annual fee of between $7,000 and $25,000 a year, and if a corporation participates in any of the nine task forces, additional fees apply, from $2,500 to $10,000 each year. ALEC also receives direct grants

from corporations, such as $1.4 million from ExxonMobil from 1998-2009. It has also received grants from some of the biggest foundations funded by corporate CEOs in the country, such as: the Koch family Charles G. Koch Foundation, the Koch-managed Claude R. Lambe Foundation, the Scaife family Allegheny Foundation, the Coors family Castle Rock Foundation, to name a few. Less than 2% of ALEC's funding comes from "Membership Dues" of $50 per year paid by state legislators, a steeply discounted price that may run afoul of state gift bans. For more, see CMD's special report on ALEC funding and spending here.

ALEC describes itself as a non-partisan, non-profit organization. The facts show that it currently has one Democrat out of 104 legislators in leadership positions. ALEC members, speakers, alumni, and award winners are a "who's who" of the extreme right. ALEC has given awards to: Ronald Reagan, Margaret Thatcher, George H.W. Bush, Charles and David

Koch, Richard de Vos, Tommy Thompson, Gov. John Kasich, Gov. Rick Perry, Congressman Mark Foley (intern sex scandal), and Congressman Billy Tauzin. ALEC alumni include: Speaker of the House John Boehner, House Majority Leader Eric Cantor, Congressman Joe Wilson, (who called President Obama a "liar" during the State of the Union address), former House Speaker Dennis Hastert, former House Speaker Tom DeLay, Andrew Card, Donald Rumsfeld (1985 Chair of ALEC's Business Policy Board), Governor Scott Walker, Governor Jan Brewer, and more. Featured speakers have included: Milton Friedman, Newt Gingrich, Dick Cheney, Dan Quayle, George Allen, Jessie Helms, Pete Coors, Governor Mitch Daniels and more.

 The organization boasts 2,000 legislative members and 300 or more corporate members. The unelected corporate representatives (often registered lobbyists) sit as equals with elected representatives on nine task forces where they have a "voice and a vote" on model legislation. Corporations on ALEC task forces VOTE on the "model" bills and resolutions, and sit as equals with legislators voting on the ALEC task forces and various working groups. Corporate and legislative governing boards also meet jointly each year. (ALEC says only the legislators have a final say on all model bills. ALEC has previously said that "The policies are debated and voted on by all members. Public and private members vote separately on policy. It is important to note that laws are not passed, debated or adopted during this process and therefor no lobbying takes place. That process is done at the state legislature.") The long-term representation of Koch Industries on the governing board means that Koch has had influence over an untold number of ALEC bills. Due to the questionable nature of this partnership with corporations, legislators rarely discuss the origins of the model legislation they bring home. Though thousands of ALEC-approved model bills have been publicly introduced across the country, ALEC's role facilitating the language in the bills and the corporate vote for them is not well known.

(ALEC legislators sometimes compare the organization to the National Conference of State Legislators (NCSL), yet the two organizations could not be more different. NCSL has zero corporate members. It is funded largely by state government appropriations and conference fees; it has a truly bipartisan governance structure, and there is a large role for nonpartisan professional staff; it does not vote on or promote model legislation; meetings are public and so are any agreed upon documents. Corporations do sponsor receptions at NCSL events through a separate foundation. For more information, see the document ALEC & NCSL.)

Although ALEC claims to take an ideological stance (of supposedly "Jeffersonian principles of free markets, limited government, federalism, and individual liberty"), many of the model bills benefit the corporations whose agents write them, shape them, and/or vote to approve them. These are just a few such measures:

Altria/Philip Morris USA benefits from ALEC's newest tobacco legislation -- an extremely narrow tax break for moist tobacco that would make fruit flavored tobacco products cheaper and more attractive to youngsters.

Health insurance companies such as Humana and Golden Rule Insurance (United Healthcare), benefit directly from ALEC model bills, such as the Health Savings Account bill that just passed in Wisconsin.

Tobacco firms such as Reynolds and pharmaceutical firms such as Bayer benefit directly from ALEC tort reform measures that make it harder for Americans to sue when injured by dangerous products.

Corrections Corporation of America (CCA) benefits directly from the anti-immigrant legislation introduced in Arizona and other states that requires expanded incarceration and housing of immigrants, along with other bills from ALEC's crime task force. (While CCA has stated that it left ALEC in late 2010 after years of membership on the Criminal Justice Task Force and even co-chairing it, its prison privatization bills remain ALEC "models.")

Connections Academy, a large online education corporation and co-chair of the Education Task Force, benefits from ALEC measures to privatize public education and promote private on-line schools.

Why would a legislator be interested in advancing cookie-cutter bills that are corporate giveaways for global firms located outside of their district? ALEC's appeal rests largely on the fact that legislators receive an all-expenses-paid trip that provides many part-time legislators with vacations that they could not afford on their own, along with the opportunity to rub shoulders with wealthy captains of industry (major prospective out-of-state donors to their political campaigns). For a few hours of work on a task force and a couple of indoctrination sessions by ALEC experts, part-time legislators can bring the whole family to ALEC's annual convention, work for a few hours, then stay in swank hotels, attend cool parties -- even strip clubs-- and raise funds for the campaign coffer, all heavily subsidized by the corporate till. In 2009, ALEC spent $251,873 on childcare so mom and dad could have fun.

 In most ordinary people's view, handing bills to legislators so they can introduce them is the very definition of lobbying. ALEC says "no lobbying takes place." The current chairman of ALEC's corporate board is W. Preston Baldwin III, until recently a lobbyist and the Vice President of State Government Affairs at UST Inc., a tobacco firm now owned by Altria/Phillip Morris USA. Altria is advancing a very short, specific bill to change the way moist tobacco products (such as fruit flavored "snus") are taxed-- to make it cheaper and more attractive to young tobacco users according to health experts. In fact, 20 of the 24 corporate representatives on ALEC's "Private Enterprise Board" are lobbyists representing major firms such as Koch Industries, Bayer, GlaxoSmithKline, Wal-Mart and Johnson and Johnson.

ALEC makes old-fashioned lobbying obsolete. Once legislators return to their state with corporate-sponsored ALEC legislation in hand, the legislators themselves become "super-lobbyists" for ALEC's corporate agenda, cutting out the middleman. Yet ALEC enjoys a 501(c)(3) classification, which allows it to keep its tax-exempt status while accepting grants from foundations, corporations, and other donors. In our view, the activities that corporate members engage in should be considered lobbying by the IRS, and the entity that facilitates that effort to influence state law, ALEC, should also be considered to be engaged predominantly in lobby-related activities, not simply "educational" activities. Re-classifying ALEC as primarily engaged in lobbying facilitation would mean that donations to it would not count as tax-deductible for businesses and foundations. Common Cause filed a complaint with the IRS on July 14, 2011, setting forth evidence supporting its complaint that ALEC is engaged in lobbying despite its claims to do no lobbying.

ALEC's operating model raises many ethical and legal concerns. Each state has a different set of ethics laws or rules. The presence of lobbyists alone may cause ethics problems for some state legislators. Wisconsin, for instance, generally requires legislators who go to events with registered lobbyists to pay on their own dime, yet in many states, legislators use public funds to attend ALEC meetings. According to one study, $3 million in public funds was spent to attend ALEC meetings in one year. Some legislators use their personal funds and are reimbursed by ALEC. Such "scholarships" may be disclosed if gifts are required to be reported. But should the legislators be allowed to accept this money when lobbyists are present at the meeting? Still other legislators use their campaign funds to go and are again reimbursed by ALEC; in some states, campaign funds are only allowed to be used to attend campaign events.

In short, many state ethics codes might consider the free vacation, steeply discounted membership fees, free day care or travel scholarships to be "gifts" that should be disallowed or disclosed.

So where did ALEC come from, and how did it become so influential in the American politics?

ALEC was founded in 1973 in Chicago as the "Conservative Caucus of State Legislators", a project initiated by Mark Rhoads, an Illinois state house staffer, to counter the Environmental Protection Agency, wage and price controls, and the defeat of Barry Goldwater in the 1964 presidential election. Conservative legislators felt the word "conservative" was unpopular with the public at the time, however, and the organization was renamed as the American Legislative Exchange Council. In 1975, with the support of the American Conservative Union, ALEC registered as a federal non-profit agency. Bill Moyers and Greenpeace have attributed the establishment of ALEC to the influential Powell Memorandum, which led to the rise of a new business activist movement in the 1970s.

Conservative activist Paul Weyrich helped the new group find a meeting room. Henry Hyde, who later became a U.S. Congressman, and Lou Barnett, who later became National Political Director of Ronald Reagan's Political Action Committee, also helped to found ALEC. Early members included a number of state and local politicians who went on to statewide office, including Bob Kasten, Tommy Thompson, and Scott Walker of Wisconsin, John Engler of Michigan, Terry Branstad of Iowa, Mitch Daniels of Indiana, and John Boehner and John Kasich of Ohio. Several members of Congress were also involved in the organization during its early years, including Sen. John Buckley and Rep. Jack Kemp of New York, Sen. Jesse Helms of North Carolina, Rep. Phil Crane of Illinois, and Rep Eric Cantor of Virginia.

In the 1980s, ALEC opposed U.S. disinvestment from South Africa, a movement to put pressure on the South African government to embark on negotiations with a goal of dismantling of apartheid. In 1985, ALEC also published a memo that opposed "the current homosexual movement," portrayed homosexuality as a result of a conscious choice, and said that pedophilia was "one of the more dominant practices within the homosexual world".[25] After the memo was leaked in 2013, ALEC spokesman Bill Meierling said that ALEC does not draft model bills on social issues, and added, "I'm also sad that the critics would not acknowledge that organizations change over time.

Duane Parde served as the executive director from December 1996 to January 2006.[26] Lori Roman, who served in the same role from 2006 to 2008, had an imperious style that led to financial difficulties and the departure of two thirds of ALEC's staff. According to Dolores Mertz, then a Democratic Iowa state representative and chairwoman of the ALEC board, ALEC became increasingly partisan during that period, with Roman once telling Mertz "she didn't like Democrats and she wasn't going to work with them." The current executive director, Ron Scheberle, was named to the position in 2010 after acting as a lobbyist for Verizon Communications (previously GTE) and as an ALEC board member.

By 2011, the number of ALEC legislative members had reached 2,000, more than 25 percent of all state legislators nationwide. Approximately 1,000 bills based on ALEC language were being introduced in state legislatures every year, with about 20% of those bills being enacted.

In 2011, ALEC's influence was the subject of criticism among media outlets and political opponents who claimed it was secretly subverting democratic institutions to further the aims of its corporate benefactors. Responding to the criticism, ALEC senior director of membership and development Chaz Cirame said, "The hook about some conspiracy or some secret organization is a lot better story than one about bringing state legislators together to talk about best practices around the country." Oregon state representative and ALEC member Gene Whisnant said, "We're getting a lot of attention saying we're trying to destroy the earth and everything on it."

In 2011, University of Wisconsin professor and historian William Cronon created a blog during protests over the state's 2011 budget bill with an entry about the history of conservative groups, including ALEC, and alleging a link between that budget bill and ALEC. Cronon said that ALEC's activities should be examined more closely and that the organization should conduct its business with greater transparency. The blog received more than 500,000 hits, and protest signs asking about ALEC appeared at the Wisconsin State Capitol in Madison. ALEC denied such a link being behind such efforts. The Wisconsin Republican Party on March 17 made a request under Wisconsin's Open Records laws to obtain e-mail messages sent to or from Cronon's university account, and that of other apparent union supporters who are state employees, containing keywords related to various political issues that were being debated in Wisconsin at the time Paul Krugman and the American Historical Association defended Cronon against what they characterized as intimidation by Wisconsin Republicans. Mari Jo and Paul Buhle characterized the e-mail search request as an "overreaction" by Wisconsin Republicans in an attempt to hide their political connections to ALEC. Mary Bottari, deputy director of the Center for Media and Democracy, wrote a year later that Cronon's connection between Wisconsin Republicans and ALEC had been "upheld" by a report from ALEC Exposed which showed that an influential bloc of 49 of Wisconsin's 132 legislators were connected to ALEC.

In 2012, ALEC was the subject of an Occupy movement protest, an Internal Revenue Service complaint by Common Cause, and calls for investigations by several states' attorney generals.

As of December 2013, ALEC had 1,810 legislative members, as well as more than 85 members of Congress and 14 sitting or former governors who are considered "alumni". The vast majority of ALEC's legislative members belong to the Republican Party. ALEC says it also has approximately 300 corporate, foundation, and other private-sector members.[citation needed] The chairmanship of ALEC is a rotating position, with a new legislator appointed to the position each year. As of 2012, 28 out of 33 of its chairs had been Republicans. In 2013 the chair was John Piscopo, a Republican member of the Connecticut House of Representatives.

Day-to-day operations are run from ALEC's Arlington, Virginia, office by an executive director and a staff of approximately 30.ALEC By-Laws specify that, "...full membership shall be open to persons dedicated to the preservation of individual liberty, basic American values and institutions, productive free enterprise, and limited representative government, who support the purposes of ALEC, and who serve, or formerly serve, as members of a state or territorial legislature, the United States Congress, or similar bodies outside the United States."

In addition to the staff and members, ALEC has a "Board of Scholars" that advises and alerts the staff and members to upcoming issues. The board is composed of Arthur Laffer, an economist who served under Ronald Reagan's Economic Policy Advisory Board; Victor Schwartz, chair of Public Policy at Shook, Hardy & Bacon; Richard Vedder, economics professor emeritus at Ohio University and adjunct scholar at the American Enterprise Institute; and Bob Williams, founder of the Freedom Foundation.

ALEC is composed of nine "task forces": 1) Civil Justice; 2) Commerce, Insurance and Economic Development; 3) Communications and Technology; 4) Education; 5) Energy, Environment, and Agriculture; 6) Health and Human Services; 7) International Relations; 8) Justice Performance Project; and 9) Tax and Fiscal Policy. Public- and private-sector members make up each of the task forces—the public-sector members are state legislators and the private-sector members are typically corporate lobbyists or think-tank representatives. These task forces generate model bills which members can then customize for communities and introduce for debate in their own state legislatures. Reporter Alan Greenblatt wrote that private sector members have veto power over model bills drafted by the task forces.

ALEC's Public Safety and Elections Task Force, which promoted stand your ground gun laws and voter identification requirements, was disbanded in April 2012. Thereafter, the National

Center for Public Policy Research announced the creation of a voter ID task force to replace the one discontinued by ALEC.

ALEC also has ties to the State Policy Network (SPN), a national association of think-tanks. The SPN regularly sponsors annual meetings for ALEC, and a number of SPN's active affiliates are members of both organizations. Some of the think tanks in the SPN write model legislation, which is then introduced at ALEC's private meetings.

ALEC's website states that its goal is to advance "the fundamental principles of free-market enterprise, limited government, and federalism". In 2003, Donald Ray Kennard, then a Louisiana state representative and ALEC national chairman, said, "We are a very, very conservative organization...We're just espousing what we really believe in."[Craig Horn, a North Carolina state representative and ALEC member, said of ALEC in 2013, "It's a lightning rod organization because it has a decidedly conservative bent – there's no doubt about it."

Although ALEC originally focused on social issues such as abortion, which it opposed, in more recent years the group has focused more on business and regulatory matters. According to The Nation 's John Nichols, ALEC's agenda "seems to be dictated at almost every turn by multinational corporations. It's to clear the way for lower taxes, less regulation, a lot of protection against lawsuits, [and] ALEC is very, very active in [the] opening up of areas via privatization for corporations to make more money, particularly in places you might not usually expect like public education." A Brookings Institution study of state legislation introduced in 2011-2012 found that ALEC model bills that became law were most often linked to controversial social and economic issues. The study concluded that this phenomenon has hurt ALEC because, "Dirtying its hands with social issues undermines ALEC's ability to exercise influence over fiscal ones."

'Stand Your Ground' gun laws expanded to 30 states through the support of ALEC, after Florida passed its law in 2002.After the Florida law had been passed, ALEC adopted a model bill with the same wording.

On April 4, 2012, after the Trayvon Martin shooting, advocacy group Color of Change urged a boycott on The Coca-Cola Company for its support of ALEC and by implication, its involvement in Stand your Ground. Within hours, Coca-Cola announced it was ending its relationship with ALEC in apparent response to the threatened boycott. More than 60 corporations and foundations including Wendy's, Kraft Foods, McDonald's, Amazon.com, Coca-Cola, General Electric, Apple, Procter & Gamble, Walmart, the Bill & Melinda Gates Foundation, and the medical insurance group Blue Cross and Blue Shield dropped support of ALEC in the ensuing weeks or let their memberships lapse. ALEC responded with a "Statement by ALEC on the Coordinated Intimidation Campaign Against Its Members".

Prior to 2012, legislation based on ALEC models bills was introduced in many states to mandate or strengthen requirements that voters produce state-issued photo identification. The bills were passed and signed into law in six states.

The "Support Our Law Enforcement and Safe Neighborhoods Act", an Arizona law commonly known as "SB 1070", was drafted during an ALEC meeting in December 2009 and became an ALEC model bill. Enacted in 2010, SB 1070 was described as the toughest illegal immigration law in the U.S. Portions of SB 1070 were held by the Supreme Court to be preempted by federal law in 2012.

One of ALEC's model bills is the "Animal and Ecological Terrorism Act", which classifies certain property destruction, acts of intimidation, and civil disobedience by environmental and animal rights activists as terrorism. This model bill appeared across the U.S. in various forms since it was drafted in 2003. The federal "Animal Enterprise Terrorism Act" has notable similarities, and at points almost verbatim language, to ALEC's model "Animal and Ecological Terrorism Act." The Senate version of the "Animal Enterprise Terrorism Act" was sponsored by Senator James Inhofe, a long-time member of ALEC.

 Many ag-gag bills are also similar to ALEC's model "Animal and Ecological Terrorism Act", which would make it against the law to film, videotape, or take photographs on livestock farms in order to "defame the facility or its owner." People found to be in violation would be put in a "terrorist registry."

According to Governing magazine, "ALEC has been a major force behind both privatizing state prison space and keeping prisons filled." ALEC has developed model bills advancing "tough on crime" initiatives, including "truth in sentencing" and "three strikes" laws. Critics argue that by funding and participating in ALEC's Criminal Justice Task Forces, private prison companies directly influence legislation for tougher, longer sentences. Corrections Corporation of America and Wackenhut Corrections, two of the largest for-profit prison companies in the U.S. (as of 2004), have been contributors to the ALEC. ALEC has also worked to pass state laws to allow the creation of private-sector for-profit prisons.

ALEC pushed for deregulation of the electricity industry in the 1990s. Maneuvering between two private sector members, Enron, a former energy trader, and the Edison Electric Institute (EEI), a utilities trade association, led EEI to withdraw its ALEC membership. Enron's position on the matter was adopted by ALEC and subsequently by many state legislatures.

An April 2012 article in the New York Times stated that while ALEC legislation having to do with public "right to know" laws regarding what fluids are used in hydraulic fracturing (also known as "fracking") has been promoted as a victory for consumers' right to know about potential drinking water contaminants, the bill contains "loopholes that would allow energy companies to withhold the names of certain fluid contents, for reasons including that they have been deemed trade secrets."

ALEC has promoted a model bill that calls plans in 2011 by the federal Environmental Protection Agency to regulate greenhouse gas emissions a "train wreck" that would harm the economy, and has supported efforts by various states to withdraw from regional climate change compacts. ALEC has also promoted a model bill that would call on the federal government to approve the proposed Keystone XL project, which would extend a synthetic crude oil pipeline from oil sands in Alberta, Canada to Nebraska.

In December 2013, ALEC planned legislation that would weaken state clean energy regulations and penalize homeowners who install their own solar panels as "free riders".

ALEC supports deregulation of America's telecom system, and has worked with AT&T and Verizon to draft legislation on prohibiting public broadband services and "sunsetting" the Public Switched Telephone Network (PSTN).Names of its 172-member task force, agenda of a 12/2010 meeting and minutes including a resolution regarding traffic pumping have been published. In February 2014, Senate Bill 304 in Kansas was introduced, "prohibiting cities and counties from building public broadband networks and providing internet service to businesses and citizens". The bill contains an underserved area exemption for public wi-fi, but it is not met anywhere in Kansas. The city of Chanute, Kansas which has led broadband development since the 1980s, financed through its public electricity company, including free wi-fi in its college, hospital and public spaces, and a 4g mobile data network, feels under attack by the bill.

ALEC opposes the individual health insurance mandate enacted by the Patient Protection and Affordable Care Act (commonly known as the "ACA" or "Obamacare"). ALEC filed an amicus brief in National Federation of Independent Business v. Sebelius, urging the Supreme Court to strike down the ACA's individual mandate. In 2011 it published the "State Legislators Guide to Repealing ObamaCare," which has served as a roadmap for repeal efforts' has also drafted a variety of model bills designed to block the law's implementation.

 In August 2013, ALEC approved as a model bill the "Health Care Freedom Act", which would strip health insurers of their licenses to do business at the ACA's federal health care exchanges if they accepted any subsidies under the system. Sean Riley, the head of ALEC's Health and Human Services taskforce, said the aim of the proposed legislation was to protect businesses from the ACA's employer mandate.[9] Slate journalist David Weigel has called the bill a "sneak attack" on the ACA. Health insurance experts have predicted that if the bill were widely adopted by Republican-controlled states, it would seriously disrupt the exchange and threaten the ACA. Wendell Potter, former health insurance executive and CMD fellow, said, "You cannot build the healthcare system based on the free market unless you have subsidies. If they are taken away the whole thing collapses."

ALEC has worked to privatize public education. It frequently promotes model bills that expand public-private partnerships in education.

The level of influence ALEC's private-sector members hold over its public-sector members has been controversial. According to the New York Times, "special interests effectively turn ALEC's lawmaker members into stealth lobbyists, providing them with talking points, signaling how they should vote, and collaborating on bills affecting hundreds of issues like school vouchers and tobacco taxes. "The Free Lance-Star has reported that ALEC had "matured into one of Big Business's most effective lobbying tools. "Chris Taylor, a

Democratic Wisconsin state assemblyman who attended an ALEC conference in 2013, described ALEC as a "well-oiled machine" and said, "In my observation, it was the corporations and the right-wing think tanks driving the agendas. Corporations have as big a say as the legislators in the model legislation that is adopted."

ALEC legislative members generally deny being overly influenced by the organization or its model legislation. "ALEC is unique in the sense that it puts legislators and companies together and they create policy collectively," said Scott Pruitt, then an Oklahoma state representative and ALEC task force chair. Vance Wilkins, a former Republican speaker of the Virginia House of Delegates and ALEC member, said in 2002, "Just because business writes a bill doesn't make it bad. We get bills from all angles. And we still have to debate the issue. "Harvey Morgan, another former Virginia delegate and ALEC member, said of ALEC conferences, "You know before you go that the big-business view will prevail, and that's not necessarily bad. I still would like them to be a little more objective."

Experts agree that, regardless of its propriety, the ALEC model has been very effective. Alan Rosenthal, a former Rutgers University political science professor and expert on state legislatures and lobbying,[96] said of ALEC, "You've had the interest groups having access and sitting on other task forces, but here you've really perfected it.... You've not only got them gaining access and interacting with legislators but you have them shaping policy together. It seems to me that's a pretty major advance. "Edwin Bender, executive director of the nonpartisan National Institute on Money in State Politics, has said, "What makes ALEC different is its effectiveness in not just bringing the people together but selling a piece of legislation that was written by the industry and for the industry and selling it as a piece of mainstream legislation."

1. In April 2012, Common Cause filed a complaint with the Internal Revenue Service objecting to ALEC's tax status as a non-profit organization and alleged that lobbying accounted for more than 60% of its expenditures. ALEC formally denied lobbying, although Delores Mertz, who had previously served as chairwoman of the ALEC board, said she was "concerned about the lobbying that's going on, especially with [ALEC's] 501(c)3 status. "Reporting on the allegations, Bloomberg Businessweek compared ALEC's work to that of lobbyists, noting, "part of ALEC's mission is to present industry-backed legislation as grass-roots

work", and that being a non-profit rather than a lobby group allows deductibility of membership dues, and the freedom not to disclose the names of legislators who attend its educational seminars or the executives who give presentations to those legislators. William Schluter, vice chairman of the New Jersey Ethics Commission and a former Republican state senator, said of ALEC's activities, "When you get right down to it, this is not different from lobbying. It is lobbying. Any kind of large organization that adds to public policy or has initiatives involving public policy should be disclosed—not only their name, but who is backing them. "According to Governing magazine, ALEC legislators often have their travel expenses paid as "scholarships" and are "wined and dined and golf-coursed" by private sector members. In July 2013 Common Cause submitted a supplemental brief to the IRS complaining about these practices.

 ALEC responded to the original Common Cause complaint by denying it engaged in lobbying, while saying that liberal groups were attacking ALEC because "they don't have a comparable group that is as effective as ALEC in enacting policies into law." In 2013 ALEC created a 501(c)(4) organization called the "Jeffersonian Project" that, according to The Guardian, "would allow Alec to be far more overt in its lobbying activities than its current charitable status as a 501(c)(3)."

 According to ALECwatch, ALEC received 95% of its funding from 1994 to 2000 from foundations, corporations, other nonprofits, meeting revenue and the sale of its publications. Legislators pay $100 in biennial membership dues, or $50 per year, while corporations pay $7,000 to $25,000 to join, and more to participate in the task forces. In 2010 NPR reported that tax records showed that corporations had collectively paid as much as $6 million a year. ALEC's total revenue in 2011 was $9 million.

 Koch Industries Inc. was one of 14 "Vice Chairman" level sponsors at ALEC's 2010 annual meeting, which requires a $25,000 donation. According to tax records, the Charles G. Koch Charitable Foundation gave $75,858 to ALEC in 2009. According to Greenpeace, ALEC has received $525,858 from Koch foundations from 2005 to 2011. According to the Center for Public Integrity, ALEC received $150,000 from Charles and David Koch in 2011.

Exxon Mobil's foundation donated $30,000 in both 2005 and 2006. Alan Jeffers, an Exxon Mobil spokesman, said the company paid $39,000 in dues in 2010 and sponsored a reception at the annual meeting in San Diego for $25,000. In August 2011, Exxon spent $45,000 to sponsor a workshop on natural gas.

According to a December 2013 article appearing in The Guardian, ALEC is facing a funding shortfall after losing more than a third of its projected income. Some 400 state legislators have left its membership along with more than 60 corporate donors.

Does a name suddenly jump out at you? The name Koch? The Koch brothers, Charles and David, happen to own Koch Industries, the second largest privately owned company in the United States. If you have bought Brawny paper towels, any lumber product from Georgia-Pacific, or a whole host of other products, you have put money in the Koch's pockets. You've also helped financed Americans for Prosperity, The Heritage Foundation, People for the American Way, and a bunch of other Koch funded right wing think tanks. It should also be noted that Charles and David's father Fred Koch, not did business with Adolf Hitler prior to World War I I, but he also accumulated the majority of his wealth by providing Stalin with oil equipment after the second world war. Just another side bar to history, their uncle, Erich Koch, was a high ranking officials in the German Nazi Party leading up to World War II and his wife was especially proud of the lamps with the shades makes out of Jewish skins. Kind of nice lineage, eh?

Anyway, the Koch's have a long history of supporting both conservative as well as libertarian causes. In fact, David ran as the Libertarian party's Vice-presidential candidate in 1980. His ticket did not stand a snowball's chance in Hell of winning primarily due to their party's platform, which called for such things as abolishment of the FAA, privatization of the United States Postal Service, abolishment of Social Security and Medicare, and an abolishment of the Internal Revenue Service as well as a massive reduction of all forms of taxation. But they also called for the abolishment of the Occupational Safety and Health Administration, the Departments of Health and Human Services, Education as well as Labor and the Environmental Protection Agency.

But enough bashing the Koch's. They get kicked around enough by the media, my book is not going to cause them to lose one wink of sleep. So I'm going to move on to the next subject. I just wanted to give you all a face (or two) to let you know exactly who is out there trying to take away your rights.

Chapter 7

I think that predatory capitalism is one of the most important issues I can bring to people's attention. So much so that I want to dedicate an entire chapter to it. But before we get started, I need to explain something to you, you are going to hear a lot about the term, neoliberal used in the next few pages. Neoliberal, as defined here is not the typical political left versus right as we think of in terms of American politics. Neoliberal in this term is an economic term closely related to libertarian philosophy.

Contemporary capitalism is characterized by a political economy which revolves around finance capital, is based on a savage form of free market fundamentalism, and thrives on a wave of globalizing processes and global financial networks that have produced global economic oligarchies with the capacity to influence the shaping of policymaking across nations.

As a result, contemporary advanced capitalist societies are plagued by dangerous levels of income and wealth inequality, mass unemployment, rising poverty rates, social polarization, and collapsing social provisions. Furthermore, democracy and the social contract are under constant attack by the current system and there is an ongoing pressure by the corporate and financial elite to convert all public goods and services into private goods and services.

The rising inequality in advanced capitalist countries is well documented. Most recently, Thomas Piketty's publishing sensation Capital in the Twentieth-First Century, translated into English and published by Harvard University Press, provides massive data showing a widening gap between the rich and the poor, thus questioning not only the claim that the capitalist economy works for all but also underscoring the point of how dangerous the current system is to democracy itself. Indeed, a few years ago, Larry M. Bartels's Unequal Democracy: The Political Economy of the New Gilded Age, published by Princeton University Press, pointed to the same gap between the rich and poor in the United States under Republican administrations.

The way wealth has changed in the United States over the last few decades, with those in Generation X and Generation Y accumulating "less wealth than their parents did at the same age 25 years ago", is also demonstrated in a study produced by Eugene Steuerle, et.

al. on behalf of the Urban Institute in Washington DC. And in a recent Strategic Analysis released just this past spring by the Levy Economics Institute with the title "Is Rising Inequality a Hindrance to the US Economic Recovery?", the authors, Dimitri B. Papadimitriou, et al., demonstrate through macro modeling simulations that the current processes of inequality in the United States are unsustainable and that, if they continue, will result in weak growth and increased unemployment.

As for the problem of mass unemployment, the facts speak for themselves. Five years after the alleged end of the global financial crisis, the official unemployment rate in the US remains as of May at 6.3% (it averaged 5.8% from 1948 until 2014) while in the eurozone the official unemployment rate as of May 2014 stood at 11.6%. In the periphery of the eurozone, which has been hard hit by austerity policies conceived in Brussels, Frankfurt and Washington as part of the international bail-out programs that went into effect when several eurozone periphery countries reached the brink of bankruptcy after the global financial crisis of 2008-09 reached Europe's shores, the official unemployment rates has reached stratospheric levels: 27% for Greece; 25% for Spain; 15% for Portugal; and 12% for Ireland, the nation with the highest emigration rate in all of Europe and whose government was actually asking the unemployed as of recently to leave and take jobs in other European countries.

In Greece, six years of an austerity-caused depression have shrunk the nation's GDP by a quarter. Yet, both European Union (EU) officials and their lackeys in Athens have been trying hard to convince Greek citizens that a "success story" is under way because the enforcement of a draconian fiscal adjustment which dropped the standard of living back to 1960 levels produced a primary surplus. In the meantime, the debt-to-GDP ratio has reached an all-time high, rising from less than 139% in 2009 to nearly 180%.

Ireland's public debt, which stood at 25% of GDP in 2008, grew to nearly 65% by 2010 and climbed to over 125% by the end of 2013. Yet German Chancellor Angela Merkel also hailed Ireland's experience with austerity as a "tremendous success story". Portugal's public debt, which was slightly less than 70% in 2008, jumped to over 100% by 2011 and then to over 130% by 2013. That's another "success story". And Spain's public debt has surged to nearly

95% of GDP, standing at close to 1 trillion euros – three times as much as it was at the start of the crisis in 2008 – and is projected to go over 100% by the end of 2014.

In short, all the bailed-out eurozone countries are sinking under the weight of debt while unemployment spreads like the plague – the result of the "voodoo" economics that the witch doctors of the EU and the International Monetary Fund cooked up in order to formulate the so-called "rescue" plans. However, according to national government and EU propaganda, everything in the periphery is working in compliance with the strategic plan for helping those countries exit the crisis.

Denial of reality, deception and distortion are traditional tactics used by the powers-that-be and their elite intellectual acolytes. We also saw this in the reaction of major media outlets like The Financial Times, Bloomberg, and Forbes Magazine, to name but just a few, to the publication of Piketty's book. The Frenchman either adopted a flawed methodology, or got his data wrong, or is simply engaging in anti-capitalist propaganda. Indeed, as yet another commentator of the Financial Times stressed, with the belief that he hit a gold vein, upon reviewing Capital in the Twentieth-First Century, even if Mr. Piketty's data about increasing inequality in capitalist societies are correct, he is not telling us why inequality is bad! In other words, Mr. Martin Wolf was essentially pondering about just what is so wrong with predatory capitalism making the rich richer and the poor poorer?

As actually existing capitalism has given up any pretext of being a "socially responsible" socioeconomic system and caters almost solely to the needs and interests of the rich and powerful by enforcing policies that are detrimental to the rest of society, the defenders of the status quo will get even more dangerous by denying the ugly truth about predatory capitalism. They don't want to hear that actually existing capitalism is a system that favors passionately and defends ruthlessly the interests of the 1% over those of the rest of society. Doing so might jeopardize the goal of the elite to roll back the course of history to the detriment of the working populations so they can further enrich themselves and act like the new rulers of the world.

The world is returning to the predatory laissez-faire capitalism that immiserated millions in the early 20th century and is predicated on neoliberal "voodoo economics," void of empirical reference.

Since the late 1970s, most capitalist economies have been marching to the tunes of neoliberalism - a term originally coined in the 1930s as a moderate alternative to classical liberalism but used in our own times to signify preference for a set of economic policies favoring privatization, deregulation and a "minimal" state. This is the version of neoliberalism developed by Milton Friedman and the so-called Chicago School and is usually associated with the Pinochet regime in Chile and later on with the so-called "free-market" policies of Margaret Thatcher and Ronald Reagan. In more popular usage, it can simply be referred to as predatory capitalism.

The neoliberal transition is associated with financial capital's rise to dominance and sharp changes in the social structure of capital accumulation, with developments in the US economy leading the way among advanced capitalist economies. The economic slowdown in the 1970s and the inflationary pressures that went along with the first major postwar systemic capitalist crisis created a window of opportunity for anti-statist economic thinking, which had been around since the 1920s but was spending most of its time hibernating because it lacked support among government and policy-making circles and had very few followers among the members of the chattering classes. The postwar capitalist era was dominated by the belief that the government had a crucial role to play in economic and societal development. It was the Keynesian legacy, even though Keynesian economics was never fully and consistently applied in any capitalist country.

Industrial capitalism, the production of real goods and services for the benefit of most members of a society, required extensive government intervention, both as a means to sustain capital accumulation and as a way to ensure that the toiling population improved its standards of living so it could purchase the goods and services that its own members produced in the great factories of the western industrial corporations. The rise of the middle class in the West takes place predominantly in the first few decades after World War II, and it is an outcome brought about by the combination of a thriving western capitalist industrial economic base and interventionist government policies. Governments and the industrial capitalist classes understood only too well that economic growth and social prosperity went hand in hand if the system of industrial capitalism was to survive. Maintaining "social peace," a long sought after objective of governments and economic elites throughout the world, mandated that the wealth of a nation actually trickle down to the members of the toiling population. The improvement of the standards of living for the working class was essential to the further growth of industrial capital accumulation.

To be sure, it took at least a couple of centuries before industrial capitalism reached a stage where its own survival and future growth was predicated on a steady increase of the standards of living among a nation's general population. In postwar capitalist economies, providing the working classes with the means for their reproduction meant constantly improving their economic purchasing power and providing them with access to educational opportunities so they could make a substantially greater contribution to productivity as well as become potential consumers. In all this, the government had a key role to play, as it was the only agent with the capability of providing the opportunities and the resources needed for the materialization of a society of plenty, where the fruits of labor were not the exclusive domain of the class that owned the means of production.

All this comes to a rather abrupt end sometime around the mid-to-late 1970s, when advanced capitalism finds itself in the grip of a major systemic crisis brought about by new technological innovations, declining rates of profit, and the dissolution of the social structures of accumulation that had emerged after the Second World War.

The new world order initiated in the aftermath of the 1973 crisis takes the form of a new wave of globalization, actually not very dissimilar to what had taken place from the 1870s up to the start of World War I: a cycle of upswing in the movement toward the global integration of national economies enforced by the market liberalization policies of leading and ascending states.

The difference in this new era of globalization is that it is finance capital that has now gained the upper hand in spite of the fact that the sector represents a very small share of the GDP. With the "financialization" of the economy and the adoption of neoliberalism as the preferred model of economic governance, financial markets begin to dominate economic decision making processes and the financial elite exercise enormous influence on government policies. In the United States, the adoption of neoliberalism as an economic model coincides with the deindustrialization period, which undermined the economy's industrial base and undercut the power and influence of the labor movement. Thus, the "financialization" of the economy is directly related to developments in the real economy. In the 1970s, it reflected the crisis that industrial capitalism had entered after nearly 25 years of continuous growth and expansion.

In this sense, the much-talked about globalization phenomenon of the 1980s and 1990s is neither a novel nor a progressive development. It had its roots in the restructuring of the process of capitalist accumulation due to inevitable crises in the workings of the capitalist economy and the squeeze in the rate of profit. But it is not the "logic of the market" nor the new technologies that provided the impetus for the new wave of globalization. The push toward globalization came from domestic institutions (core and ascending capitalist states), powerful economic players (industry and finance) and international organizations (International Monetary Fund, World Bank). The new information technologies have facilitated the drive toward globalization. Decisions about the future direction of the economy are political in nature and highly antidemocratic. Labor's voice is totally ignored. But that should not be surprising. Capitalism is antithetical to economic democracy.

In fact, the expansion of capitalism takes place with the financial (and even political and military) support of the state through subsidies and the facilitation of internal exploitation, which includes the transfer of valuable resources from domestic society for the reproduction of capitalist accumulation abroad. Opening new markets and creating investment sites has always been a key role of the capitalist state - and this has been no less true under the global neoliberal order initiated after the 1973 crisis. Far from being anti-government, big business and finance capital demand an interventionist state - but one that rolls back the standard of living for the working populations and dismantles the welfare state in favor of market liberalization and globalization. Policies that increase the upward flows of income and the availability of public property for private exploitation rest at the core of the global neoliberal project, where predatory capitalism reigns supreme. So does privatizing profits and socializing losses.

Contrary to neoliberal discourse, the state has not disappeared under the process of globalization; nor has it become weaker. It has merely been refocused so it can perform activities more amenable to the needs and demands of the global financial elite. The state, as a social institution, does retain a certain degree of relative autonomy, and thus it can be recaptured by progressive forces determined enough to work toward the realization of a just and decent society, instead of standing idly by and watching elected public officials squander the common good (officials often eager to get into office to serve big business interests so they can later pursue lucrative private-sector roles). But that is another story. The point underlined here is that the spread of neoliberal capitalism is deeply rooted in changes in the correlation of class forces. The near collapse of industrial labor and the subsequent weakening of trade unions ensured the success of the transition from managed capitalism to global neoliberalism. So did the shift to the right of the Democratic Party in the United States and of the social democratic parties in Europe.

In sum, the post-1973 global and neoliberal version of capitalist development basically iterates the policy context of finance-led capitalism and includes (a) changes in the postwar social structure of capital accumulation; (b) the shift in the balance of power between industrial capital and finance capital and the consolidation of monopolistic interests across the capitalist economy; and (c) the declining influence of organized labor, mainly through ideological and political historic defeats by the forces of global capitalism. As such, the global neoliberal transition in the world economy is a reflection of fundamental changes in the "movement of capital," but also the outcome of specific class policies pursued by international financial organizations, such as the International Monetary Fund (IMF) and the World Bank, and domestic agents and institutions (the national corporate/financial/cultural elite and the state).

At the heart of the neoliberal vision is a societal and world order based on the prioritization of corporate power, laissez-faire markets and the abandonment of public services. The neoliberal claim is that capitalist economies would perform more effectively, producing greater wealth and economic prosperity for all, if markets are allowed to perform their functions without government intervention. This mainly Hayekian claim is predicated on the idea that unregulated markets are inherently just and can create effective low-cost ways to produce consumer goods and services. Conversely, an interventionist or state-managed economy is wasteful and inefficient, choking off growth and expansion by constraining innovation and the entrepreneurial spirit.

Neoliberal economics is, of course, plain "voodoo economics." The intellectual foundations of neoliberal economic discourse are couched in profusely vague claims and ahistorical terms. Notions such as "free markets," "economic efficiency" and "perfect competition" are so devoid of any empirical reference that they belong to a discourse on metaphysics, not economics. More important, the facts debunk the stubborn myths built around the efficiency of neoliberal economics.

During the period known as "state-managed capitalism" (roughly from 1945-1973, and otherwise known as the classical Keynesian era), the western capitalist economies were growing faster than any other time in the 20th century, and wealth was reaching those at the bottom of the social pyramid more effectively than ever before. OECD (Organization for Economic Co-operation and Development) countries experienced real GDP growth rates averaging "over 4 percent annually in the 1950s and near 5 percent in the 1960s, compared with 3 percent in the 1970s and 2 percent in the 1980s."[2] Economic performance in the world's biggest capitalist economy was particularly impressive: "From the late 1940s to the early 1970s, the US economy grew at an average annual rate of nearly 4%. The annual unemployment rate only exceeded 6% twice in the 25 years between 1949 and 1973. The annual inflation rate, too, only topped 6% twice and was actually under 2% for 14 of the 25 years in this period. The real average hourly earnings of production workers increased at an average rate of over 2% per year."

The extent to which capitalism is capable of maintaining constant rates of growth is of course highly debatable. We also know that the reproduction of capitalism means ever-increasing damage to natural resources and the environment. But seen from a purely political economy perspective, what neoliberalism represents is a counterrevolution to the postwar regime in the area of economic and social rights that serves the interests of the rich, corporations and the needs of the dominant form of capital in contemporary capitalism, finance. It is a socio-economic and political project that stands for the systematic attempt to roll back the course of history - a return journey to the age of predatory capitalism when labor power was completely "free," nature at the mercy of unrestrained capital exploitation, state policies catering exclusively to the interests and needs of the plutocrats, and philanthropy serving as a means to disguise the exploitation of the poor and deny the structural problems of the capitalist system. In sum, neoliberalism is a new form of laissez-faire capitalism wrapped up in old-fashioned class warfare.

It is thus hardly surprisingly that the neoliberal capitalist order has given rise to a "Great U-Turn," an amazing growth in the spread between rich and poor that has accumulated in the course of the past 35 years largely as a result of sharp distortions that have taken place in the real economy. Neoliberalism has allowed the castration of labor rules, privatization of state assets, budget cuts in social programs, public education and public health. It has enacted and protected sharp tax cuts for the rich, real estate, banks and financial transactions. It has worked to strengthen the penal state. It has supported the penalization of poverty and criminalization of many social movements resisting the collapse of the public sphere.

Neoliberalism has turned out to be the new dystopia of the contemporary world, as British philosopher John Gray powerfully argued at a time when mass media and most academics were raving about the virtues of globalization and the alleged superiority of "free markets,"[4] with the unfolding crisis in southern Europe representing the latest episode of the catastrophic impact that "free market" fundamentalism and financial capitalism have on contemporary economies and societies. During the last three to four years, several southern European nations, under the management of debt crises, have been subjected to a brutal experiment in neoliberal social engineering, not unlike the ones that many Latin American and African countries were subjected to back in the 1980s. The debt crisis is being used as an opportunity to dismantle the social state, to sell off profitable public enterprises and state assets at bargain prices, to deprive labor of even its most basic rights after decades of hard-fought struggles against management, and to substantially reduce wages and rob pensions. This is predatory capitalism at its best.

Over the last several decades, both government policy and private sector labor relations have evolved to reduce the sharing of the economic risks involved in managing lives, caring for families, and safeguarding futures. Instead, individual Americans are increasingly being asked to plan for and guarantee their own educations, health care, and retirements. If today's families want a safety net to catch them when they fall, they need to weave their own.

 Underlying this shift in risk is neoliberal political ideology, often identified with leaders like Ronald Reagan and Margaret Thatcher, which holds that people will work harder and make better decisions if they must defend themselves against the vicissitudes of life. Neoliberal doctrine views dependence in a negative light (arguing that "coddling" by government undermines individual initiative) and actually celebrates risk and uncertainty as sources of self-reliance. In this new paradigm, the individual is encouraged to gain greater control over his or her life by making personal risk-management choices within the free market (and living with the consequences of any misjudgments). In this "ownership society," individuals must learn to be secure with insecurity; the goal is to amass security on our own rather than look to government help or collective action as sources of support.

 With the rise of neoliberalism, the ethic of sharing risk among workers, employers, and the federal government that emerged after the New Deal was replaced by an aggressively free-market approach that pushed deregulation and privatization in order to minimize the role of government in economic life. At the same time, responsibility for social welfare has steadily devolved from the federal government to states, localities, and even the private sector. The push toward privatizing social services reached a new level when President George W. Bush, through his establishment of the office of faith-based organizations, sought to formally create public-private partnerships in which welfare provision would increasingly be supplied not by the government but by religious organizations. The result of this devolution of social services has been the replacement of a relatively stable, consistent system of safety-net programs with a patchwork of state, local, and private programs, all of which scramble to find funding.

 Though many Americans may be unfamiliar with the risk shift story, the results are widely known. From 1980 to 2004, the number of workers covered by a traditional defined-benefit retirement pension decreased from 60 percent to 11 percent. In contrast, the number of workers covered by a defined-contribution retirement benefit like a 401(k) plan, in which the worker is fully responsible for saving and managing his or her savings, grew from 17 percent in 1980 to 61 percent in 2004.

Traditional employer-provided health-care coverage began to erode as well. From 1979 to 2004, coverage dropped from 69 percent to 55.9 percent. In 2010, 49 million Americans were uninsured, an increase of close to 13 million people since 2000. For workers who continue to receive coverage, their share of the costs has increased drastically. A survey conducted by the Employee Benefit Research Institute found that to cover medical costs, 45 percent have decreased their contributions to other savings, 35 percent have had difficulty paying other bills, and 24 percent have had difficulty paying for basic necessities.

The Affordable Care Act, passed in 2010 and upheld by the Supreme Court in 2012, will greatly expand affordable health care. As a result of the legislation, it is estimated that by 2019, 29 million Americans will gain health insurance coverage. However, an equal number will still be uninsured. And the number of uninsured may rise depending on how many states opt out of expanding Medicaid eligibility. Currently twenty states will not participate in the Medicaid expansion. Analysis of states that won't expand Medicaid has found that, as a result, about 5.3 million people will earn too much under their state's Medicaid eligibility level to qualify but will earn too little to be eligible for tax credits that help offset the cost of insurance. Of the top ten least-insured metropolitan areas in the United States, seven are in states that will not expand Medicaid eligibility.

When it comes to aid for higher education, federal funding has grown, but that aid has mostly come in the form of loans rather than grants. Over the last decade, grants have made up between 22 and 28 percent of federal aid for education, while loans have made up between 61 and 70 percent. Moreover, even though there has been a 15 percent increase in the number of low-income students who receive a Pell Grant, the maximum award these students can receive now covers only about a third of the costs of a college education, as compared to around three-quarters in the 1970s.

The high price of a college degree is linked with a significant decline in the number of low- and moderate-income students who enroll in and graduate from college. Between 1992 and 2004, the percentage of low-income students enrolled in a four-year college decreased from 54 to 40 percent and the percentage of middle-income students decreased from 59 to 53 percent. For low-income children, the college completion rate has increased by only 4 percentage points between the generation born in the early 1960s and the generation born in the early 1980s. In contrast, among high-income children the college graduation rate increased 18 percentage points between generations. If education is the ladder by which less-advantaged Americans can hope to rise to the middle class and beyond, the rungs of that ladder are increasingly out of reach—yet another way in which the traditional system of shared social responsibility has been gradually dismantled over the past forty years.

Predatory capitalism is pushing societies to a breaking point. After having caused the biggest financial crisis since the crash of 1929 and having already rolled back the progress made under the Keynesian order of capitalism, global neoliberalism has put millions in Europe and the United States into unemployment and poverty and is digging even bigger graves for the generations to follow.

So far, resistance to the deadly effects of predatory capitalism have had rather limited effect. Progressive forces worldwide remain fragmented and largely unorganized while economic elites have hijacked national governments. In this context, representative democracy has deteriorated to a political instrument used to maintain, promote and legitimize plutocracy.

The challenges ahead are daunting. Predatory capitalism has created the synergy needed for the exploitation of labor at national, regional and global levels. Developing types of international organization should become therefore a top priority for labor and the progressive forces - an old vision of the left, but more vital today than ever before - while resistance on the home front should be intensified. How this ought to be done is, of course, not yet clear.

What? Globalization was a liberal idea? Actually in this sense, political liberalism. Indeed, once upon a time globalization was an idea hit upon immediately after World War II, by David Rockefeller as well as the Council of Foreign Relations came upon the idea that if all the world's economies were somehow interconnected the probability of war would greatly be reduced if not totally eliminated. Sounds like a wonderful idea, but a pipe dream. You see, in his farewell speech in 1960, President Eisenhower warned of the gaining power of the "military industrial complex," which has over the years increased in power and influence in the halls of Congress over the past 50 years. Corporations like Raytheon, Boeing, Lockheed-Martin, Halliburton, and a host of other U.S. Corporations have secured literally trillions upon trillions of taxpayer dollars and raping them ever since. They were responsible for the troop build-up in Vietnam, the Kuwait war, the actions in both in Iraq and Afghanistan. Sad part about spending so much about weapons of war, is that once you have them, you are always looking for a place to use them. However, as stated in the beginning of this chapter, this is more a case of neoliberalism, more aligned to the European model of liberalism.

Each time a military conflict occurs and the guns are silenced. The veterans come home, but they are not the same people that left home. I remember a Vietnam-era vet I used to work with, and his name is lost to me after twenty plus years since I have seen him, but he suffered from severe PTSD, and he suffered an attack while we were having lunch. He got a faraway look in his eyes, and I just sat there with him. When he returned to reality, he told me what had happened and apologized for his behavior. I just told him he had nothing to apologize for. Just another unsung hero and another faceless victim in a long ago conflict.

 Beginning in the mid-to-late 1970s, U.S. firms began to face dramatically increased competition from around the world. To compete, American companies sought to lower labor costs, in part by outsourcing work to lower-wage countries. Technological advances aided this outsourcing process, as the growth in electronic tools for communication and information management meant that goods, services, and people could be coordinated and controlled from anywhere around the globe, enabling businesses to more easily move their operations to exploit cheap labor sources abroad.

Perhaps the most far-reaching effect of globalization has been a renegotiation of the unwritten social contract between American employers and employees. Managers now demand greater flexibility to quickly adapt and survive in an increasingly competitive global marketplace. In this context, the traditional employment relationship, in which work is steady and full-time, workers are rarely fired except for incompetence, working conditions are generally predictable and fair (often defined by union-negotiated contracts), and good employees can expect to climb a lifetime career ladder in the service of one employer, has come to seem unrealistic and onerous to business leaders. Today that traditional arrangement has largely disappeared, replaced by nonstandard, part-time, contract, and contingent work, generally offering reduced wages and scanty benefits. Mass layoffs are no longer an option of last resort but rather a key restructuring strategy used to increase short-term profits by reducing labor costs in both good times and bad.

Chapter 8

Slash expenses! Raise Revenues! Improve the dividends to the stockholders!

These have been the battle cries from the executive suites ever since the mid-1980s. In general, investors and stock analysts have acted favorably to such news, bidding up the prices of shares in companies where they have perceived management, particularly upper management, that have what appears to have a relentless commitment to the bottom line. However, it has become increasingly evident that most American corporations have behaviors similar to that of some misguided adolescent girls. By that I mean they both suffer from a body demographic disorder, namely anorexia, an all-consuming obsession with food in case of the teenagers and a relentless shedding of workers as it reduces its products, services or entire divisions in the case of corporations. Moderation, in both cases, goes by the way of reason. Such cost cutting measures, if taken to an extreme, will ultimately stifle growth and in turn stockholder value. It creates in a business an atmosphere of uneasiness where neither productivity nor profits are enhanced. Also, it creates a culture of fear amongst the workers, a culture where new ideas are never explored, mediocrity is expected, and after a while the business will either eventually go under or never grow.

The word "downsizing" may have a ring of fiscal responsibility to it and may conjure up visions of huge savings of corporate expenses and shareholder returns, and a salvation from whatever monetary woes, either real or imagined, a company may be suffering, but today's saving may eventually be the source of tomorrow's financial suffering. I am reminded of an exchange between Henry Ford and Walter Ruther, then President of the United Auto Workers. Henry Ford was rumored to have to Mr. Ruther that one day all the automobiles in Ford's plants would be manufactured by machines and how would be collect Union dues from them? Walter Ruther then turned the question around and asked Mr. Ford who would buy his automobiles?

As a result, something dangerous is occurring in both our economy and in our society. While corporations have and continue to rake in record to near record profits, the benefits of those profits are being enjoyed by fear Americans. Wages, which have, in the past, normally gone up when a company enjoyed profitable years, are remaining stagnant or have increased at a rate of a little over 2 percent. The specter which haunted the working poor for decades, a lack of decent paying jobs has slowly creeper into working and middle-class realms. I'll use a town in which I work as an example: Huntington, West Virginia. For over a century, Huntington, the second largest city in West Virginia, was an industrial powerhouse, home to steel mills, glass works, railcar repair shops, chemical manufacturers and a multitude of other industries. Today, all have either shut down or greatly downsized. Today, the largest employers are either the two medical centers, Marshall University, or one of the server call centers located within the city limits. Little heavy industry, all service based industries. Some make good money, but most do not. How can an economy expect to survive under these conditions? Simply put, and I have been saying this for years, both as a businessman and as a social worker, that a service-oriented economy cannot feed upon itself. Eventually, that type of economy will begin to cannibalize on itself and it becomes a rapid slide to the bottom. Legal scholar Derrick Bell, foresees, if this trend continues, to a return to the dark days of the Reconstruction, when the sharpest of class divisions hurt all the poor, and where racist appeals from opportunistic politicians galvanized whites against blacks and immigrants.

The term ""Downsizing" is an interesting one. A comparably interesting term could be "post-traumatic stress disorder." It is very hard to overreact to the seriousness to what is happening to Americans and their jobs as well as their livelihoods.

Income inequality has increased considerably. Between 1979 and 2004, the mean after-tax income of the top percentile increased 167%, versus 69% for the top quintile overall, 29% for the fourth quintile, 21% for the middle quintile, 17% for the second quintile and 6% for the bottom quintile. While wages for women have increased greatly, median earnings of male wage earners have remained stagnant since the late 1970s. Household income, however, has risen due the increasing number of household with more than one income earners and women's increased presence in the labor force. Half of the U.S. population lives in poverty or is low-income, according to U.S. Census data. On the other hand, some members of the U. S. population have earned a considerable income: the top earner in

2011, hedge fund manager John Paulson, earned "$4.9 billion", according to Business Insider.

In our "new" economy, it is all too easy for those displaced to become some faceless statistics. However, these are real people of all shapes, colors and creeds. Their job lossless that these people become unemployed, unhoused, uninsured, unempowered and unable to live the American Dream. Their loss represents the failed hopes and dreams of honest, hardworking people. A failure that will eventually impact us all in a negative fashion. As these unemployed draw out their unemployment insurance or severance package, then they begin to draw out their personal savings. After all their resources have been exhausted, they begin to fade into the ever growing population of non-persons of this country and it impacts their family, relatives and kin of those displaced. Because of the ever shrinking employment base, displaced workers find themselves two options.

First, is what is called underemployment. To put it another way, lose your job today, and tomorrow, maybe the next day, week, month, year or in some cases two years from that day, you might find another job, but chances are it will pay 10, 20, 30, up 50 percent less than your old one. I saw folks that I used to work with as Steelworkers, years later working as janitors, mopping floors and cleaning up vomit at wages far less than they used to make. But hey, it a job, right? Right, but is it a living? But in addition to less pay, the job they get will probably have less benefits, if they are lucky to even to have benefits. I was always taught by both my grandfather and my father that, "if you take care of your job, your job would take care of you." And, being the idiot that I was, I taught my children the same die hard work ethic. As I said in *"All our Hands are Stained,"* I am not against work. In fact, I believe hard work builds character and a solid work ethic of dependability and responsibility. Something I think is sometimes lacking in some people of **ALL** socio-economic classes. We have been conditioned to have instant gratification. We want what we want, and we want it **NOW!** Second is to become dependent upon government programs, charities, and handouts for their basic existence. Given the changes in the welfare laws, more and more downsized workers will lose everything they have worked for and accumulated. If this continues unchecked, we will have unemployment to such magnitude that the unemployment rate during the Great Depression would look like a drop in the bucket. But it is not just established workers who are feeling the impact of the "new" economy. Veronique De Rugy, a senior research fellow at the Mercuatus Center of George Mason University recently published an article which gave a glimpse on how downsizing and massive unemployment has impacted a large, young segment of our economy:

"Until recently, a bad job market was nearly always bad news for political incumbents. Unemployed and anxious voters have a habit of throwing the bums out. But headed into the 2016 election season, one large demographic group is still likely to vote Democratic: millennials.

Which is weird, because when it comes to the labor market, it sucks to be young. To be sure, it has always been hard to enter the workforce during a recession. But this recession has not only been particularly severe; it has been made longer and deeper than necessary by the Obama administration's policies. Washington's burdensome regulations, "stimulus" spending, and health insurance mandates have given us a slow recovery, high uncertainty, and a pathetic job market.

According to the Bureau of Labor Statistics (BLS), some 1.2 million unemployed millennials with little or no job experience are trying to find jobs for the first time right now. Their unemployment rate is 12.2 percent, more than twice the rate for 25- to 54-year-olds. And if those first-time job seekers don't find employment soon, some of them may actually never work. "It is even more depressing," says my Mercatus Center colleague Keith Hall, a former BLS commissioner, "when you know that some 400,000 young long-term unemployed have never worked before." That's much higher than anything we have seen in the last 45 years.

It gets worse. In June testimony before the Senate Committee on Banking, Housing, and Urban Affairs' subcommittee on economic policy, Hall explained that "job prospects have been so bad that many have withdrawn from the labor force and do not even show up in the official unemployment rate statistics." According to his calculations, some 2 million young workers are simply missing from the labor force, and "if not left uncounted in the official unemployment rate, these 2 million would raise the youth unemployment rate from its current 10.9 percent rate to 15.4 percent-well above their highest rate in over 65

years." Only 63.4 percent of youth aged 18 to 29 are employed today, a pathetic and alarming figure.

Teenagers face even more abysmal prospects. The unemployment rate for 16- to 19-year-olds is 21 percent, down from its 27.3 percent peak in 2009 but up from 14.8 percent at the beginning of 1990. They are also more disengaged from the labor force than their slightly older peers, with a labor force participation rate of a very low 33.9 percent. Only 26.8 percent of older teens are employed, compared with 46.7 percent in January 1990, or even 37 percent at the end of 2006.

Joblessness is costly, especially for young adults who have invested time and resources in career-specific knowledge and skills. Studies consistently show that the longer people are unemployed, the less likely they are to find new work. They may lose their job skills over time, have less connections with informal professional networks, or face potential employers more reluctant to hire the long-term unemployed.

Those who finally do get a job after looking for a long time will continue to face a disadvantage. It can take as long as 20 years for re-employed workers to catch up on lost earnings, mostly due to skill mismatches between the jobs lost and the new jobs created in the economy. These losses occur for workers with different lengths of previous job tenure, across all major industries, and of any age, including millennials. Hall notes that recent estimates have found that the losses "range from 1.4 years of earnings in good times to 2.8 years during times of high unemployment."

And none of those ugly figures capture the problem of underemployment: part-time and/or lower-paying jobs. Currently employed seniors tend to hang on to their jobs rather than retire, as they work to rebuild some of the assets they lost during the Great Recession, so younger workers are finding it hard to move up the work ladder.

Older workers also don't quit their jobs as often as they used to. The number of quits, defined by the BLS as "generally voluntary separations initiated by the employees," serves as an indicator of the health of the labor market. A high quits number tells us that people are willing or able to leave their jobs for better opportunities. Five years after the recession ended, the quits rate hasn't grown as fast as one would hope. At a 1.8 percent

level, it is still lower than it was at the beginning of 2007. The consequence is stalled careers for younger Americans.

While millennials struggle to find jobs and grow their wages, previous generations continue to expect them to foot the bill for trillions of dollars of unfunded liabilities and entitlement promises. Add that tab to their student debts, and the situation looks unsustainable.

So why aren't these kids more freaked out about their future? Why did the youth-driven Occupy Wall Street movement fizzle out instead of becoming the new normal? The July Reason-Rupe poll suggests one possibility: Millennials define themselves politically in cultural terms rather than economic terms. This aversion to economics may be a product of growing up in a time when the economic headlines have always been bad.

If the economy doesn't improve, reality will catch up with this generation. When that happens, let's hope they demand the same freedom in their economic lives that they have grown to expect in their social lives."

Of course, this presents New motivation for the remaining workers in the workforce. The fear of being turned out into an economy where falling real wages and job instability is the order of the day. The fear is a natural reaction to our current economic situation. As a result, corporations have made a sudden imposition of a new, tougher social contract between the corporations and its workers.

In the old post World War II social contract paid what economists call "efficiency wages." Wages were higher than necessary to obtain a work force with the right skills. Above-market wages gave workers an incentive to cooperate with their employers, an incentive to work hard and not to quit - taking their skills with them to some other employer, possibly another competitor within the same field. Today, most employers have new employers have new employees sign "non-competitive" agreements when they hire on, threatening legal action against the worker if they would go to work for a competitor within a certain time frame, usually two years. TWO YEARS! Give me a fucking break! Not only has small businesses as well as multinational corporations have a lock on wages, but they also attempt to control the free flow of labor! This one aspect should have you, my reader friend, so angry you shouldn't be able to see straight, but you're probably not though. Admit it, you are scared, confused, don't know what to do, and are probably grasping at straws looking for answers. Answers to questions so economically complex, you need a PhD in economics to understand it all. So why am I tackling it. I'm glad you ask. You see, social work, was explained to me and my cohorts during one of our first lectures in social work school was, "the applied social science." We take, as social workers information from all the fields of the social sciences, economics being one of those, an apply them within our practice. Plus the social issues of worker rights and income inequality are near and dear to me, because I believe that if we are to continue to enjoy the standard of living in this country, we have to make sure that everyone has the opportunity to make a decent living wage.

Once upon a time, workers were part of the capitalistic team. But, without the ever present threat of Communism or the economic threat from other competitive units within a market (these were pretty much done away with during the mergers and acquisitions craze of the 1980s,) and being able to integrate foreign low-wage, high-skill workers into corporate activities, efficiency wages are not needed anymore. Therefore, the shift in motivation moved away from having workers play a part in economic growth to a system where workers are frightened into producing more products for less wages, all the while their bosses all the way up the corporate hierarchy rake in obscene compensation while the investors reap benefits from inflated stock prices and dividends. And if a downsized worker has 15 or more years' experience, lives in a low-cost region of the country, and is forced to switch jobs, he or she could lose as much as 50 percent of their previous wages. Those workers who are 55 years of age or older are typically thrown out of the workforce entirely. Mainly to have their position refilled by younger employees, typically fresh out of college, who will perform the work for one-third to one-half of what the previous employee was being paid.

Then there are "survivor" employees, who are often overlooked as a component of the negative effects of downsizing and job elimination. In practically every downsizing -- the remaining employees are faced with uncertainty about their futures and future role with the company. Layoffs, restructuring, and new assignments often send staff into a turmoil.

Even after the layoffs are completed and the smoke finally clears, the remaining employees remain ever suspicious and wary of the company motives and work under the constant stress and fear of yet another round of job cuts and being terminated themselves. Whether that specter is real or imagined.

Chapter 9

Simply put, downsizing and job elimination are way to eliminate and reduce wages and labor costs. The high wages and benefits are downsized into non-existence, saving the corporation money and greatly improving their profit margins by replacing them with lower wage replacements, once the job eliminations are completed, many of the laid off workers will be replaced by a "contingent" workforce comprised of involuntary part-time, "temps," and limited term contract employees. With contingent employees, companies receive lower labor costs and greater deployment flexibility. Workers receive lower wages, few if any benefits, and face greater economic uncertainty. It should be said that is behaviors creates an economic paradox. How can American businesses survive and provide goods and services to consumers while reducing their workforce 10 to 30 percent? Simply put, they are just shuffling employees as well as employment costs. Raw materials are exported to areas in the world were labor and regulatory costs are at a minimum, manufactured at costs which are pennies on the dollar, and then imported into this country and American consumers are charged a greatly inflated price. Hence, not only do the American worker get the screw, but the American consumer ends up buying cheap goods which not only wastes valuable resources, but are soon discarded for the latest thing which is "New and improved" or has more whistles and bells than last year's model.

From a social policy perspective, public policy and corporate policy *actually share* common ground. I'm going reach back to one of my old social work classes, Introduction to Public Policy, to define these decisions. In doing so, I am going to use two of Dye's models: Elitist and Institutional, to further explain my position. (Note: If you are unfamiliar with Dye's models, Google them, so you can enlighten yourself.)

Elitist: Dye States that the Elite Theory is "Public policy is viewed as the preferences and values of a governing elite. It suggests that the masses are passive and ill informed. The elites shape public policy. Naturally, if you are either uninformed or a conspiracy theorist, it would be easy to think that downsizing and job elimination is some evil conspiracy by the CEO's of American Corporations to make us all wage slaves and load us all into Oscars and transfer us to FEMA Camps to work as mindless drones for our corporate overlords. However, it is neither evil nor a conspiracy. It could be better termed a consensus, to find the most profitable means of doing business, even if it means going to where the wage and occupational safety laws are far more liberal than those of the United States.

<u>Institutional:</u> Dye States in the Institutional Model of public policy, "A policy is not a policy unless it is implemented by some level of government. Several laws and treaties have attributed to the downsizing of the American workforce. As I discussed previously, NAFTA, CAFTA (The Central American Free Trade Agreement,) GATT, and the currently being negotiated TPP have either decimated or has the potential to further decimate American jobs. Each one of these agreements create "tariff-free" zones in which tariffs were reduced or completely eliminated on everything from textiles to clothing to steel. Each one of these agreements have promised new jobs and new job opportunities for American workers. How? ***<u>Exports!</u>*** Or at least that has been what every President and Congress for the past thirty years has been telling us. It has become an enduring article of faith in our Capitol that if U.S. manufacturers can sell more goods through unrestricted free global trade, then the American workforce will have a bright and sunny future, right? ***WRONG!***

It doesn't quite work like that.

For the past three decades, policies have been directed to the dream of "free trade" -- and the American workforce has steadily lost ground as a result. Blue collar wages have eroded, and middle management have dwindled as well. These groups formed the backbone of the middle-class, are slowly disappearing. With that, America is becoming a society of have-mores and have-nots. The main problem with our government's policy of free trade is that it does not take calculate into the equation the negative impact of imports. To put it another way, for every $1 billion dollars of exports creating 20,000 jobs, $1 billion dollars in imports eliminates a like number of jobs. That is the down side of the free trade policy. Under our government's blind following of free trade, imports have far and away outpaced exports. American companies are creating jobs -- in third world countries. In fact, there is an agency of the U.S. State Department, The Agency for International Development (AID,) that is assigned to encourage economic growth among poorer third world nations. Nations such Mexico, Honduras, Malaysia, India, and Vietnam which do not have the same laws as the United States does governing minimum wages, child labor, occupational health and safety, and other worker rights.

Boeing manufactured the B-17 Flying Fortress and B-29 Superfortress during World War II. The B-17 was produced in Boeing's home State of Washington; but the manufacturing of the B-29 involved factories in Renton Washington, Wichita Kansas, Marietta Georgia and Omaha Nebraska.

On Oct. 26, 1958 history was made when Pan Am flew a new commercial Boeing 707 jetliner from New York to Paris. That was when manufacturing had been the backbone of the U.S. economy --- when only 8 percent of all cars sold in the United States were imports.

Also that year, a small Japanese company sold its first vehicle in California. Toyota had sold 288 Toyopet sedans to American consumers in 1958. By comparison, General Motors produced 2.1 million cars in the U.S. that same year -- and the 1958 Chevy Impala had been one of the best-selling cars in America.

According the U.S. Bureau of Labor Statistics, manufacturing in the U.S. peaked in 1979 when we had over 19.6 million manufacturing jobs --- but it has been on a downward trend ever since. As of 2012, that number stood around 11.8 million --- for net difference of 7.8 million manufacturing jobs --- jobs that we could use today with 11.8 million unemployed (not to mention, all the exponentially created jobs that we could have also realized.)

And it's also no coincidence that today the labor force participation rate is also the lowest it's been since 1979. And 1979 is also when the U.S. broke off formal diplomatic relations with Taiwan and established full diplomatic relations with China.

Since 1979, the collapse of the manufacturing sector due to globalization not only increased unemployment dramatically, but also created urban decay and ghettos. In some cases, whole towns were left to ruin. The year 1979 could have been the peak year for America's middle-class, before it's long slide into decline.

Since 1979, the massive U.S. trade deficit has been a major cause of the decline of U.S. manufacturing over the past several decades, the cause of the current high unemployment rate, and the debilitating budget deficit. Domestic suppliers have watched with utter dismay as large manufacturers have outsourced work and good-paying jobs to foreign countries.

Ten years ago Boeing had a unit of 1,200 engineers in their home State of Washington designing electronic controls for all its airplanes, and a plant in Texas where another 1,200 people built the hardware. When Boeing launched the 787 Dreamliner program in 2003, management dispersed all those engineers, outsourced their work, then sold off the Texas plant.

Data shows there were 398,887 private manufacturing establishments of all sizes in the United States during the first quarter of 2001. By the end of 2010, the number declined to 342,647, a loss of 56,190 facilities. Just over that short span of 10 years, that equates to an average yearly loss of 5,619 factories --- or more than 15 factory closings per day.

Robert Reich recently wrote, "If we had a strategy designed to increase jobs and wages...it would focus on raising the productivity of all Americans through better education." But what does that have to do with manufacturing jobs? After all, we can't all be IT or mechanical engineers. Have you ever heard of the saying, "Too many chiefs and not enough Indians." And supposedly, Americans are already the most productive workers in the world.

Although I do agree with Robert Reich when he says, "We should also unionize low-wage service workers in order to give them bargaining power to get better wages." But then again, we can't all be expected to work in the fast food or retail industry either --- which means, we need more manufacturing jobs (less imports and more exports).

Robert Reich also says, "Companies should spend at least 2 percent of their earnings upgrading the skills of their lower-wage workers." I don't know about that --- two percent sounds like a huge investment to me; but just exactly what other skills are needed for manufacturing

(excluding automation and robotics) besides: tool-and-die makers, assembly line workers, machinists, fork-lift operators, truck drivers and janitors to sweep the factory floor? Exactly what skills do the Foxconn workers in China possess that Americans don't have or can't obtain? And besides, whatever became of "on-the-job" training?

In their book, Producing Prosperity, Harvard Business School professors Gary Pisano and Willy Shih write, "For years--even decades--in response to intensifying global competition, companies decided to outsource their manufacturing operations in order to reduce costs. But we are now seeing the alarming long-term effect of those choices. In many cases, once manufacturing capabilities go away, so does much of the ability to also innovate and compete. Manufacturing, it turns out, really matters in an innovation-driven economy. Companies must reinvest in new product and process development in the US industrial sector. Only by reviving this "industrial commons" can the world's largest economy build the expertise and manufacturing muscle to regain competitive advantage."

Edward Alden at the Council of Foreign Relations writes, "They [Gary Pisano and Willy Shih] demolish the comforting story that many economists have offered to dismiss concerns over the shrinking role of manufacturing in the U.S. economy. The conventional argument goes like this: It makes more economic sense to locate the actual production of goods in lower-wage countries, while the United States maintains the skilled parts of the supply chain (R&D, branding, marketing, etc.) The classic example here is Apple: most of the value of an iPhone or iPad comes from the design, software, branding and retailing, not from the assembly. Therefore, U.S.-headquartered Apple can become the most valuable company in the world even while making virtually nothing in the United States."

Forbes reports that a number of recent initiatives are seeking to pump muscle into U.S. manufacturing as fresh data on industrial activity is giving M&A (mergers and acquisitions) professionals reason for some optimism. Three investment bankers who focus on industrials said M&A could increase if U.S. manufacturing goes up.

The initiative that has attracted the most interest from Wall Street is the Reshoring Initiative.

According to their website, the mission of the Reshoring Initiative is to bring good, well-paying manufacturing jobs back to the United States by assisting companies to more accurately assess their total cost of offshoring, and shift collective thinking from "offshoring is cheaper" to "local reduces the total cost of ownership".

Reshoring is an efficient way to reduce imports, increase exports and regain manufacturing jobs in the United States. It's also the fastest and most efficient way to strengthen the U.S. economy. For the nation, reshoring brings back desirable jobs that have been lost to decades of offshoring. Reshoring also helps manufacturers recover from offshoring's poor quality, trade secret thefts (industrial espionage), supply chain disruptions and lengthy delivery times -- all while staying cost competitive.

Earlier this year Forbes reported that about 220 to 250 companies have brought manufacturing back to the U.S., with the heaviest migration from China. This represented about 50,000 jobs, which is only 10% of job growth in manufacturing since January 2010. Key reasons for returning to the U.S. include rising wages offshore, better quality of goods produced in the U.S., easier access to repairs and lower delivery costs.

But Harry Moser, the president and founder of the Reshoring Initiative, has called the 50,000 reshored jobs "a trickle" --- and also noted that U.S. companies continue to offshore jobs, saying that there has been a net loss of 3 million jobs since offshoring started decades ago. But Moser estimated that 6 million jobs could be created if certain scenarios, such as an increase in Chinese wages, continue.

The offshoring of manufacturing jobs is a result of the corporate strategy of "lean manufacturing", a production practice that considers the expenditure of resources for any goal (other than the creation of value for the end customer) to be wasteful, and thus a target for elimination. Essentially, "lean" is centered on preserving value with less work.

Lean manufacturing is a philosophy derived mostly from the Toyota Production System (TPS) and was identified as "lean" in the 1990s. TPS is renowned for its focus on reduction of the original Toyota "seven wastes" to improve overall customer value: Transportation, Inventory, Motion, Waiting, Over-processing, Over-production, and Defects.

The steady growth of Toyota, from a small company in 1958 to the world's largest automaker, has focused attention on how it has achieved this success. In 2007, for the first time, Toyota passed General Motors to become the #1 automaker.

In 2012 the three-way race between Toyota, GM and Volkswagen was tight, but Toyota held onto its status as the world's top-selling automaker in the first quarter of 2013.

Sub-note: In the last 10 years, Airbus has received 7,714 orders while delivering 4,503, and Boeing has received 7,312 orders while delivering 4,091 --- competition is intense.

So, while the Elite Theory of public policy could be utilized to explain downsizing and job elimination as a matter of policy, but I believe that the Institutional Model provides a far better explanation. While it is a corporate decision to eliminate higher paying American jobs in favor of cheaper foreign labor in third world countries where workers are exploited and paid nearly slave wages, it is done with the blessing and encouragement of the Federal government.

Chapter 10

SO WHERE DO WE GO FROM HERE?

Corporations merge to form giant corporations which exert influence over in the governmental halls of power. Workers work longer hours just to make ends meet. The gap between rich and poor widens at an alarming pace. The government taxes it's working and middle-classes obscenely, while imposing little or no tax burden upon its wealthiest citizens. Sounds like the America of today, right?

Wrong! The America I just described was of the late 19th and early 20th century. That was before President Theodore Roosevelt and the Progressive movement started making proposals and laws to give safeties and protections to the workers and the American public in general. I am reminded of the muckrakers, particularly Upton Sinclair and his book, "The Jungle," which exposed the horrors and poor conditions of the Chicago backyards and meat processing plants. This one book led to the creation of the Pure Food and Drug Act of 1906, and the Food and Drug Administration, charged with making sure America's food and medicines are safe and effective.

To understand what the future might hold for us as a nation, we could look to see how our ancestors dealt with similar situations. Similar situations which social workers could play a vital role. It was through the work of such people as Mother Jones. Jane Addams, Senator Wagner and countless other people who believed America could be better, that legislation and policy was enacted to protect the average Citizen from big business, special interests, and others who used the government for their own personal gains. In time, these policy frameworks fostered the creation of the largest middle-class in the history of this country.

Granted, Capitalism by its very nature has always dealt the cards unevenly, with very few winners, and a whole lot of losers, but in this country almost everyone has enjoyed some freedom and *some* prosperity by living under this system. But today in America, there is a certain of *angst* when it concerns the future. There is nothing new concerning the cyclic nature of the economy in this country, a cycle which caused moves from farm to factory. In fact, there have been 11 such economic downturns in the economy since World War II. As the "patron saint" of corporate downsizing, Austrian economist and Harvard professor in the 1930s and 1940s, Josef Schupeter, stated that Capitalism embodies the process of "creative destruction "which old and outdated enterprises give way to new.

However, there is something new and troubling about the current state of affairs in the "new" economy. The middle and upper middle-classes -- the very groups which have benefited the most from the education and training that have for decades been a path upwards -- are for the first time experiencing the massive layoffs and job losses previously experienced by their blue collar cousins. Many of them have been forced to accept less secure positions with reduced pay and benefits. What is most disturbing to me is that the majority of the layoffs and downsizing occupied during the last 20 or so years occurred during what could be considered "good" times, and companies with strong profits and excellent Price/Earnings ratios have created an atmosphere of insecurity as employees work for less, and upper management accumulates more of the profits, resulting in a leveling off and even a decline in real wages as a result of inflation, the longest since the Civil War.

Even though every President since Reagan has tried to convince the American people that their situation in regards to job creation is rather rosy and upbeat would have a hard time convincing them that a new "morning in America" is dawning.

However, with the advent of predatory capitalism, where corporations seek places to do business , that have the highest levels of misery and the lowest levels of both wages and governmental oversight, that framework has been weakened -- pitting one socio-economic class against another, creating an ever widening gap between the haves and have-nots. Social workers, who have a long history of helping the poor and underprivileged, now have a new battleground opening up before them: assisting and advocating for the working and middle-classes to keep and maintain their economic foothold in this country.

Chapter 11

With instability and uncertainty figuring prominently in people's lives, it is important to ask if these social and economic trends are reflected in the way Americans feel. Do Americans feel more insecure? Have they become more worried? This question turns out to be a difficult one to answer.

The first obstacle to figuring out the answer is that we lack rich, long-term survey data that would enable us to tease out an in-depth answer. As a recent Rockefeller Foundation report noted, efforts to assess and measure people's sense of security are rare. And the surveys we do have focus almost exclusively on job loss, which is just one risk among many that needs to be explored.

A second obstacle to measuring perceptions of security and insecurity across the decades is whether or not, over time, people continue to judge and evaluate their situations by the same criteria. In other words, can we assume that year in and year out people use the same yardstick to measure whether or not they are having a good or bad year? If assessments and meanings change over time and surveys don't capture these subjective changes, then it's not clear what our assessments are really measuring.

Analysis by Richard Curtin, the director of the Survey of Consumers at the University of Michigan, addresses the subjective nature of evaluation in his analysis of changes in the standards by which consumers have judged the economy over the last fifty years. For example, during the 1960s people had high expectations and were very confident about the government's ability to control the economy and keep things on track. Such optimism about rising affluence ran into a brick wall during the economic shocks of the 1970s and early 1980s. Initially, dissatisfaction ensued as people continued to hold on to the economic aspirations from the past. By the mid-1980s, however, after repeated economic setbacks, consumers lowered their expectations about achievable growth rates and became more tolerant of high inflation and high unemployment. By the early 1990s, fears about job security grew as Americans became skeptical about the government's ability to use economic policy to prevent downturns.

At this point expectations were so diminished that it took one of the longest economic expansions in U.S. history to reset high levels of optimism. Fueled by the dot-com boom, aspirations soared. In 2000, consumer confidence hit a new peak. With expectations high, consumers in the early 2000s cited high unemployment as an issue even though it was only around 6 percent, half as much as it had been in the early 1980s. The optimism of the late 1990s soon gave way to pessimism because of the successive recessions of 2001 and late 2007. In fact, between January 2007 and mid-2008, the Index of Consumer Sentiment fell by 42 percent, the greatest percentage decline compared to any other recession.

By mapping out historical shifts in consumers' assessments of the economy, Curtin illustrates how "the same level of economic performance, say in terms of the inflation or unemployment rate, can be evaluated quite differently depending on what was thought to be the expected standard." Moreover, changes in standards of evaluation usually occur very slowly and therefore can be difficult to detect. And since different groups of Americans have fared differently as a result of macroeconomic changes, it stands to reason that some Americans may have altered their standards and expectations sooner than others, and some may have altered their aspirations more significantly, and perhaps more permanently. In all likelihood, for example, those employed in the waning manufacturing sector, like autoworkers, had to let go of their expectations for a secure economic life long before and to a much larger degree than have college-educated Americans employed in the expanding service sector.

With this in mind, when sociologists Katherine Newman and Elisabeth Jacobs looked at survey data from the late 1970s to just before the Great Recession that examined people's economic perceptions, they found something interesting. Their analysis revealed that, despite a few peaks and valleys, overall trends during this period suggest that Americans came to see themselves as more secure and in better financial shape, with about the same likelihood of losing their job. As we might expect, their analysis found that those with the lowest incomes and least education expressed the most vulnerability to employment insecurity and financial hardship, while those with higher incomes and more education expressed lower levels of concern.

Yet, despite their lower levels of concern overall, Americans with higher earnings, bachelor's degrees, and managerial jobs have nonetheless exhibited the biggest increase in worry. Over the last thirty years, the proportions of college graduates and managers who said that they are likely to lose their jobs next year and the proportions who said they did worse financially this year than last year have gone up. The rise in concern about job security and financial stability among this group reflects new realities. During this period, the rate of job loss for the most educated went up faster than the rate of job loss for less-educated Americans. And when these workers lost their jobs and found new ones, the new jobs often didn't pay as much. By 2001, workers with a bachelor's degree experienced about a 23 percent drop in their earnings after losing a job. Such trends stand at odds with a long-standing belief among Americans with college degrees that their skills and credentials will translate into a solid footing. If discontent emerges when there is a gap between expectations and outcomes, then it would make sense for concern to increase more among the group that still thought it was well positioned to maintain a good, secure life. When this kind of an expectation smacks into job loss and downward mobility, people will start to worry.

For Americans with less education and lower earnings, it is very possible that worry as measured by feelings about job insecurity and financial hardship did not increase as much over a sustained period because they altered their expectations sooner and more permanently than did better-off Americans. As Newman and Jacobs point out, when those at the bottom lose a job, there is not as far to fall. For such families, their economic situation doesn't change much from year to year; it's always bad. Alternatively, other families may have taken on debt in order to hold on to their standards for security. The lack of a consistent and steep increase in worry among less well-off Americans thus does not necessarily signal that they feel more secure than they used to feel. To be sure, it could actually mean that they have gotten used to having less or gotten used to the high levels of debt required for them to hold on to traditional conceptions of security amid declining fortunes. What is also likely going on is that people's frame of reference for what security even means has undergone a transformation. Finally, it could also be the case that our standard measures for these issues (concern about job security and whether or not we are worse off this year than last) don't allow us to accurately assess people's feelings.

We do not have the kind of comprehensive longitudinal survey data that would enable us to detect subjective changes in Americans' views about what constitutes security and insecurity and whether such definitions shape trends in worry and concern over time. But other measures point to increases in insecure feelings among Americans. For example, even before the Great Recession started, about half of those surveyed worried somewhat about their economic security, with one-quarter "very" or "fairly" worried. By 2009, just over half of those surveyed were now "very" or "fairly" worried. A Pew Research survey done in 2011 found that only 56 percent of those polled felt that they were better off financially than their own parents were when they were the same age, which is the lowest percentage since the question was first asked in 1981, when 69 percent said they felt better off. In 2012, the General Social Survey (GSS) found that less than 55 percent of Americans agreed that "people like me and my family have a good chance of improving our standard of living," the lowest reported level since 1987. That same year, the GSS also found that a record number of Americans (8.4 percent) identified themselves as "lower class," which is the highest percentage reported in the forty years that the GSS has asked this question.

And we may be seeing changes in the definition of the American dream. The American dream has long been equated with moving up the class ladder and owning a home, but recent surveys have noted shifts away from such notions. When Joel Benenson, chief pollster for President Obama, examined voters' thoughts about economic security and the American dream in 2011, he found something new. His polling discovered that middle-class Americans were more concerned about keeping what they have than they were with getting more. Another 2011 survey found the same thing. When asked which is more important to them, 85 percent of those surveyed said "financial stability" and only 13 percent said "moving up the income ladder." In 2007, a survey found that owning a home defined the American dream for 35 percent of those surveyed. By 2013, the top two definitions of the American dream were "retiring with financial security" (28 percent) and "being debt free" (23 percent). Only 18 percent of those surveyed defined the American dream as owning a home.

As the economy experienced wide-reaching transformations, meanings and feelings have likely changed along with it. A National Journal article noted how even the definition of being middle class has undergone adjustment, especially in light of the rise of contract workers or "permatemps," those who may make a good wage but receive no benefits and can expect no job security. Capturing this adjustment, the article asks, "If they make a decent income, are permatemps middle class? Not by the standards of the past. But by the diminished redefinition, maybe they are: earning a middle-class living—for the moment."

Amid these shifting economic tides and morphing definitions, many have lost their way. While old beliefs such as that hard work will lead to security and prosperity have fallen by the wayside, it's unclear to many Americans what new truths lay in their stead. As President Obama's pollster Joel Benenson discovered, this lack of direction causes a great deal of unease. "One of the big sources of concern for the people we talked with," Benenson said, "was that they didn't recognize any new rules in this environment. All of the rules they had learned about how you succeed, how you get ahead—those rules no longer apply, and they didn't feel there was a set of new rules." These kinds of examinations suggest that in the age of insecurity, Americans are not just trying to weather an economic storm, but they are also feeling their way through the dark.

In the throes of the Great Depression, Americans decided that there had to be a better way to organize government and society, one that would allow individuals and families to enjoy greater stability and security. This philosophical shift from "rugged individualism" to "united we stand, divided we fall" paved the way for the New Deal, the Great Society, and the forging of an unwritten but pervasive social contract between employers and employees that rested on mutual loyalties and protections. The government invested in its citizens, employers invested in their employees, and individuals worked hard to make the most of those investments. As a result, in the decades immediately following World War II, prosperity reigned, inequality decreased, and a large and thriving middle class was born.

Beginning in the 1970s, this system began to unravel. Large-scale changes from globalization and the rise of the service economy to a philosophical shift toward free-market ideology and a celebration of risk changed the landscape of security in America. Against this backdrop, the government curtailed its investments in and protections of its citizens, and employers rewrote the social contract to increase their own flexibility and demand greater risk bearing by workers. Individuals continued to work hard, but instead of getting ahead, more Americans struggled harder and harder just to get by.

 Insecurity now defines our world. The secure society has become the "risk society." The belief that we are all in this together has been replaced with the assumption that we are each on our own. Cut adrift, Americans are struggling to forge security in an insecure age. Which goes back to a message I said in, All our Hands are Stained," parents now send the message to their children before sending them at arm's length into the world, "THE WORLD IS NOT SAFE AND SECURE ANYMORE." And most people are willing to trade everything including their freedoms, just to feel safe. Look around, over my lifetime, I have seen our rights and liberty curtailed in the name of freedom, and the world looks more Orwellian by the day.

Corporations for years have advocated for years that occupational and environmental regulations were detrimental for the business and their profitability. For your reading pleasure I have included just a few of some of the more recent industrial accidents caused by corporations either a.) Ignoring current U.S. occupational and environmental regulations or, b.) Moving jobs off-slingshot to another country to sidestep U.S. occupational and environmental regulations:

March 23, 2005: Texas City Refinery explosion. An explosion occurred at a BP refinery in Texas City, Texas. It is the third largest refinery in the United States and one of the largest in the world, processing 433,000 barrels of crude oil per day and accounting for 3% of that nation's gasoline supply. Over 100 were injured, and 15 were confirmed dead, including employees of the Fluor Corporation as well as BP. BP has since accepted that its employees contributed to the accident. Several level indicators failed, leading to overfilling of a knock out drum, and light hydrocarbons concentrated at ground level throughout the area. A nearby running diesel truck set off the explosion

February 7, 2010: 2010 Connecticut power plant explosion. A large explosion occurred at a Kleen Energy Systems 620-megawatt, Siemens combined cycle gas- and oil- fired power plant in Middletown, Connecticut, United States. Preliminary reports attributed the cause of the explosion to a test of the plant's energy systems.[6] The plant was still under construction and scheduled to start supplying energy in June 2010.[7] The number of injuries was eventually established to be 27.[8] Five people died in the explosion.[9]

April 20, 2010: Deepwater Horizon oil spill in the Gulf of Mexico. 11 oil platform workers died in an explosion and fire that resulted in a massive oil spill in the Gulf of Mexico, considered the largest offshore spill in U.S. history.

(Author's note: British Petroleum (BP) pled guilty to 11 counts of manslaughter and during a bench trial (a trial before a judge,) the judge that BP was guilty of negligence and the penalty phase of the trial would commence in January 2015.)

February 7, 2008: The 2008 Georgia sugar refinery explosion in Port Wentworth, Georgia, United States. Thirteen people were killed and 42 injured when a dust explosion occurred at a sugar refinery owned by Imperial Sugar

September 11, 2012: Karachi, Pakistan, 289 people died in a fire at the Ali Enterprises garment factory, which made ready-to-wear clothing for Western export.

November 24, 2012: Dhaka Tasreen Fashions fire. A seven story factory fire outside of Dhaka, the capital of Bangladesh, killed at least 112 people, 12 from jumping out of windows to escape the blaze.

April 24, 2013: 2013 Savar building collapse. An eight-story factory building collapse on the outskirts of Dhaka, the capital of Bangladesh, killed 1129 people.[16] The building contained five garment factories that were manufacturing clothing for the western market

April 5, 2010: Upper Big Branch Mine disaster, West Virginia, United States. An explosion occurred in Massey Energy's Upper Big Branch coal. Twenty-nine out of thirty-one miners at the site were killed.

April 17, 2013: Fertilizer plant explosion in West, Texas, an explosion occurred at the West Fertilizer Company storage and distribution facility in West, Texas, 18 miles (29 km) north of Waco while emergency services personnel were responding to a fire at the facility. At least 14 people were killed, more than 160 were injured and more than 150 buildings were damaged or destroyed.

The only problem with **_ANY_** disasters is that none of the corporate executives were sent to prison for these crimes. They were fined and in the instance of BP was banned from bidding on any drilling contracts on federal lands for four years. But there were injuries and moreover, in each case, multiple loss of life. If corporations want the status of personhood, the individuals responsible for the operation of that corporation must be held to account for behaviors which put profits over people. But the corporate hierarchy always argue that there were multiple people responsible for the decision, hence no one should be heard accountable. I disagree. They should **_ALL_** be held accountable, both criminally and financially. Once that occurs, just once, the corporate oligarchy would rethink or at least give a second thought to their decisions for the greater good rather than for the bottom line.

CHAPTER 12

So the question begs what started this whole mess and how did corporations get so damn powerful? First, we have to examine what is called the Powell Memorandum or the Powell Manifesto, written in 1971, by the late Supreme Court justice Lewis Powell, two months before his appointment to the high court by President Nixon. I discovered this during my research for this book. I was surprised of the amount of folks that did not know the existence of this document. I did not know of its existence. So here it is:

The Powell Memo (also known as the Powell Manifesto)

The Powell Memo was first published August 23, 1971

Introduction

In 1971, Lewis Powell, then a corporate lawyer and member of the boards of 11 corporations, wrote a memo to his friend Eugene Sydnor, Jr., the Director of the U.S. Chamber of Commerce. The memorandum was dated August 23, 1971, two months prior to Powell's nomination by President Nixon to the U.S. Supreme Court.

The Powell Memo did not become available to the public until long after his confirmation to the Court. It was leaked to Jack Anderson, a liberal syndicated columnist, who stirred interest in the document when he cited it as reason to doubt Powell's legal objectivity. Anderson cautioned that Powell "might use his position on the Supreme Court to put his ideas into practice...in behalf of business interests."

Though Powell's memo was not the sole influence, the Chamber and corporate activists took his advice to heart and began building a powerful array of institutions designed to shift public attitudes and beliefs over the course of years and decades. The memo influenced or inspired the creation of the Heritage Foundation, the Manhattan Institute, the Cato Institute, Citizens for a Sound Economy, Accuracy in Academe, and other powerful organizations. Their long-term focus began paying off handsomely in the 1980s, in coordination with the Reagan Administration's "hands-off business" philosophy.

*Most notable about these institutions was their focus on education, shifting values, and movement-building — a focus we share, though often with sharply contrasting goals. * (See our endnote for more on this.)*

So did Powell's political views influence his judicial decisions? The evidence is mixed. Powell did embrace expansion of corporate privilege and wrote the majority opinion in First National Bank of Boston v. Bellotti, a 1978 decision that effectively invented a First Amendment "right" for corporations to influence ballot questions. On social issues, he was a moderate, whose votes often surprised his backers.

Confidential Memorandum: Attack of American Free Enterprise System

DATE: August 23, 1971

TO: Mr. Eugene B. Sydnor, Jr., Chairman, Education Committee, U.S. Chamber of Commerce

FROM: Lewis F. Powell, Jr.

This memorandum is submitted at your request as a basis for the discussion on August 24 with Mr. Booth (executive vice president) and others at the U.S. Chamber of Commerce. The purpose is to identify the problem, and suggest possible avenues of action for further consideration.

Dimensions of the Attack

No thoughtful person can question that the American economic system is under broad attack. This varies in scope, intensity, in the techniques employed, and in the level of visibility.

There always have been some who opposed the American system, and preferred socialism or some form of statism (communism or fascism). Also, there always have been critics of the system, whose criticism has been wholesome and constructive so long as the objective was to improve rather than to subvert or destroy.

But what now concerns us is quite new in the history of America. We are not dealing with sporadic or isolated attacks from a relatively few extremists or even from the minority socialist cadre. Rather, the assault on the enterprise system is broadly based and consistently pursued. It is gaining momentum and converts.

Sources of the Attack

The sources are varied and diffused. They include, not unexpectedly, the Communists, New Leftists and other revolutionaries who would destroy the entire system, both political and economic. These extremists of the left are far more numerous, better financed, and increasingly are more welcomed and encouraged by other elements of society, than ever before in our history. But they remain a small minority, and are not yet the principal cause for concern.

The most disquieting voices joining the chorus of criticism come from perfectly respectable elements of society: from the college campus, the pulpit, the media, the intellectual and literary journals, the arts and sciences, and from politicians. In most of these groups the movement against the system is participated in only by minorities. Yet, these often are the most articulate, the most vocal, the most prolific in their writing and speaking.

Moreover, much of the media-for varying motives and in varying degrees-either voluntarily accords unique publicity to these "attackers," or at least allows them to exploit the media for their purposes. This is especially true of television, which now plays such a predominant role in shaping the thinking, attitudes and emotions of our people.

One of the bewildering paradoxes of our time is the extent to which the enterprise system tolerates, if not participates in, its own destruction.

The campuses from which much of the criticism emanates are supported by (i) tax funds generated largely from American business, and (ii) contributions from capital funds controlled or generated by American business. The boards of trustees of our universities overwhelmingly are composed of men and women who are leaders in the system.

Most of the media, including the national TV systems, are owned and theoretically controlled by corporations which depend upon profits, and the enterprise system to survive.

Tone of the Attack

This memorandum is not the place to document in detail the tone, character, or intensity of the attack. The following quotations will suffice to give one a general idea:

William Kunstler, warmly welcomed on campuses and listed in a recent student poll as the "American lawyer most admired," incites audiences as follows:

"You must learn to fight in the streets, to revolt, to shoot guns. We will learn to do all of the things that property owners fear."2 The New Leftists who heed Kunstler's advice increasingly are beginning to act — not just against military recruiting offices and manufacturers of munitions, but against a variety of businesses: "Since February, 1970, branches (of Bank of America) have been attacked 39 times, 22 times with explosive devices and 17 times with fire bombs or by arsonists."3 Although New Leftist spokesmen are succeeding in radicalizing thousands of the young, the greater cause for concern is the hostility of respectable liberals and social reformers. It is the sum total of their views and influence which could indeed fatally weaken or destroy the system.

A chilling description of what is being taught on many of our campuses was written by Stewart Alsop:

"Yale, like every other major college, is graduating scores of bright young men who are practitioners of 'the politics of despair.' These young men despise the American political and economic system . . . (their) minds seem to be wholly closed. They live, not by rational discussion, but by mindless slogans."4 A recent poll of students on 12 representative campuses reported that: "Almost half the students favored socialization of basic U.S. industries."5

A visiting professor from England at Rockford College gave a series of lectures entitled "The Ideological War Against Western Society," in which he documents the extent to which members of the intellectual community are waging ideological warfare against the enterprise system and the values of western society. In a foreword to these lectures, famed Dr. Milton Friedman of Chicago warned: "It (is) crystal clear that the foundations of our free society are under wide-ranging and powerful attack — not by Communist or any other conspiracy but by misguided individuals parroting one another and unwittingly serving ends they would never intentionally promote."6

Perhaps the single most effective antagonist of American business is Ralph Nader, who — thanks largely to the media — has become a legend in his own time and an idol of millions of Americans. A recent article in Fortune speaks of Nader as follows:

"The passion that rules in him — and he is a passionate man — is aimed at smashing utterly the target of his hatred, which is corporate power. He thinks, and says quite bluntly, that a great many corporate executives belong in prison — for defrauding the consumer with shoddy merchandise, poisoning the food supply with chemical additives, and willfully manufacturing unsafe products that will maim or kill the buyer. He emphasizes that he is not talking just about 'fly-by-night hucksters' but the top management of blue chip business."7

A frontal assault was made on our government, our system of justice, and the free enterprise system by Yale Professor Charles Reich in his widely publicized book: "The Greening of America," published last winter.

The foregoing references illustrate the broad, shotgun attack on the system itself. There are countless examples of rifle shots which undermine confidence and confuse the public. Favorite current targets are proposals for tax incentives through changes in depreciation rates and investment credits. These are usually described in the media as "tax breaks," "loop holes" or "tax benefits" for the benefit of business. As viewed by a columnist in the Post, such tax measures would benefit "only the rich, the owners of big companies."8

It is dismaying that many politicians make the same argument that tax measures of this kind benefit only "business," without benefit to "the poor." The fact that this is either political demagoguery or economic illiteracy is of slight comfort. This setting of the "rich" against the "poor," of business against the people, is the cheapest and most dangerous kind of politics.

The Apathy and Default of Business

What has been the response of business to this massive assault upon its fundamental economics, upon its philosophy, upon its right to continue to manage its own affairs, and indeed upon its integrity?

The painfully sad truth is that business, including the boards of directors' and the top executives of corporations great and small and business organizations at all levels, often have responded — if at all — by appeasement, ineptitude and ignoring the problem. There are, of course, many exceptions to this sweeping generalization. But the net effect of such response as has been made is scarcely visible.

In all fairness, it must be recognized that businessmen have not been trained or equipped to conduct guerrilla warfare with those who propagandize against the system, seeking insidiously and constantly to sabotage it. The traditional role of business executives has been to manage, to produce, to sell, to create jobs, to make profits, to improve the standard of living, to be community leaders, to serve on charitable and educational boards, and generally to be good citizens. They have performed these tasks very well indeed.

But they have shown little stomach for hard-nose contest with their critics, and little skill in effective intellectual and philosophical debate.

A column recently carried by the Wall Street Journal was entitled: "Memo to GM: Why Not Fight Back?"9 Although addressed to GM by name, the article was a warning to all American business. Columnist St. John said:

"General Motors, like American business in general, is 'plainly in trouble' because intellectual bromides have been substituted for a sound intellectual exposition of its point of view." Mr. St. John then commented on the tendency of business leaders to compromise with and appease critics. He cited the concessions which Nader wins from management, and spoke of "the fallacious view many businessmen take toward their critics." He drew a parallel to the mistaken tactics of many college administrators: "College administrators learned too late that such appeasement serves to destroy free

speech, academic freedom and genuine scholarship. One campus radical demand was conceded by university heads only to be followed by a fresh crop which soon escalated to what amounted to a demand for outright surrender."

One need not agree entirely with Mr. St. John's analysis. But most observers of the American scene will agree that the essence of his message is sound. American business "plainly in trouble"; the response to the wide range of critics has been ineffective, and has included appeasement; the time has come — indeed, it is long overdue — for the wisdom, ingenuity and resources of American business to be marshalled against those who would destroy it.

Responsibility of Business Executives

What specifically should be done? The first essential — a prerequisite to any effective action — is for businessmen to confront this problem as a primary responsibility of corporate management.

The overriding first need is for businessmen to recognize that the ultimate issue may be survival — survival of what we call the free enterprise system, and all that this means for the strength and prosperity of America and the freedom of our people.

The day is long past when the chief executive officer of a major corporation discharges his responsibility by maintaining a satisfactory growth of profits, with due regard to the corporation's public and social responsibilities. If our system is to survive, top management must be equally concerned with protecting and preserving the system itself. This involves far more than an increased emphasis on "public relations" or "governmental affairs" — two areas in which corporations long have invested substantial sums.

A significant first step by individual corporations could well be the designation of an executive vice president (ranking with other executive VP's) whose responsibility is to counter-on the broadest front-the attack on the enterprise system. The public relations department could be one of the foundations assigned to this executive, but his responsibilities should encompass some of the types of activities referred to subsequently in this memorandum. His budget and staff should be adequate to the task.

Possible Role of the Chamber of Commerce

But independent and uncoordinated activity by individual corporations, as important as this is, will not be sufficient. Strength lies in organization, in careful long-range planning and implementation, in consistency of action over an indefinite period of years, in the scale of financing available only through joint effort, and in the political power available only through united action and national organizations.

Moreover, there is the quite understandable reluctance on the part of any one corporation to get too far out in front and to make itself too visible a target.

The role of the National Chamber of Commerce is therefore vital. Other national organizations (especially those of various industrial and commercial groups) should join in the effort, but no other organizations appear to be as well situated as the Chamber. It enjoys a strategic position, with a fine reputation and a broad base of support. Also — and this is of immeasurable merit — there are hundreds of local Chambers of Commerce which can play a vital supportive role.

It hardly need be said that before embarking upon any program, the Chamber should study and analyze possible courses of action and activities, weighing risks against probable effectiveness and feasibility of each. Considerations of cost, the assurance of financial and other support from members, adequacy of staffing and similar problems will all require the most thoughtful consideration.

The Campus

The assault on the enterprise system was not mounted in a few months. It has gradually evolved over the past two decades, barely perceptible in its origins and benefiting (sic) from a gradualism that provoked little awareness much less any real reaction.

Although origins, sources and causes are complex and interrelated, and obviously difficult to identify without careful qualification, there is reason to believe that the campus is the single most dynamic source. The social science faculties usually include members who are unsympathetic to the enterprise system. They may range from a Herbert Marcuse, Marxist faculty member at the University of California at San Diego, and convinced socialists, to *the ambivalent liberal critic who finds more to condemn than to commend. Such faculty members need not be in a majority. They are often personally attractive and magnetic; they are stimulating teachers, and their controversy attracts student following; they are prolific writers and lecturers; they author many of the textbooks, and they exert enormous influence — far out of proportion to their numbers — on their colleagues and in the academic world.*

Social science faculties (the political scientist, economist, sociologist and many of the historians) tend to be liberally oriented, even when leftists are not present. This is not a criticism per se, as the need for liberal thought is essential to a balanced viewpoint. The difficulty is that "balance" is conspicuous by its absence on many campuses, with relatively few members being of conservatives or moderate persuasion and even the relatively few often being less articulate and aggressive than their crusading colleagues.

This situation extending back many years and with the imbalance gradually worsening, has had an enormous impact on millions of young American students. In an article in Barron's Weekly, seeking an answer to why so many young people are disaffected even to the point of being revolutionaries, it was said: "Because they were taught that way."10 Or, as noted by columnist Stewart Alsop, writing about his alma mater: "Yale, like every other major college, is graduating scores' of bright young men ... who despise the American political and economic system."

As these "bright young men," from campuses across the country, seek opportunities to change a system which they have been taught to distrust — if not, indeed "despise" — they seek employment in the centers of the real power and influence in our country, namely: (i) with the news media, especially television; (ii) in government, as "staffers" and consultants at various levels; (iii) in elective politics; (iv) as lecturers and writers, and (v) on the faculties at various levels of education.

Many do enter the enterprise system — in business and the professions — and for the most part they quickly discover the fallacies of what they have been taught. But those who eschew the mainstream of the system often remain in key positions of influence where they mold public opinion and often shape governmental action. In many instances, these "intellectuals" end up in regulatory agencies or governmental departments with large authority over the business system they do not believe in.

If the foregoing analysis is approximately sound, a priority task of business — and organizations such as the Chamber — is to address the campus origin of this hostility. Few things are more sanctified in American life than academic freedom. It would be fatal to attack this as a principle. But if academic freedom is to retain the qualities of "openness," "fairness" and "balance" — which are essential to its intellectual significance — there is a great opportunity for constructive action. The thrust of such action must be to restore the qualities just mentioned to the academic communities.

What Can Be Done About the Campus?

The ultimate responsibility for intellectual integrity on the campus must remain on the administrations and faculties of our colleges and universities. But organizations such as the Chamber can assist and activate constructive change in many ways, including the following:

Staff of Scholars

The Chamber should consider establishing a staff of highly qualified scholars in the social sciences who do believe in the system. It should include several of national reputation whose authorship would be widely respected — even when disagreed with.

Staff of Speakers

There also should be a staff of speakers of the highest competency. These might include the scholars, and certainly those who speak for the Chamber would have to articulate the product of the scholars.

Speaker's Bureau

In addition to full-time staff personnel, the Chamber should have a Speaker's Bureau which should include the ablest and most effective advocates from the top echelons of American business.

Evaluation of Textbooks

The staff of scholars (or preferably a panel of independent scholars) should evaluate social science textbooks, especially in economics, political science and sociology. This should be a continuing program.

The objective of such evaluation should be oriented toward restoring the balance essential to genuine academic freedom. This would include assurance of fair and factual treatment of our system of government and our enterprise system, its accomplishments, its basic relationship to individual rights and freedoms, and comparisons with the systems of socialism, fascism and communism. Most of the existing textbooks have some sort of comparisons, but many are superficial, biased and unfair.

We have seen the civil rights movement insist on re-writing many of the textbooks in our universities and schools. The labor unions likewise insist that textbooks be fair to the viewpoints of organized labor. Other interested citizens groups have not hesitated to review, analyze and criticize textbooks and teaching materials. In a democratic society, this can be a constructive process and should be regarded as an aid to genuine academic freedom and not as an intrusion upon it.

If the authors, publishers and users of textbooks know that they will be subjected — honestly, fairly and thoroughly — to review and critique by eminent scholars who believe in the American system, a return to a more rational balance can be expected.

Equal Time on the Campus

The Chamber should insist upon equal time on the college speaking circuit. The FBI publishes each year a list of speeches made on college campuses by avowed Communists. The number in 1970 exceeded 100. There were, of course, many hundreds of appearances by leftists and ultra-liberals who urge the types of viewpoints indicated earlier in this memorandum. There was no corresponding representation of American business, or indeed by individuals or organizations who appeared in support of the American system of government and business.

Every campus has its formal and informal groups which invite speakers. Each law school does the same thing. Many universities and colleges officially sponsor lecture and speaking programs. We all know the inadequacy of the representation of business in the programs.

It will be said that few invitations would be extended to Chamber speakers.11 This undoubtedly would be true unless the Chamber aggressively insisted upon the right to be heard — in effect, insisted upon "equal time." University administrators and the great majority of student groups and committees would not welcome being put in the position publicly of refusing a forum to diverse views, indeed, this is the classic excuse for allowing Communists to speak.

The two essential ingredients are (i) to have attractive, articulate and well-informed speakers; and (ii) to exert whatever degree of pressure — publicly and privately — may be necessary to assure opportunities to speak. The objective always must be to inform and enlighten, and not merely to propagandize.

Balancing of Faculties

Perhaps the most fundamental problem is the imbalance of many faculties. Correcting this is indeed a long-range and difficult project. Yet, it should be undertaken as a part of an overall program. This would mean the urging of the need for faculty balance upon university administrators and boards of trustees.

The methods to be employed require careful thought, and the obvious pitfalls must be avoided. Improper pressure would be counterproductive. But the basic concepts of balance, fairness and truth are difficult to resist, if properly presented to boards of trustees, by writing and speaking, and by appeals to alumni associations and groups.

This is a long road and not one for the fainthearted. But if pursued with integrity and conviction it could lead to a strengthening of both academic freedom on the campus and of the values which have made America the most productive of all societies.

Graduate Schools of Business

The Chamber should enjoy a particular rapport with the increasingly influential graduate schools of business. Much that has been suggested above applies to such schools.

Should not the Chamber also request specific courses in such schools dealing with the entire scope of the problem addressed by this memorandum? This is now essential training for the executives of the future.

Secondary Education

While the first priority should be at the college level, the trends mentioned above are increasingly evidenced in the high schools. Action programs, tailored to the high schools and similar to those mentioned, should be considered. The implementation thereof could become a major program for local chambers of commerce, although the control and direction — especially the quality control — should be retained by the National Chamber.

What Can Be Done About the Public?

Reaching the campus and the secondary schools is vital for the long-term. Reaching the public generally may be more important for the shorter term. The first essential is to establish the staffs of eminent scholars, writers and speakers, who will do the thinking, the analysis, the writing and the speaking. It will also be essential to have staff personnel who are thoroughly familiar with the media, and how most effectively to communicate with the public. Among the more obvious means are the following:

Television

The national television networks should be monitored in the same way that textbooks should be kept under constant surveillance. This applies not merely to so-called educational programs (such as "Selling of the Pentagon"), but to the daily "news analysis" which so often includes the most insidious type of criticism of the enterprise system.12 Whether this criticism results from hostility or economic ignorance, the result is the gradual erosion of confidence in "business" and free enterprise.

This monitoring, to be effective, would require constant examination of the texts of adequate samples of programs. Complaints — to the media and to the Federal

Communications Commission — should be made promptly and strongly when programs are unfair or inaccurate.

Equal time should be demanded when appropriate. Effort should be made to see that the forum-type programs (the Today Show, Meet the Press, etc.) afford at least as much opportunity for supporters of the American system to participate as these programs do for those who attack it.

Other Media

Radio and the press are also important, and every available means should be employed to challenge and refute unfair attacks, as well as to present the affirmative case through these media.

The Scholarly Journals

It is especially important for the Chamber's "faculty of scholars" to publish. One of the keys to the success of the liberal and leftist faculty members has been their passion for "publication" and "lecturing." A similar passion must exist among the Chamber's scholars.

Incentives might be devised to induce more "publishing" by independent scholars who do believe in the system.

There should be a fairly steady flow of scholarly articles presented to a broad spectrum of magazines and periodicals — ranging from the popular magazines (Life, Look, Reader's Digest, etc.) to the more intellectual ones (Atlantic, Harper's, Saturday Review, New York, etc.)13 and to the various professional journals.

Books, Paperbacks and Pamphlets

The newsstands — at airports, drugstores, and elsewhere — are filled with paperbacks and pamphlets advocating everything from revolution to erotic free love. One finds almost no attractive, well-written paperbacks or pamphlets on "our side." It will be difficult to compete with an Eldridge Cleaver or even a Charles Reich for reader attention, but unless the effort is made — on a large enough scale and with appropriate imagination to assure some success — this opportunity for educating the public will be irretrievably lost.

Paid Advertisements

Business pays hundreds of millions of dollars to the media for advertisements. Most of this supports specific products; much of it supports institutional image making; and some fraction of it does support the system. But the latter has been more or less tangential, and rarely part of a sustained, major effort to inform and enlighten the American people.

If American business devoted only 10% of its total annual advertising budget to this overall purpose, it would be a statesman-like expenditure.

The Neglected Political Arena

In the final analysis, the payoff — short-of revolution — is what government does. Business has been the favorite whipping-boy of many politicians for many years. But the measure of how far this has gone is perhaps best found in the anti-business views now being expressed by several leading candidates for President of the United States.

It is still Marxist doctrine that the "capitalist" countries are controlled by big business. This doctrine, consistently a part of leftist propaganda all over the world, has a wide public following among Americans.

Yet, as every business executive knows, few elements of American society today have as little influence in government as the American businessman, the corporation, or even the millions of corporate stockholders. If one doubts this, let him undertake the role of "lobbyist" for the business point of view before Congressional committees. The same situation obtains in the legislative halls of most states and major cities. One does not exaggerate to say that, in terms of political influence with respect to the course of legislation and government action, the American business executive is truly the "forgotten man."

Current examples of the impotency of business, and of the near-contempt with which businessmen's views are held, are the stampedes by politicians to support almost any legislation related to "consumerism" or to the "environment."

Politicians reflect what they believe to be majority views of their constituents. It is thus evident that most politicians are making the judgment that the public has little sympathy for the businessman or his viewpoint.

The educational programs suggested above would be designed to enlighten public thinking — not so much about the businessman and his individual role as about the system which he administers, and which provides the goods, services and jobs on which our country depends.

But one should not postpone more direct political action, while awaiting the gradual change in public opinion to be effected through education and information. Business must learn the lesson, long ago learned by labor and other self-interest groups. This is the lesson that political power is necessary; that such power must be assiduously (sic) cultivated; and that when necessary, it must be used aggressively and with determination — without embarrassment and without the reluctance which has been so characteristic of American business.

As unwelcome as it may be to the Chamber, it should consider assuming a broader and more vigorous role in the political arena.

Neglected Opportunity in the Courts

American business and the enterprise system have been affected as much by the courts as by the executive and legislative branches of government. Under our constitutional system, especially with an activist-minded Supreme Court, the judiciary may be the most important instrument for social, economic and political change.

Other organizations and groups, recognizing this, have been far more astute in exploiting judicial action than American business. Perhaps the most active exploiters of the judicial system have been groups ranging in political orientation from "liberal" to the far left.

The American Civil Liberties Union is one example. It initiates or intervenes in scores of cases each year, and it files briefs amicus curiae in the Supreme Court in a number of cases during each term of that court. Labor unions, civil rights groups and now the public interest law firms are extremely active in the judicial arena. Their success, often at business' expense, has not been inconsequential.

This is a vast area of opportunity for the Chamber, if it is willing to undertake the role of spokesman for American business and if, in turn, business is willing to provide the funds.

As with respect to scholars and speakers, the Chamber would need a highly competent staff of lawyers. In special situations it should be authorized to engage, to appear as counsel amicus in the Supreme Court, lawyers of national standing and reputation. The greatest care should be exercised in selecting the cases in which to participate, or the suits to institute. But the opportunity merits the necessary effort.

Neglected Stockholder Power

The average member of the public thinks of "business" as an impersonal corporate entity, owned by the very rich and managed by over-paid executives. There is an almost total failure to appreciate that "business" actually embraces — in one way or another — most Americans. Those for whom business provides jobs, constitute a fairly obvious class. But the 20 million stockholders — most of whom are of modest means — are the real owners, the real entrepreneurs, the real capitalists under our system. They provide the capital which fuels the economic system which has produced the highest standard of living in all history. Yet, stockholders have been as ineffectual as business executives in promoting a genuine understanding of our system or in exercising political influence.

The question which merits the most thorough examination is how can the weight and influence of stockholders — 20 million voters — be mobilized to support (i) an educational program and (ii) a political action program.

Individual corporations are now required to make numerous reports to shareholders. Many corporations also have expensive "news" magazines which go to employees and stockholders. These opportunities to communicate can be used far more effectively as educational media.

The corporation itself must exercise restraint in undertaking political action and must, of course, comply with applicable laws. But is it not feasible — through an affiliate of the

Chamber or otherwise — to establish a national organization of American stockholders and give it enough muscle to be influential?

A More Aggressive Attitude

Business interests — especially big business and their national trade organizations — have tried to maintain low profiles, especially with respect to political action.

As suggested in the Wall Street Journal article, it has been fairly characteristic of the average business executive to be tolerant — at least in public — of those who attack his corporation and the system. Very few businessmen or business organizations respond in kind. There has been a disposition to appease; to regard the opposition as willing to compromise, or as likely to fade away in due time.

Business has shunted confrontation politics. Business, quite understandably, has been repelled by the multiplicity of non-negotiable "demands" made constantly by self-interest groups of all kinds.

While neither responsible business interests, nor the United States Chamber of Commerce, would engage in the irresponsible tactics of some pressure groups, it is essential that spokesmen for the enterprise system — at all levels and at every opportunity — be far more aggressive than in the past.

There should be no hesitation to attack the Naders, the Marcuses and others who openly seek destruction of the system. There should not be the slightest hesitation to press vigorously in all political arenas for support of the enterprise system. Nor should there be reluctance to penalize politically those who oppose it.

Lessons can be learned from organized labor in this respect. The head of the AFL-CIO may not appeal to businessmen as the most endearing or public-minded of citizens. Yet, over many years the heads of national labor organizations have done what they were paid to do very effectively. They may not have been beloved, but they have been respected — where it counts the most — by politicians, on the campus, and among the media.

It is time for American business — which has demonstrated the greatest capacity in all history to produce and to influence consumer decisions — to apply their great talents vigorously to the preservation of the system itself.

The Cost

The type of program described above (which includes a broadly based combination of education and political action), if undertaken long term and adequately staffed, would require far more generous financial support from American corporations than the Chamber has ever received in the past. High level management participation in Chamber affairs also would be required.

The staff of the Chamber would have to be significantly increased, with the highest quality established and maintained. Salaries would have to be at levels fully comparable to those paid key business executives and the most prestigious faculty members. Professionals of the great skill in advertising and in working with the media, speakers, lawyers and other specialists would have to be recruited.

It is possible that the organization of the Chamber itself would benefit from restructuring. For example, as suggested by union experience, the office of President of the Chamber might well be a full-time career position. To assure maximum effectiveness and continuity, the chief executive officer of the Chamber should not be changed each year. The functions now largely performed by the President could be transferred to a Chairman of the Board, annually elected by the membership. The Board, of course, would continue to exercise policy control.

Quality Control is Essential

Essential ingredients of the entire program must be responsibility and "quality control." The publications, the articles, the speeches, the media programs, the advertising, the briefs filed in courts, and the appearances before legislative committees — all must meet the most exacting standards of accuracy and professional excellence. They must merit respect for their level of public responsibility and scholarship, whether one agrees with the viewpoints expressed or not.

Relationship to Freedom

The threat to the enterprise system is not merely a matter of economics. It also is a threat to individual freedom.

It is this great truth — now so submerged by the rhetoric of the New Left and of many liberals — that must be re-affirmed if this program is to be meaningful.

There seems to be little awareness that the only alternatives to free enterprise are varying degrees of bureaucratic regulation of individual freedom — ranging from that under moderate socialism to the iron heel of the leftist or rightist dictatorship.

We in America already have moved very far indeed toward some aspects of state socialism, as the needs and complexities of a vast urban society require types of regulation and control that were quite unnecessary in earlier times. In some areas, such regulation and control already have seriously impaired the freedom of both business and labor, and indeed of the public generally. But most of the essential freedoms remain: private ownership, private profit, labor unions, collective bargaining, consumer choice, and a market economy in which competition largely determines price, quality and variety of the goods and services provided the consumer.

In addition to the ideological attack on the system itself (discussed in this memorandum), its essentials also are threatened by inequitable taxation, and — more recently — by an inflation which has seemed uncontrollable.14 But whatever the causes of diminishing economic freedom may be, the truth is that freedom as a concept is indivisible. As the experience of the socialist and totalitarian states demonstrates, the contraction and denial of economic freedom is followed inevitably by governmental restrictions on other cherished rights. It is this message, above all others, that must be carried home to the American people.

Conclusion

It hardly need be said that the views expressed above are tentative and suggestive. The first step should be a thorough study. But this would be an exercise in futility unless the

*Board of Directors of the Chamber accepts the fundamental premise of this paper,
namely, that business and the enterprise system are in deep trouble, and the hour is late.*

Footnotes (Powell's)

*Variously called: the "free enterprise system," "capitalism," and the "profit system." The
American political system of democracy under the rule of law is also under attack, often
by the same individuals and organizations who seek to undermine the enterprise system.*

Richmond News Leader, June 8, 1970. Column of William F. Buckley, Jr.

N.Y. Times Service article, reprinted Richmond Times-Dispatch, May 17, 1971.

Stewart Alsop, Yale and the Deadly Danger, Newsweek, May 18. 1970.

Editorial, Richmond Times-Dispatch, July 7, 1971.

*Dr. Milton Friedman, Prof. of Economics, U. of Chicago, writing a foreword to Dr. Arthur A.
Shenfield's Rockford College lectures entitled "The Ideological War Against Western
Society," copyrighted 1970 by Rockford College.*

*Fortune. May, 1971, p. 145. This Fortune analysis of the Nader influence includes a
reference to Nader's visit to a college where he was paid a lecture fee of $2,500 for
"denouncing America's big corporations in venomous language . . . bringing (rousing and
spontaneous) bursts of applause" when he was asked when he planned to run for
President.*

The Washington Post, Column of William Raspberry, June 28, 1971.

Jeffrey St. John, The Wall Street Journal, May 21, 1971.

*Barron's National Business and Financial Weekly, "The Total Break with America, The Fifth
Annual Conference of Socialist Scholars," Sept. 15, 1969.*

*On many campuses freedom of speech has been denied to all who express moderate or
conservative viewpoints.*

Sounds pretty damn scary, doesn't it? That one corporate attorney laid the foundation for the shit storm all of America is currently experiencing. Thanks, asshole. This guy, while a very intelligent and articulate attorney, but with this one act (or memo,) he set the stage for a massive screwing of the American workforce. As a result of this memo, the U.S. Chamber of Commerce moved its headquarters from the seat of Commerce in the United States (New York City) to the very center of American political power Washington, D.C., All in order to be able to peddle influence and lobby for their causes and agendas. They used their power and influence, particularly with the Republican party, a party which the 1890s became notoriously associated with the wants and needs of the rich and powerful, and to hell with the common man.

Anyone remember during the 2012 campaign, when the Republican candidate Mitt Romney was at a campaign stop and was being heckled about something and he said, "Hey, corporations are people too, you know." And shortly thereafter just about every liberal I knew lost their collective minds. But, Mr. Romney was absolutely 100% correct, a corporation, through a series of Supreme Court rulings based upon the 14th Amendment to the Constitution, corporations enjoy a concept what is known as " Corporate Personhood."

Corporate personhood is an American legal concept that a corporation may be recognized as an individual in the eyes of the law. This doctrine forms the basis for legal recognition that corporations, as groups of people, may hold and exercise certain rights under the common law and the U.S. Constitution. For example, corporations may contract with other parties and sue or be sued in court in the same way as natural persons or unincorporated associations of persons. The doctrine does not hold that corporations are flesh and blood "people" apart from their shareholders, executives, and managers, nor does it grant to corporations all of the rights of citizens.

 Since at least Trustees of Dartmouth College v. Woodward – 17 U.S. 518 (1819), the U.S. Supreme Court has recognized corporations as having the same rights as natural persons to contract and to enforce contracts. In Santa Clara County v. Southern Pacific Railroad – 118 U.S. 394 (1886), the court reporter, Bancroft Davis, noted in the headnote to the opinion that the Chief Justice Morrison Waite began oral argument by stating, "The court does not wish to hear argument on the question whether the provision in the Fourteenth Amendment to the Constitution, which forbids a State to deny to any person within its jurisdiction the equal protection of the laws, applies to these corporations. We are all of the opinion that it does." While the headnote is not part of the Court's opinion and thus not precedent, two years later, in Pembina Consolidated Silver Mining Co. v. Pennsylvania – 125 U.S. 181 (1888), the Court clearly affirmed the doctrine, holding, "Under the designation of 'person' there is no doubt that a private corporation is included [in the Fourteenth Amendment]. Such corporations are merely associations of individuals united for a special purpose and permitted to do business under a particular name and have a succession of members without dissolution." This doctrine has been reaffirmed by the Court many times since.

As a matter of interpretation of the word "person" in the Fourteenth Amendment, U.S. courts have extended certain constitutional protections to corporations. Opponents of corporate personhood seek to amend the U.S. Constitution to limit these rights to those provided by state law and state constitutions.

The basis for allowing corporations to assert protection under the U.S. Constitution is that they are organizations of people, and the people should not be deprived of their constitutional rights when they act collectively. In this view, treating corporations as "persons" is a convenient legal fiction which allows corporations to sue and to be sued, provides a single entity for easier taxation and regulation, simplifies complex transactions that would otherwise involve, in the case of large corporations, thousands of people, and protects the individual rights of the shareholders as well as the right of association.

Generally, corporations are not able to claim constitutional protections that would not otherwise be available to persons acting as a group. For example, the Supreme Court has not recognized a Fifth Amendment right against self-incrimination for a corporation, since the right can be exercised only on an individual basis. In United States v. Sourapas and Crest Beverage Company, "[a]ppellants [suggested] the use of the word "taxpayer" several times in the regulations requires the fifth-amendment self-incrimination warning be given to a corporation." The Court did not agree.

Since the Supreme Court's ruling in Citizens United v. Federal Election Commission in 2010, upholding the rights of corporations to make political expenditures under the First Amendment, there have been several calls for a U.S. Constitutional amendment to abolish Corporate Personhood, even though the Citizens United majority opinion makes no reference to corporate personhood or to the Fourteenth Amendment.

During the colonial era, British corporations were chartered by the crown to do business in North America. This practice continued in the early United States. They were often granted monopolies as part of the chartering process. For example, the controversial Bank Bill of 1791 chartered a 20-year corporate monopoly for the First Bank of the United States. Although the Federal government has from time to time chartered corporations, the general chartering of corporations has been left to the states. In the late 18th and early 19th centuries, corporations began to be chartered in greater numbers by the states, under general laws allowing for incorporation at the initiative of citizens, rather than through specific acts of the legislature.

The degree of permissible government interference in corporate affairs was controversial from the earliest days of the nation. In 1790, John Marshall, a private attorney and a veteran of the Continental Army, represented the board of the College of William and Mary, in litigation that required him to defend the corporation's right to reorganize itself and in the process remove professors, The Rev John Bracken v. The Visitors of Wm & Mary College (7 Va. 573; 1790 Supreme Court of Virginia). The Supreme Court of Virginia ruled that the original crown charter provided the authority for the corporation's Board of Visitors to make changes including the reorganization.

As the 19th century matured, manufacturing in the U.S. became more complex as the Industrial Revolution generated new inventions and business processes. The favored form for large businesses became the corporation because the corporation provided a mechanism to raise the large amounts of investment capital large business required, especially for capital intensive yet risky projects such as railroads.

The Civil War accelerated the growth of manufacturing and the power of the men who owned the large corporations. Businessmen such as Mark Hanna, sugar trust magnate Henry O. Havemeyer, banker J. P. Morgan, steel makers Charles M. Schwab and Andrew Carnegie, and railroad owners Cornelius Vanderbilt and Jay Gould created corporations which influenced legislation at the local, state, and federal levels as they built businesses that spanned multiple states and communities. After the adoption of the 14th Amendment in 1868, there was some question as to whether the Amendment applied to other than freed slaves, and whether its protections could be invoked by corporations and other organizations of persons.

The primary purpose of the 14th Amendment was undoubtedly to protect freed slaves.[10] However, the Amendment applies to all Americans, not only freed slaves and their descendants.

Following the reasoning of the Dartmouth College case and other precedents (see below, Case law in the United States), corporations could exercise the rights of their shareholders and these shareholders were entitled to some of the legal protections against arbitrary state action. Their cause was strengthened by the adoption of general incorporation statutes in the states in the late 19th century, most notably in New Jersey and Delaware, which allowed anyone to form corporations without any particular government grant or authorization, and thus without the government-granted monopolies that had been common in charters granted by the Crown or by acts of the legislature. See Delaware General Corporation Law. In Santa Clara County v. Southern Pacific Railroad (1886), the Supreme Court held, ipse dixit, that the Fourteenth Amendment applied to corporations. Since then the Court has repeatedly reaffirmed this protection.

In 1818, the United States Supreme Court decided Dartmouth College v. Woodward, 17 U.S. 518 (1819), writing: "The opinion of the Court, after mature deliberation, is that this corporate charter is a contract, the obligation of which cannot be impaired without violating the Constitution of the United States. This opinion appears to us to be equally supported by reason, and by the former decisions of this Court."

 Seven years after the Dartmouth College opinion, the Supreme Court decided Society for the Propagation of the Gospel in Foreign Parts v. Town of Pawlet (1823), in which an English corporation dedicated to missionary work, with land in the U.S., sought to protect its rights to the land under colonial-era grants against an effort by the state of Vermont to revoke the grants. Justice Joseph Story, writing for the court, explicitly extended the same protections to corporate-owned property as it would have to property owned by natural persons. Seven years later, Chief Justice Marshall stated; "The great object of an incorporation is to bestow the character and properties of individuality on a collective and changing body of men."

In the 1886 case Santa Clara v. Southern Pacific, the Chief Justice Waite of the Supreme Court orally directed the lawyers that the Fourteenth Amendment equal protection clause guarantees constitutional protections to corporations in addition to natural persons, and the oral argument should focus on other issues in the case.

The 14th Amendment does not insulate corporations from all government regulation, any more than it relieves individuals from all regulatory obligations. Thus, for example, in Northwestern Nat Life Ins. Co. v. Riggs (203 U.S. 243 (1906)), the Court accepted that corporations are for legal purposes "persons," but still ruled that the Fourteenth Amendment was not a bar to many state laws which effectively limited a corporation's right to contract business as it pleased. However, this was not because corporations were not protected under the Fourteenth Amendment - rather, the Court's ruling was that the Fourteenth Amendment did not prohibit the type of regulation at issue, whether of a corporation or of sole proprietorship or partnership.[citation needed]

Opinions by two long serving Supreme Court judges, Hugo Black and William O. Douglas, indicate the extent to which corporate personhood is not an all-or-nothing doctrine, but rather relates to the purpose of government regulation and the underlying rights of the individuals making up the corporation. In a case challenging corporate tax rates, Justice Black wrote:

If the people of this nation wish to deprive the states of their sovereign rights to determine what is a fair and just tax upon corporations doing a purely local business within their own state boundaries, there is a way provided by the Constitution to accomplish this purpose. That way does not lie along the course of judicial amendment to that fundamental charter. An amendment having that purpose could be submitted by Congress as provided by the Constitution. I do not believe that the Fourteenth Amendment had that purpose, nor that the people believed it had that purpose, nor that it should be construed as having that purpose.

(Hugo Black, dissenting, Connecticut General Life Insurance Company v. Johnson (303 U.S. 77, 1938).)

Justice Douglas, dissenting in Wheeling Steel Corp. v. Glander (337 U.S. 562, 1949), gave an opinion similar to, but shorter than, the one quoted above, to which Justice Black concurred.

By the time of those opinions, political contributions to candidates in federal races by corporations had been prohibited since the Tillman Act of 1907, even though individual contributions remained unlimited. Yet both Justice Black and Justice Douglas dissented from the Supreme Court's 1957 decision in United States v. United Auto Workers, 352 U.S. 567

(1957), in which the Court, on procedural grounds, overruled a lower court decision striking down the prohibition on corporate and union political expenditures:

We deal here with a problem that is fundamental to the electoral process and to the operation of our democratic society. It is whether a union can express its views on the issues of an election and on the merits of the candidates, unrestrained and unfettered by the Congress. The principle at stake is not peculiar to unions. It is applicable as well to associations of manufacturers, retail and wholesale trade groups, consumers' leagues, farmers' unions, religious groups, and every other association representing a segment of American life and taking an active part in our political campaigns and discussions. It is as important an issue as has come before the Court, for it reaches the very vitals of our system of government. Under our Constitution, it is We the People who are sovereign. The people have the final say. The legislators are their spokesmen. The people determine through their votes the destiny of the nation. It is therefore important -- vitally important -- that all channels of communication be open to them during every election, that no point of view be restrained or barred, and that the people have access to the views of every group in the community.

Thus the two justices would have adjudicated the case and upheld the lower court opinion striking down the ban on corporate and union spending.

Although it is now well settled law that the 14th Amendment extends to corporations, the extent to which it should attach to corporations has continued to draw criticism from liberal legal theorists.

The laws of the United States hold that a legal entity (like a corporation or non-profit organization) shall be treated under the law as a person except when otherwise noted. This rule of construction is specified in 1 U.S.C. §1 (United States Code),[14] which states:

In determining the meaning of any Act of Congress, unless the context indicates otherwise--

the words "person" and "whoever" include corporations, companies, associations, firms, partnerships, societies, and joint stock companies, as well as individuals;

This federal statute has many consequences. For example, a corporation is allowed to own property and enter contracts. It can also sue and be sued and held liable under both civil and criminal law. As well, because the corporation is legally considered the "person," individual shareholders are not legally responsible for the corporation's debts and damages beyond their investment in the corporation. Similarly, individual employees, managers, and directors are liable for their own malfeasance or lawbreaking while acting on behalf of the corporation, but are not generally liable for the corporation's actions. Among the most frequently discussed and controversial consequences of corporate personhood in the United States is the extension of a limited subset of the same constitutional rights.

Corporations as legal entities have always been able to perform commercial activities, similar to a person acting as a sole proprietor, such as entering into a contract or owning property. Therefore, corporations have always had a 'legal personality' for the purposes of conducting business while shielding individual shareholders from personal liability (i.e., protecting personal assets which were not invested in the corporation).

Broadcaster Thom Hartmann has argued that the Santa Clara County case was not intended to extend equal protection to corporations. Chief Justice Waite wrote in private correspondence; "we avoided meeting the [Constitutional] question." Hartmann claims that correspondence between Waite and Bancroft Davis (available in the Library of Congress) demonstrates Waite did not intend to create a legal precedent. The question of whether corporations were persons within the meaning of the Fourteenth Amendment had been argued in the lower courts and briefed for the Supreme Court, but in this interpretation, the Waite Court did not explicitly decide upon this issue. Whatever the merits of Hartmann's theory about the Santa Clara County case, in numerous cases since the Court has reiterated that corporations are protected in many activities by the equal protection clause of the Fourteenth Amendment to the Constitution. The extent of the protection is what continues to be at issue. Generally speaking, corporations may invoke rights that groups of individuals may invoke, such as the right to petition, to speech, to enter into contracts and to hold property, to sue and to be sued, to hold religious beliefs. However, they may not exercise rights which are exclusive to individuals and cannot be exercised by other associations of individuals, including the right to vote and the right against self-incrimination.

Ralph Nader, Phil Radford and others have argued that a strict originalist philosophy should reject the doctrine of corporate personhood under the Fourteenth Amendment.[15] Indeed, Chief Justice William Rehnquist repeatedly criticized the Court's invention of corporate constitutional "rights," most famously in his dissenting opinion in the 1978 case First National Bank of Boston v. Bellotti; though, in Bellotti, Justice Rhenquist's objections are based on his "views of the limited application of the First Amendment to the States" and not on whether corporations qualify as "persons" under the Fourteenth Amendment.[16][17] Nonetheless, these justices' rulings have continued to affirm the assumption of corporate personhood, as the Waite court did, and Justice Rehnquist himself eventually endorsed the right of corporations to spend in elections (the majority view in Bellotti) in his dissenting opinion in McConnell v. FEC.

A central point of debate in recent years has been what role corporate money plays and should play in democratic politics. This is part of the larger debate on campaign finance reform and the role which money may play in politics.

In the United States, legal milestones in this debate include:

Tillman Act of 1907, banned corporate political contributions to national campaigns.

Federal Election Campaign Act of 1971, campaign financing legislation.

1974 Amendments to Federal Election Campaign Act provided for first comprehensive system of regulation, including limitations on the size of contributions and expenditures and prohibitions on certain entities from contributing or spending, disclosure, creation of the Federal Election Commission as a regulatory agency, and government funding of presidential campaigns.

Buckley v. Valeo (1976) upheld limits on campaign contributions, but held that spending money to influence elections is protected speech by the First Amendment.

First National Bank of Boston v. Bellotti (1978) upheld the rights of corporations to spend money in non-candidate elections (i.e. ballot initiatives and referendums).

Austin v. Michigan Chamber of Commerce (1990) upheld the right of the state of Michigan to prohibit corporations from using money from their corporate treasuries to support or oppose candidates in elections, noting: "[c]corporate wealth can unfairly influence elections."

Bipartisan Campaign Reform Act of 2002 (McCain–Feingold), banned corporate funding of issue advocacy ads which mentioned candidates close to an election.

McConnell v. Federal Election Commission (2003), substantially upheld McCain–Feingold.

Federal Election Commission v. Wisconsin Right to Life, Inc. (2007) weakened McCain–Feingold, but upheld core of McConnell.

Citizens United v. Federal Election Commission (2010) the Supreme Court of the United States held that corporate funding of independent political broadcasts in candidate elections cannot be limited under the First Amendment, overruling Austin (1990) and partly overruling McConnell (2003).

Western Tradition Partnership, Inc. v. Attorney General of Montana (2012). U.S. Supreme Court summary reversal of a decision by the Montana Supreme Court holding that Citizens United did not preclude a Montana state law prohibiting corporate spending in elections.

The corporate personhood aspect of the campaign finance debate turns on Buckley v. Valeo (1976) and Citizens United v. Federal Election Commission (2010): Buckley ruled that political spending is protected by the First Amendment right to free speech, while Citizens United ruled that corporate political spending is protected, holding that corporations have a First Amendment right to free speech. Opponents of these decisions have argued that if all corporate rights under the Constitution were abolished, it would clear the way for greater regulation of campaign spending and contributions. It should be noted, however, that neither decision relied on the concept of corporate personhood, and the Buckley decision in particular deals with the rights of individuals and political committees, not corporations.

So you are now looking at every major corporation in America asking, no, make that demanding, that they have their voices be heard through either campaign donations or commercials on every media outlet contributing to the dumbing down of the American populace. But the problem is they don't want to pay for the privilege. They demand to pay little or no taxes, given the fact the fact they continue to demand an ever diminishing tax burden while demanding ever increasing profits via decreased labor costs.

Of course, I also stated previously, the multinational corporations in this country want a loosening of environmental as well as occupational health and safety regulations because it is "bad and costly" to do business in the various states. Most corporations target during every Congresspersons and Senators who support protections as "job killers," with hard working men and women lamenting how a certain pieces of legislation did away with their job and their way of life. This is really evident in my home evident in my area of Appalachian America. Right now, conservative political action groups are claiming that the Environmental Protection Agency's new regulations concerning emissions from coal fired power plants in an effort to reduce greenhouse gas emissions. The folks who mine coal both underground and surface miners, lost their fucking minds. Protests were staged, commercials were aired, naturally the Republican candidates tried to tie the Democratic candidate to President Obama and naturally blamed him for the whole thing. These people would not even consider the possibility of converting the flat tops of all the mountains they destroyed to wind farms for electricity. Renewable energy could be the future for America. It could not only reduce America's dependence upon fossil fuels, it could also provide many thousands of good paying technical jobs.

Unfortunately, one of the biggest growth industries in the United States right now is the corrections industry. The term "prison–industrial complex" (PIC) is used to attribute the rapid expansion of the US inmate population to the political influence of private prison companies and businesses that supply goods and services to government prison agencies. The term is derived from the "military–industrial complex" of the 1950s. Such groups include corporations that contract prison labor, construction companies, surveillance technology vendors, companies that operate prison food services and medical facilities, private probation companies, lawyers, and lobby groups that represent them. Activists[who?] have argued that the prison-industrial complex is perpetuating a flawed belief that imprisonment is an effective solution to social problems such as homelessness, unemployment, drug addiction, mental illness, and illiteracy.

The term 'prison industrial complex' has been used to describe a similar issue in other countries' prisons of expanding populations.

The promotion of prison-building as a job creator and the use of inmate labor are also cited as elements of the prison-industrial complex. The term often implies a network of actors who are motivated by making profit rather than solely by punishing or rehabilitating criminals or reducing crime rates. Proponents of this view, including civil rights organizations such as the Rutherford Institute and the American Civil Liberties Union (ACLU),believe that the desire for monetary gain has led to the growth of the prison industry and the number of incarcerated individuals.

The signing of the Rockefeller drug laws in May 1973 by New York's Governor Nelson Rockefeller is considered to be the beginning of the Prison Industrial Complex. The laws established strict mandatory prison sentences for the sale or possession of illegal narcotics. Federal Judge Mark W. Bennett stated that mandatory sentencing destroys families and perpetuates the cycle of poverty and addiction, with no evidence that it works.

"The Prison Industrial Complex" is the title of a recorded 1997 speech by social activist Angela Davis, later released as an audio CD that served as the basis for her book of the same title. Davis also co-founded the prison abolition group, Critical Resistance, which held its first conference in 1998. Her article entitled "Masked Racism: Reflections on the Prison Industrial Complex," published in the Fall 1998 issue of ColorLines, stated: "Homelessness, unemployment, drug addiction, mental illness, and illiteracy are only a few of the problems that disappear from public view when the human beings contending with them are relegated to cages," Davis says. "Taking into account the structural similarities of business-government linkages in the realms of military production and public punishment, the expanding penal system can now be characterized as a 'prison industrial complex.' "

A few months later, Eric Schlosser wrote an article published in Atlantic Monthly in December 1998 stating that:

"The 'prison-industrial complex' (PIC) is not only a set of interest groups and institutions; it is also a state of mind. The lure of big money is corrupting the nation's criminal-justice system, replacing notions of safety and public service with a drive for higher profits. The eagerness of elected officials to pass tough-on-crime legislation – combined with their unwillingness to disclose the external and social costs of these laws – has encouraged all sorts of financial improprieties."

Schlosser defined the prison industrial complex as "a set of bureaucratic, political, and economic interests that encourage increased spending on imprisonment, regardless of the actual need."[5]

Another writer of the era who covered the expanding prison population and attacked "the prison industrial complex" was Christian Parenti, who later disavowed the term before the publication of his book, Lockdown America (2000). "How, then, should the left critique the prison buildup?" asked The Nation in 1999:

"Not, Parenti stresses, by making slippery usage of concepts like the 'prison–industrial complex.' Simply put, the scale of spending on prisons, though growing rapidly, will never match the military budget; nor will prisons produce anywhere near the same 'technological and industrial spin-off.'"

Others argue that while prison reform is necessary, economic reform through equality for people of color is first necessary before real change can be realized.

As the prison population grows, a rising rate of incarceration feeds small and large businesses such as providers of furniture, transportation, food, clothes and medical services, construction and communication firms. Prison activists who buttress the notion of a prison industrial complex have argued that these parties have a great interest in the expansion of the prison system since their development and prosperity directly depends on the number of inmates. They liken the prison industrial complex to any industry that needs more and more raw materials, prisoners being the material.

The prison industrial complex has also been said to include private businesses that benefit from the exploitation of the prison labor; prison mechanisms remove "unexploitable" labor, or so-called "underclass", from society and redefine it as highly exploitable cheap labor. Scholars using the term "prison industrial complex" have argued that the trend of "hiring out prisoners" is a continuation of the slavery tradition. Prisoners perform a great array of jobs and are exploited in the following ways: minimal payments, no insurances, no strikes, all workers are full-time and never arrive late. Cynthia Young states that prison labor is "employers' paradise". Because of the high profits possible, new businesses involving the import and export of prisoners were developed. Also the prison industry enables to close the gap between free and coerced labor. Prison labor can soon deprive the free labor of jobs in a number of sectors, since the organized labor turns out to be uncompetitive compared to the prison counterpart.

Journalist Jonathan Kay in the National Post defined the "prison industrial complex" as a corrupt human-warehousing operation that combines the worst qualities of government (its power to coerce) and private enterprise (greed). He states that inmates are kept in inhuman conditions and that the need to preserve the economic advantage of a full prison leads prison leaders to thwart any effort or reforms that might reduce recidivism and incarcerations.

The private prison industry has been accused of incarcerating people in mainly impoverished communities for minor crimes so as to use them for free labor. In a study by Doug McDonald, Ph.D. and Scott Camp, Ph.D., known as the "Taft studies", privatized prisons were compared side-to-side with the public prisons on economic, performance, and quality of life for the prisoner scales. They found that in a tradeoff for allowing prisons to be more cheaply run and operated, the degree of reform for the prisoners was going down. Because the privatized prisons were so much larger than the public-run prisons, they were subject to economies of scale. With more prisoners in a single prison, the day-to-day cost to hold the prisoner goes down as the initial startup costs of the prison are already taken care of. Furthermore, with more prisoners comes more free labor. When having larger, privatized prisons makes it cheaper to incarcerate each individual and the only side effect is having more free labor, it is extremely beneficial for companies to essentially rent out their facilities to the state and the government

A response to the prison industrial complex is the prison abolition movement, which seeks to end the social problems that fuel the need for prisons and punishment. The goal of prison abolition is to end the prison industrial complex by eliminating prisons. Prison abolitionists aim to do this by changing the socioeconomic conditions of the communities that are affected the most by the prison-industrial complex. They propose increasing funding of social programs in order to lower the rate of crimes, and therefore eventually end the need for police and prisons. The movement gained momentum in 1997, when a group of prison abolition activists, scholars, and former prisoners collaborated to organize a three-day conference to examine the prison-industrial complex in the U.S. The conference, Critical Resistance to the prison-industrial complex, was held in September 1998 at the University of California, Berkeley and was attended by over 3,500 people of diverse academic, socioeconomic and ethnic backgrounds. Two years after the conference, a political grassroots organization was founded bearing the same name with the mission to challenge and dismantle the prison-industrial complex.

Funding of the Immigration and Naturalization Service (INS) is increasing as about a total of $4.27 billion was allotted to the INS in the 2000 fiscal budget. This is 8% more than in the 1999 fiscal budget. This expansion, experts claim, has been too rapid and thus has led to an increased chance on the part of faculty for negligence and abuse. Lucas Guttengag, director of the ACLU Immigrants' Rights Project stated that, "immigrants awaiting administrative hearings are being detained in conditions that would be unacceptable at prisons for criminal offenders. "Such examples include "travelers without visas" (TWOVs) being held in motels near airports nicknamed "Motel Kafkas" that are under the jurisdiction of private security officers who have no affiliation to the government, often denying them telephones or fresh air, and there are some cases where detainees have been shackled and sexually abused according to Guttengag. Similar conditions arose in the ESMOR detention center at Elizabeth, New Jersey where complaints arose in less than a year, despite having a "state-of-the-art" facility.

The number of undocumented immigrants in the U.S. is over 12 million in total. Those that argue against the PIC claim that effective immigration policy has failed to pass since private detention centers profit from keeping undocumented immigrants detained. They also claim that despite having the incarceration rate grow "10 times what it was prior to 1970", "it has not made this country any safer." Since the September 11 attacks in 2001, the budget for Customs and Border Protection (CBP), and U.S. Immigration and Customs Enforcement (ICE), have nearly doubled from 2003 to 2008, with CBP's budget increasing from $5.8 billion to $10.1 billion and ICE from $3.2 billion to $5 billion and even so there has been no significant decrease in immigrant population. Professor Wayne Cornelius even argued that it is so ineffective that "(92-97%)" of immigrants who attempt to cross in illegally "keep trying until they succeed," and that such measures actually increase the risk and cost of travel, leading to longer stays and settlement in the US.

There are around 400,000 immigrant detainees per year, and 50% are housed in privatized facilities. Over half of the prison industry's yearly revenue comes from immigrant detention centers. For some small communities in the Southwestern United States, these facilities serve as an integral part of the economy. According to Chris Kirkham, this constitutes part of a growing immigration industrial complex: "Companies dependent upon continued growth in the numbers of undocumented immigrants detained have exerted themselves in the nation's capital and in small, rural communities to create incentives that reinforce that growth."

Both the Corrections Corporation of America and The GEO Group have been members of the American Legislative Exchange Council, which has been a factor driving nation-wide adoption of laws, like mandatory minimums for non-violent drug offenders. Investors inquired about Arizona SB 1070 during a conference call with GEO Group executives, in which company president Wayne Calabrese said to them:

"This is Wayne. I can only believe the opportunities at the federal level are going to continue apace as a result of what's happening. Those people coming across the border and getting caught are going to have to be detained and that for me, at least I think, there's going to be enhanced opportunities for what we do."

The reason I bring up the "prison industrial complex," is twofold. First, the fact that the United States has the highest number of incarcerated individuals of any industrialized country on earth. The majority of those incarcerated are both a minority and guilty of nonviolent drug offenses. After they are released, their chances of getting a decent job to provide for their families are slim to none. Secondly, I used to work at a Halfway house for convicted felons. As a social worker, I brought to the job a respect for the "guests," but the program director and higher administration of the company did not view with as much compassion as I did. The prevailing view of "once a criminal, always a criminal," was very pervasive throughout the organization. It did not matter what they were convicted of, each resident was required to undergo intensive drug and alcohol counseling, even if their offense was burglary. I would always explain then they would benefit from the educational experience. I found this a very disgusting experience. So much for them being a social service organization. I noted that they were more interested in keeping the beds full in order to keep payments from the Department of Corrections flowing into their coffers.

But now the "prison industrial complex" has another monetary motivation to keep the beds full. Recently was watching a show on CNBC called "Billions Behind Bars," which profiled some prisons in the state of Colorado which built cabinets, made license plates (the usual prison industry,) parts for guided missiles, and farm raised Tilapia fish for sale in stores. The reason for this rush to capitalize on prison labor? The proponents of this says it teaches the inmates valuable job skills and helps in rehabilitation. Bullshit. The primary reason for the use of inmates in manufacturing in the fact that "state pay" (which when I worked at the halfway house was $1.25 *a day.*) So pretty much the labor costs associated with these prison industries amounts to slave wages. The company's which exploit these inmates are utilizing the 21st century version of slavery. Since the majority of the inmates in this country are either African-American or Latinos, the bear the brunt of the prison industrial complex.

But the conservative noise machine and the talking heads on the evening news are constantly hammering the point home that our streets are not safe. Around every corner there is a drug dealer, crack house, pedophile, rapist or some other ner-do-well. We demand our legislators make tougher and tougher laws all in the name in "law and order." As a result, our police departments look more like an occupying army than one who's primary charge is to "serve and protect." In fact, with the Occupy movement and the protests in Ferguson, Missouri as well as other cities, it is becoming evident that the police departments in this country is more interested in protecting properties and serving the interests of the oligarchy than it is the average citizens.

Take a look at every major empire that has ever existed on planet Earth, which usually lasts about 200 years. Two events generally occur which leads to their downfall. Either by conquest (the Roman Empire,) or by revolt (The French Revolution.) But the course is always the same, ruling class generally get laws (or rulings) which enhanced and cemented their positions while they took advantage of the working and the lower classes. Is America headed down the same path? Is the Tea Party, Sovereign States, and other militia movements which always rise up every time a liberal President is elected to office been duped into thinking that they are being "patriotic" when they are merely being pawns in the games of the oligarchy? America does have its problems, but we always have those of us who believe in the little guy will never give up advocating for their best interests. Of course, the current power structure is set up to hold the workers under the thumb under the corporate hierarchy in an effort for them to maximize their own personal earnings as well as the profits of the corporate masters they have chosen to serve. But the one thing most forget, corporations are immortal; while people are not. So despite all the years of service a person puts into a corporation, they will age, retire and/or die. But the corporation will live on. That is why corporation has the luxury when they lose a lawsuit, they can appeal in perpetuity, knowing full well all they have to do is wait, because, as The Rolling Stones song goes, "Time is on my side."

One aspect which could prevent this obvious abuse of unbridled greed and power, is to give corporations a life span, like any other being on planet Earth. A modest proposal would be to follow the conservative's lead and follow the Holy Bible. Since the Bible says that a measure of a man's years on earth is "three score and ten (or seventy) years.

Another thing conservatives wish to do away with is "entitlements," in particularly Social Security and Medicare. First thing, those are not "entitlements," they are insurance policies, paid for by both the employees and their employers. Whoa, wait a minute. Did I say employer? Who am I to expect a "job creator" to pay for insurance for their wage slaves, Err, I mean their employees. Just kidding, that is exactly what I am expecting. According to current laws, Social Security contributions for individuals are capped out at $117,000. Now most people never reach the cap out, but millionaires and billionaires usually reach that amount on January 2 of the calendar year. Senator Bernie Saunders (I-VT.) Has proposed removing the cap on Social Security insurance on individuals entirely. He stated that this would make Social Security solvent for the next 75 years.

Well, that would solve one problem. Now onto the next. Raise the Damn taxes back to what they were back to the levels in the levels in the 1950s. You remember the 1950's, when the United States citizenry went into a decade long coma and only woke up to enjoy a three year love affair with a youthful President Kennedy before descending into an almost 50 year nightmare of the Vietnam conflict (sorry, it was never declared a war by Congress,) the Presidencies of Nixon and Ford, out of control inflation under President Carter, Reagan and Bush and their economic and military policies. Clinton and his trade agreements, The George W. Bush and his "War on Terror," as well as his economic policies, and the current President Obama, who runs into constant obstructionist roadblocks for the Republican led in Congress. In fact, since World War II, only two Presidents have not only balanced budget, but reported a surplus. President Eisenhower and President Clinton. In Eisenhower's time the top tax rate was 90%.90%! Most conservatives would literally shit a brick at a 90% tax bracket. And i would hate what their supporters would do, burn them at the stake? Probably. But during that time, we were able to build the interstate highway system, and other multiple infrastructure improvements and creations which are now falling into disrepair.

During the 2012 campaign, President Obama made a statement which was taken way out of context, when he said, "You didn't build that." What he actually said was:

"There are a lot of wealthy, successful Americans who agree with me—because they want to give something back. They know they didn't—look, if you've been successful, you didn't get there on your own... If you were successful, somebody along the line gave you some help. There was a great teacher somewhere in your life. Somebody helped to create this unbelievable American system that we have that allowed you to thrive. Somebody invested in roads and bridges. If you've got a business—you didn't build that. Somebody else made that happen.

If you were successful, somebody along the line gave you some help. There was a great teacher somewhere in your life. Somebody helped to create this unbelievable American system that we have that allowed you to thrive. Somebody invested in roads and bridges. If you've got a business – you didn't build that. Somebody else made that happen. The Internet didn't get invented on its own. Government research created the Internet so that all the companies could make money off the Internet."

The point is, is that when we succeed, we succeed because of our individual initiative, but also because we do things together. There are some things, just like fighting fires, we don't do on our own. I mean, imagine if everybody had their own fire service. That would be a hard way to organize fighting fires."

Obama then cited the funding of the G.I. Bill, the creation of the middle class, the construction of the Golden Gate Bridge and Hoover Dam, creation of the Internet, and landing on the moon as examples of what he was talking about.

Although the remark was not initially seen as significant, it soon gained traction. And it became a hashtag on Twitter. According to David Weigel of Slate, the first news story regarding the speech was done by Fox News. The phrase was used by the Republicans to build a political meme. The Washington Post identified the quote in full in the Top 10 political quotes of 2012 in their article of December 28, 2012.

An opinion piece in The Wall Street Journal on July 17, 2012, stated that the speech is a "burst of ideological candor" and that the statement meant that "the self-made man is an illusion". In another Wall Street Journal piece, James Taranto wrote that "The president's remark was a direct attack on the principle of individual responsibility, the foundation of American freedom." Later Kimberley Strassel, wrote that the portion of the speech that spoke about Obama's views on the relationship between business and government was similar to statements made by Massachusetts Senate candidate Elizabeth Warren and that the effect of the speech was to "suck away the president's momentum".

In The Washington Post, Jennifer Rubin wrote that the statement showed that Obama "revealed a level of resentment toward the private sector that was startling, even to his critics", and that the speech reflects that "the anti-business assaults become the campaign.

Meanwhile, his affection for government becomes a chip on his shoulder, prompting him to dare those private-sector wise guys to deny the centrality of government in their success." Later, Glenn Kessler said that the Obama statement was taken out of context and that he was speaking about higher taxes for the wealthy, comparing individual initiative to the system of many people working to create supporting infrastructure.

In The Atlantic, Andrew Cline wrote that what Obama said was an "enormous controversy — a philosophical rewriting of the American story" and that "With his Roanoke speech, Obama turned Jefferson on his head. In Obama's formulation, government is not a tool for the people's use, but the very foundation upon which all of American prosperity is built. Government is not dependent upon the people; the people are dependent upon the government." This, Cline writes, is fundamentally non-Jeffersonian.[29] Earlier in the same publication, Clive Crook wrote that Obama's statements did not mean what his critics wrote they meant, but that the caricature resonates due to it being recognizable as part of his theme of the "rich aren't paying their fair share". Jonah Goldberg, in the National Review, wrote that Obama's "gaffe" was at best truism, and the reason for Obama's supporters attacking others, for taking Obama's words and progressive roots seriously, is because they do not portray Obama as a pragmatist and a moderate.

Guy Benson, on Townhall.com, wrote that the Romney campaign did not take Obama's words out of context since "Obama essentially posits that no private or individual success is possible in America without the government's help." Rachael Larimore, in Slate, wrote that it does not matter what Obama meant to say, as conservatives heard "You didn't get credit for your hard work" and even with the context of the entire speech, the reaction would be largely the same, more importantly it resonated with small-business owners. Rush Limbaugh has commented that business owners did build the roads and bridges through their taxes, and that Obama wants to socialize private profit. Mark Levin, in reaction to the speech, said that Obama was "disrespecting the American people" and that "he despises the capitalist system." Josh Barro, in Bloomberg, wrote that Obama's speech was needlessly insulting, and that the statement resonates badly with people of all income levels; later he quoted Sam Seaborn in the television show The West Wing in regards to progressive taxation.

In researching the 2002 Winter Olympics, NBC News' Domenico Montanaro found that Romney made a similar statement during his speech during those game's opening ceremony, where he said:

"Tonight we cheer the Olympians, who only yesterday were children themselves. As we watch them over the next 16 days, we affirm that our aspirations, and those of our children and grandchildren, can become reality. We salute you Olympians – both because you dreamed and because you paid the price to make your dreams real. You guys pushed yourself, drove yourself, sacrificed, trained and competed time and again at winning and losing.

You Olympians, however, know you didn't get here solely on your own power. For most of you, loving parents, sisters or brothers, encouraged your hopes, coaches guided, communities built venues in order to organize competitions. All Olympians stand on the shoulders of those who lifted them. We've already cheered the Olympians, let's also cheer the parents, coaches, and communities. All right!"

In The Huffington Post, Michael Smerconish wrote that the Romney campaign did take the words out of context, and that the message of the importance of social contracts were better worded by Elizabeth Warren. Nelson Davis, president of Nelson Davis Productions, rebuked the conservatives' take on what Obama had said in Roanoke, saying that the reason why the United States has become great is due to business and government working together. Keeping with the "You didn't build that" meme, Alan Colmes wrote that Romney will not have sewed his suit, would not have built the stage used during the 2012 Republican National Convention in Tampa Bay, Florida, and that his success at Bain Capital would not have been possible without government assistance. Additionally, Anthony Gregory of The Independent Institute, wrote that the implication of the speech was "The state protects business interests, so taxpayers have a partial claim on the wealth produced. "Michael Cohen writing for the Guardian stated that the Republican's usage of the phrase exemplifies that they "not only toil in their own narrowly and misleadingly constructed world, but really are just making stuff up."

In the New York Magazine, Jonathan Chait wrote that Romney use of the words from the Roanoke speech as a "plan of blatantly lying" about it, and the reason why it works is because of a "broader subtext" of the speech due to Obama not using his normal voice, but speaking with a "black dialect". In Bloomberg Businessweek, Charles Kenny of the Center for Global Development also criticized the Romney campaign for taking the word out of context, and went on to state that American businesses benefit from infrastructure, and other elements of the "system" that Obama was speaking about in the speech. Media Matters has made several post targeting Fox News, and other news source who they view as using Obama's words out of context through "deceptive" editing. Ezra Klein, on The Rachel Maddow Show, said that the political statements made in the Roanoke speech were not particularly controversial and that people rely on others and themselves.

There is a lot of people, particularly conservatives who fail, or even live in a state of denial, on they have become a success. Granted, hard work, timeless hours and luck played a factor in their success. But they fail to recognize their workers, teachers, and countless others who along the way. No doubt they have the idea of the rugged individual "pull themselves up by their bootstraps" attitude. No wonder they are resistant to changes. That is why they are called conservatives. They long to preserve the status quo, even if it means harming themselves in the process.

Chapter 13

I want to talk for a few minutes about another attack on worker rights, this time from the state legislatures sworn to serve the public, not set obstacles in place of them. Naturally, conservatives argue that the Declaration of Independence allows people the " pursuit of happiness," not it's attainment. But whose happiness are we discussing, the workers or their employers? Anyway, I digress. Right to work legislation are designed to keep employees and unions from entering into relationships. While unions are not completely outlawed, the union is prohibited from collecting union dues from them, should the employee chose not to pay them. Right to work states usually are in Southern states, but recently it has made inroads into such past union strongholds as Indiana and Michigan.

A "right-to-work" law is a statute in the United States that prohibits union security agreements, or agreements between labor unions and employers, that govern the extent to which an established union can require employees' membership, payment of union dues, or fees as a condition of employment, either before or after hiring. Right-to-work laws do not aim to provide general guarantee of employment to people seeking work, but rather are a government regulation of the contractual agreements between employers and labor unions that prevents them from excluding non-union workers, or requiring employers to pay a fee to unions that have negotiated the labor contract all the employees work under.

 Right-to-work provisions (either by law or by constitutional provision) exist in 24 U.S. states, mostly in the southern and western United States, but also including, as of 2012, the midwestern states of Michigan and Indiana. Business interests represented by the Chamber of Commerce have lobbied extensively to pass right-to-work legislation. Such laws are allowed under the 1947 federal Taft–Hartley Act. A further distinction is often made within the law between those employed by state and municipal governments and those employed by the private sector with states that are otherwise union shop (i.e., pay union dues or lose the job) having right to work laws in effect for government employees.

Before Congress passed the Taft–Hartley Act over President Harry S. Truman's veto in 1947, unions and employers covered by the National Labor Relations Act could lawfully agree to a closed shop, in which employees at unionized workplaces must be members of the union as a condition of employment. Before the Taft-Hartley amendments, an employee who ceased being a member of the union for whatever reason, from failure to pay dues to expulsion from the union as an internal disciplinary punishment, could also be fired even if the employee did not violate any of the employer's rules.

The Taft–Hartley Act outlawed the closed shop. The union shop rule, which required all new employees to join the union after a minimum period after their hire, is also illegal. Under the law, it is illegal for any employer to force an employee to join a union.

A similar arrangement to the union shop is the agency shop, under which employees must pay the equivalent of union dues, but need not formally join such union.

Section 14(b) of the Taft–Hartley Act goes further and authorizes individual states (but not local governments, such as cities or counties) to outlaw the union shop and agency shop for employees working in their jurisdictions. Under the open shop rule, an employee cannot be compelled to join or pay the equivalent of dues to a union, nor can the employee be fired if he joins the union. In other words, the employee has the right to work for a willing employer, regardless of whether or not he is a member or financial contributor to the union.

The Federal Government operates under open shop rules nationwide, though many of its employees are represented by unions. Unions that represent professional athletes have written contracts that include exclusive representation provisions (for example in the National Football League), but their application is limited to "wherever and whenever legal," as the Supreme Court has clearly held that the application of a Right to Work law is determined by the employee's "predominant job situs." Hence, players on professional sports teams in states with Right to Work laws are protected by those laws, and cannot be required to pay any portion of union dues as a condition of continued employment.

Twenty-six states and the District of Columbia do not have right-to-work laws.

Proponents

The first arguments concerning the right to work centered around the rights of a dissenting minority with respect to an opposing majoritarian collective bargain. President Franklin

Roosevelt's "New Deal" had prompted many U.S. Supreme Court challenges, among which, were challenges regarding the constitutionality of the National Industry Recovery Act of 1933 (NIRA). In 1935, as a part of its ruling in Schechter Poultry Corp. v. United States the Court ruled against mandatory collective bargaining, stating: "[t]he effect, in respect to wages and hours, is to subject the dissenting minority... to the will of the stated majority... To 'accept' in these circumstances, is not to exercise choice, but to surrender to force. The power conferred upon the majority is, in effect, the power to regulate the affairs of an unwilling minority. This is legislative delegation in its most obnoxious form; for it is not even delegation to an official or an official body... but to private persons... [A] statute which attempts to confer such power undertakes an intolerable and unconstitutional interference with personal liberty and private property. The delegation is so clearly arbitrary, and so clearly a denial of rights safeguarded by the due process clause of the Fifth Amendment, that it is unnecessary to do more than refer to decisions of this Court which foreclose the question."(However this and other findings in Schechter Poultry were overturned in later Court decisions.)

Besides the U.S. Supreme Court, other proponents of right-to-work laws also point to the Constitution and the right to freedom of association. They argue that workers should both be free to join unions or to refrain, and thus, sometimes refer to non-right-to-work states as forced unionism states. These proponents argue that by being forced into a collective bargain, what the majoritarian unions call a fair share of collective bargaining costs is actually "financial coercion and a violation of freedom of choice." An opponent to the union bargain is forced to "financially support an organization they did not vote for, in order to receive monopoly representation, they have no choice over."

Proponents such as the Mackinac Center for Public Policy contend that it is unfair that unions can require new and existing employees to either join the union or pay fair share fees for collective bargaining expenses as a condition of employment under union security agreement contracts.

Opponents

Some opponents (such as Richard Kahlenberg and Moshe Z. Marvit) have argued that while a wonderfully effective political slogan, "right-to-work" is a misnomer because the lack of such a law does not deprive anyone of the right to work; a right-to-work law simply "gives employees the right to be free riders--to benefit from collective bargaining without paying for it". Khalenberg and Marvit also argue that at least in efforts to pass a right-to-work law in Michigan, the exclusion of police and firefighter unions—traditionally more friendly to Republicans—from the law, belied claims that the law was simply an effort to improve Michigan's businesses climate, not to seek partisan advantage.

Opponents argue that right-to-work laws restrict freedom of association, and limit on the sorts of agreements individuals acting collectively can make with their employer, by prohibiting workers and employers from agreeing to contracts that include "fair share fees". This creates a free rider problem among non-union employees who find the union contract beneficial. Thus, union members may end up subsidizing non-union members. Moreover, American law imposes a duty of fair representation on unions; consequently, non-members in right to work states can and do force unions to provide without compensation grievance services that are paid for by union members. Hence right-to-work laws are not neutral, but rather impose an active and artificial burden on labor unions.

Critics from organized labor have argued since the late 1970s that while the National Right to Work Committee purports to engage in grass-roots lobbying on behalf of the "little guy", the National Right to Work Committee was formed by a group of southern businessmen with the express purpose of fighting unions, and that they "added a few workers for the purpose of public relations".

The unions also contend that the National Right to Work Legal Defense Foundation and National Right to Work Committee have received millions of dollars in grants from foundations controlled by major U.S. industrialists like the New York-based Olin Foundation, Inc., which grew out of a family manufacturing business.

In December 2012, an editorial in the libertarian publication Reason magazine wrote: "I consider the restrictions right-to-work laws impose on bargaining between unions and businesses to violate freedom of contract and association. So I'm not cheerleading for the right-to-work law just passed in Michigan, which bans closed shops in which union membership is a condition of employment. I'm disappointed that the state has, once again, inserted itself into the marketplace to place its thumb on the scale in the never-ending game of playing business and labor off against one another. ... This is not to say that unions are always good. It means that, when the state isn't involved, they're private organizations that can offer value to their members."

According to Tim Bartik of the W. E. Upjohn Institute for Employment Research, studies of the effect of right-to-work laws "abound", but are not "consistent". Studies have found both "some positive effect on job growth", and no effect. Thomas Holmes argues that it is difficult to analyze right-to-work laws by comparing states due to other similarities between states that have passed these laws. For instance, right-to-work states often have a number of strong pro-business policies, making it difficult to isolate the effect of right-to-work laws. Looking at the growth of states in the Southeast following World War II, Bartik notes that while they have right-to-work laws they have also benefited from "factors like the widespread use of air conditioning and different modes of transportation that helped decentralize manufacturing".

Economist Thomas Holmes, compared counties close to the border between states with and without right-to-work laws (thereby holding constant an array of factors related to geography and climate). He found that the cumulative growth of employment in manufacturing in the right-to-work states was 26 percentage points greater than that in the non-right-to-work states. However, given the study design, Holmes points out "my results do not say that it is right-to-work laws that matter, but rather that the 'probusiness package' offered by right-to-work states seems to matter". Moreover, as noted by Kevin Drum and others, this result may reflect business relocation rather than overall enhancement of economic growth, since "businesses prefer locating in states where costs are low and rules are lax".

A February 2011 study by the Economic Policy Institute found:

In 2009, the unemployment rate was 1.0 percentage points lower in RTW states than states without the legislation. In RTW states, it was 8.6%, In other states it was 9.6%.

Wages in right-to-work states are 3.2% lower than those in non-RTW states, after controlling for a full complement of individual demographic and socioeconomic variables as well as state macroeconomic indicators. Using the average wage in non-RTW states as the base ($22.11), the average full-time, full-year worker in an RTW state makes about $1,500 less annually than a similar worker in a non-RTW state. The study goes on to say "How much of this difference can be attributed to RTW status itself? There is an inherent "endogeneity" problem in any attempt to answer that question, namely that RTW and non-RTW states differ on a wide variety of measures that are also related to compensation, making it difficult to isolate the impact of RTW status."

The rate of employer-sponsored health insurance (ESI) is 2.6 percentage points lower in RTW states compared with non-RTW states, after controlling for individual, job, and state-level characteristics. If workers in non-RTW states were to receive ESI at this lower rate, 2 million fewer workers nationally would be covered.

The rate of employer-sponsored pensions is 4.8 percentage points lower in RTW states, using the full complement of control variables in [the study's] regression model. If workers in non-RTW states were to receive pensions at this lower rate, 3.8 million fewer workers nationally would have pensions.

A 2008 editorial in the pro-business periodical The Wall Street Journal comparing job growth in Ohio and Texas stated that from 1998 to 2008, Ohio lost 10,400 jobs, while Texas gained 1,615,000. The opinion piece suggested right-to-work laws might be among the reasons for the economic expansion in Texas, along with the North American Free Trade Agreement (NAFTA), and the absence of a state income tax in Texas.[29] Another Wall Street Journal editorial in 2012, by the president and the labor policy director of the Mackinac Center for Public Policy, reported 71% employment growth in right-to-work states from 1980 to 2011, while employment in non-right-to-work states grew just 32% during the same period.[30] The 2012 editorial also stated that since 2001, compensation in right-to-work states had increased 4 times faster than in other states.

In January 2012, in the immediate aftermath of passage of Indiana's right-to-work law, Rasmussen Reports found that 74% of U.S. voters support right-to-work laws.

In Michigan in January through March 2013, a poll found that 43 percent of those polled said the law will help Michigan's economy, while 41 percent said it will hurt.

Alabama

Arizona † (Constitution, 1912, State Constitution Article 25)

Arkansas † (Constitution, 1947, Amendment 34)

Florida † (Constitution, 1968, Article 1, Section 6) [33]

Georgia

Idaho

Indiana [3] (State law, 2012)

Iowa

Kansas † (Constitution, 1958, Article 15, Section 12)

Kentucky

Louisiana

Michigan [2] (State law, 2012)

Mississippi †

Nebraska ††

Nevada

North Carolina

North Dakota

Oklahoma †

South Carolina [34]

South Dakota

Tennessee

Texas [35]

Utah

Virginia

West Virginia

Wyoming

† An employee's right to work is established under the state Constitution, not under legislative action.

†† An employee's right to work is established under the state Constitution, and there is also a statute.

Pissed off yet? Have I made you just a little angry? I certainly hope so. I just wanted for you to understand that there is an all-out war being declared against the working, middle and poor classes in this country. A war waged by the rich and powerful who are motivated simply by their desire to control as much wealth as possible in our economy. Regardless of what or who it destroys or ruins. In the 1970s and early 1980s, it was the banking industry who decided that the steel industry was too old, too costly and, more importantly, too unionized, to be allowed to continue to operate in the United States. It was far more profitable to go to China or India and build steel mills where they could pay workers about one-sided of what they paid American steelworkers as well as those pesky environmental regulations.

Guess what? Welcome to the wonderful world of the multinational corporations. There mantra is profits, profits, PROFITS. No matter who they kill, how much damage they do to the environment, or how many towns they decimated when they moved their operations offshore, they always get away with it. How long do they keep to expect this gravy train to keep going? Well if current situation keeps going, they hope for, in perpetuity.

Back in the day, years ago before. most of us were even born, and definitely before the days of the internet, corporations actually behaved as good corporate citizens. I remember going to Carnegie Hall a few years ago and was impressed at the number of large corporations who donated to the construction of that beautiful structure for the performing arts. Would such a thing occur today? Highly doubtful, well not without a highly orchestrated public relations campaign much like we saw after the Deep Water Horizon spill with BP. I have to admit, I was impressed at the efforts of BP, even though they killed 11 people and damaged an entire ecosystem for generations to come. But hey, they keep raking in record profits, right? And in a Capitalist economy, that's all that really matters. Well, that and awesome stockholder return.

What the fuck? When I went to business school, we talked about a thing called stakeholders. You know everyone who the business has any impact upon. That not only includes the shareholders, suppliers, customers, the towns which they operate in, and yes, even their employees. Stakeholders are the lifeblood of a business. Without the stakeholders, the only group a business answers to is its shareholders, and all they are concerned with is the maximization of their investment. Kind of sad, isn't it. Money, they say is the root of all evil. No, it is the love of money which is the root of all evil. If that old saying is true, we are closely to becoming one of the most evil, callous societies which ever existed in human history. With the Chairman of the House Budget Committee, Paul Ryan (R-WI.,) will makes a point to extol the virtues of Ayn Rand, who worshiped the individual, regardless of its impact upon community or society as a whole. Rand was, in her defense an ardent Capitalist, who in her novels always showed the protagonist, them ardent Capitalists as well, were always smart, handsome, and willing to do anything to achieve their goals. The consequences be damned.

Even though we love to call ourselves a Capitalist society, we are far from it. Just as we like to call ourselves a democracy, which again, we are not. We are a Republic, at least when it comes to us sending elected representatives to vote on issues in our best interest. Yeah, right. And our society is a Democratic Socialist, more or less. The reason that I use the term socialist is because the government, not the individual, constructed the means in which to do business, but again, they do not seem to realize that they are not alone in their success.

Entrepreneurs have a different mindset than the rest of us. They do since they put in enormously long hours. Working themselves (and their employees) unmercifully. But hey, all for the fulfillment of the American Dream, right? I know I may sound a bit cynical about the individual thing, but I believe that the community is stronger than the individual. Ever since man first appeared on the face of the Earth either 250 million years ago (or 6,000 years ago, if you are a conservative,) man learned very quickly that going it alone was foolish and even suicidal. That is why we formed tribes, families, villages, communities, and eventually cities. It is these building blocks of civilization which allowed mankind to evolve and flourish on planet Earth. And what have we done with it? Pretty much exploited every resource we have gotten our hands on. Timber, coal, natural gas. And in doing so, we have polluted our streams, rivers and air. It is an established fact that the heart's climate is changing. In the Northern Hemisphere, the "polar vortex" a blast of cold article air not only impacted the Northern hemisphere during the winter of 2024, but also the summer of 2014. Of course, the climate change deniers would say that this is proof positive that global warming is nothing to be concerned about. But there have been too many scientific studies to the contrary. And I fear, as my grandson reaches adulthood, he will not only have little or no opportunities to be successful and if he will be able to go outside for fear of being burned to a crisp. I know I may be exaggerating, but I am fearful for a future I know I shall never see.

My generation, the Baby Boomers, were supposed to be the most educated generation in the history of this country. The problem is, we graduated more Master of Business Administration (MBAs,) that any other advanced degree program, including psychologists, social workers (my personal favorites,) and engineering. The people who design and build stuff. We actually have more people who shuffle paper in this country than who build things. And they are rewarded handsomely for it. We squandered our opportunities in service to the almighty Dollar. We have raped and pillaged the environment, waged wars and placed them on a credit card only to expect our children and grandchildren to pay for it. And, to add insult to injury, we take the best paying jobs and send them overseas in the name of profits. All of this was done over the past thirty years.

CHAPTER 15

So now our journey through the rise and fall of the American working class is completed. Thank you for accompanying me on it. We covered multiple issues and many complex socio-economic issues and I hoped I showed you just how truly how fucked up America has become as a result of the greedy, self-serving interests of a few rich Americans who want ALL the economic marbles for themselves. Some who read this would call this book socialistic. I would respectfully disagree with them. I do not call myself a socialist, but I do consider myself very liberal as well as very pragmatic in my approach to life. I believe that everyone should be given as much of an opportunity as possible. And we all go through tough times, but neither kicking a person when they are down nor stacking the deck against them so they cannot get ahead is not the way to do it. Everyone needs an equal opportunity to achieve the same American Dream regardless of the socio-economic status. But until attitudes and thinking towards the working poor and poor classes in this country change, I fear that this is going to be a hard sell.

My family has drifted all over the socio-economic spectrum. Except, we never broke into the upper class. Kinda hard for two social workers to do that, but we were solidly considered middle class. My wife grew up poor, and I grew up in a working class background, so both of our families were very proud of us that we used education to move up the ladder. Now our children are doing the exact same thing. My daughter, Emily, is a Critical Care Nurse and makes more money than either her mother or I ever made as social workers. Good for her! She did her parents proud. And she's not done "bettering" herself. She is currently working full-time, pursuing her BSN full time, all while being a single parent. My son is also pursuing a career as a Social Studies teacher, working after class, and attending college full-time. Both kids are working hard and exhibit the same work ethic my wife and I instilled in them long ago. But I always wonder, what kind of future will they have? Will they be successful? Will they have enough for retirement? All of these things weight on my mind, as it would any good parent.

But I do believe that the American workers are starting to realize that they do not have to sit idly by and allow themselves to be taken advantage of by both Wall Street as well as the corporate oligarchy. Recently fast food workers took to the street to protest the sorry poverty wages, but also for the right to collectively organize. This is a huge step, because multiple cities from New York City to Chicago to Los Angeles all did this. These workers took a huge chance on not only losing their jobs, but also getting arrested, which 700 workers (and a Congresswoman) did get arrested. This is a throwback to the days when union men across the nation, from the Pullman Strike in the 1880s, to the Coal Miners' Strike in the 1920s, to the Farm Workers strikes in the 1960s. All of these strikes had two things in common. First workers did NOT want to be treated just like another piece of disposable machinery. So when they became too old or too sick to continue on with their working lives, they knew that they and their families could and would be taken care of. Second, they wanted to enjoy the fruits of their labors. They wanted to enjoy a lifestyle and a life which rewarded them for THEIR hard work, and not rewarded their bosses for THEIR hard work. To put it simply, they wanted their place at the table, not shoved into the corner, or outside into the elements. Which was the way it used to be. People were kicked out of their homes, blackballed (meaning they could never work in a town again,) if a child or they got sick, their options were either come to work or die. Sounds kind of familiar, doesn't it?

This book was to make you think, which I hope it did it. Thank you for taking the time for buying and reading it.

<u>WORKS CITED AND CONSULTED</u>

Urbina, Ian (April 9, 2010). "No Survivors Found After West Virginia Mine Disaster". The New York Times.

Weiner, Juli (July 18, 2012). "The Rise of Romney's "You Didn't Build That" Meme". Vanity Fair. Retrieved September 14, 2012.

Cohen, Michael (August 29, 2012). "They built that: how a Republican lie turned into an alternate universe". The Guardian. Retrieved September 14, 2012.

"Meme of the Week: 'You Didn't Build That'". The Daily Beast. Retrieved September 14, 2012.

Kessler, Glenn (July 23, 2012). "An unoriginal Obama quote, taken out of context". The Fact Checker (Washington Post). Retrieved January 19, 2014.

"President Obama Campaign Rally in Roanoke". Road to the White House. C-SPAN. July 13, 2012. Retrieved August 13, 2012.

"Putting Mitt Romney's attacks on 'You didn't build that' to the Truth-O-Meter". Politifact. Tampa Bay Times. July 25, 2012. Retrieved August 13, 2012.

Eugene Kiely (July 24, 2012). "'You Didn't Build That,' Uncut and Unedited". The FactCheck Wire. Annenberg Public Policy Center of the University of Pennsylvania. Retrieved August 12, 2012.

Smerconish, Michael (July 30, 2012). "'You Didn't Build That!' in Context". The Huffington Post. Retrieved September 2, 2012.

Sargent, Greg (September 21, 2011). "Class warfare, Elizabeth Warren style". The Washington Post. Retrieved September 31.

Elizabeth Warren speaking in Andover, Massachusetts, on Debt Crisis and Fair Taxation

Smerconish, Michael (July 30, 2012). "The context behind Obama's 'you didn't build that'". Philadelphia Inquirer. Retrieved September 31, 2012.

Gabbay, Tiffany (September 21, 2011). "Elizabeth Warren on class warfare: 'There is nobody in this country who got rich on his own'". TheBlaze. Retrieved September 2, 2012.

Robillard, Kevin (July 25, 2012). "Scott Brown: Obama echoed Elizabeth Warren speech". Politico. Retrieved September 2, 2012.

Trumbull, Mark (July 31, 2012). "Elizabeth Warren: What will Obama's 'you didn't build that' ally say to DNC?". The Christian Science Monitor. Retrieved September 2, 2012.

Democrat Warren Tops Brown in Mass. Senate Race WBUR Fred Thys November 6, 2012 Updated Nov 7,

"Obama campaign in full swing in Virginia". San Francisco Chronicle. 13 July 212. Retrieved August 13, 2012.

Chait, Jonathan (July 20, 2012). "How 'You Didn't Build That' Violated Conservative P.C.". New York (magazine). Retrieved September 2, 2012.

"Remarks by the President at a Campaign Event in Roanoke, Virginia". Office of the Press Secretary. White House. 13 July 2012. Retrieved 13 August 2012.

Aaron Blake (July 18, 2012). "Obama's 'You didn't build that' problem". The Washington Post. Retrieved August 13, 2012.

Kathleen Hennessey (July 18, 2012). "Republicans pouncing on Obama's 'you didn't build that' remark". Los Angeles Times. Retrieved August 13, 2012.

David Weigel (July 16, 2012). "Memewatch: Did Obama Say That Successful People Didn't Earn What They Have?". Slate. Retrieved August 13, 2012.

"Obama to business owners: 'You didn't build that'". Fox News. July 16, 2012. Retrieved August 13, 2012.

Juli Weiner (July 18, 2012). "The Rise of Romney's "You Didn't Build That" Meme". Vanity Fair. Retrieved August 13, 2012.

"'You Didn't Build That'". The Wall Street Journal. July 17, 2012. Retrieved August 13, 2012.

James Taranto (July 18, 2012). "You Didn't Sweat, He Did". The Wall Street Journal. Retrieved August 13, 2012.

Kimberley A. Strassel (July 26, 2012). "Four Little Words: Why the Obama campaign is suddenly so worried". The Wall Street Journal. Retrieved August 13, 2012.

Jennifer Ruben (July 24, 2012). "Obama is losing his message like nobody's business". The Washington Post. Retrieved August 13, 2012.

Glenn Kessler (August 13, 2012). "What did Obama mean when he said, 'you didn't build that'? —Gaffe Check Video". The Washington Post. Retrieved August 13, 2012.

Andrew Cline (August 10, 2012). "What 'You Didn't Build That' Really Means—and Why Romney Can't Explain It". The Atlantic. Retrieved August 17, 2012.

Clive Crook (July 22, 2012). "There's No Such Thing as Building a Business". The Atlantic. Retrieved August 17, 2012.

Jonah Goldberg (July 20, 2012). "Co-sponsoring Your Success". National Review Online. Retrieved August 28, 2012.

Guy Benson (August 19, 2012). "No, Conservatives Aren't Taking 'You Didn't Build That' Out of Context". Townhall.com. Salem Communications. Retrieved August 19, 2012.

Rachael Larimore (August 30, 2012). ""You Didn't Build That" Isn't Going Away". Slate. Retrieved September 4, 2012.

"An Incomprehensible Defense of Obama's "You Didn't Build That" Philosophy". RushLimbaugh.com. Premiere Radio Networks. August 23, 2012. Retrieved August 20, 2012. "Right. Roads and bridges. The fact is, they did build the roads and bridges. It was their taxes who built the roads and bridges."

"The Most Telling Moment of Obama's Presidency: "You Didn't Build That"". RushLimbaugh.com. Premiere Radio Networks. August 24, 2012. Retrieved August 20, 2012. "This roads-and-bridges stuff is just liberal claptrap. What he's doing, what he's setting the stage for is trying to socialize profit so that he can claim it. What he wants people to conclude is that profit was not possible, is not possible, without government first making it possible. And, therefore, government owns it. It's government's profit. He wants to socialize the profit, and that's then the vehicle for going after everybody's money via higher taxes, a wealth tax, or whatever technique that he tries."

Mark Levin (2012). Romney Goes On Offense, Mark Levin Reacts. New York: Fox News. Event occurs at 1:30. Archived from the original on August 18, 2012. Retrieved August 28, 2012.

Josh Barro (July 30, 2012). "Why 'You Didn't Build That' Resonates". Bloomberg. Retrieved August 13, 2012.

Domenico Montanaro (23 July 2012). "Romney to Olympians: 'You didn't get here solely on your own'". NBC News. Retrieved 13 August 2012.

Michael Smerconish (July 30, 2012). "'You Didn't Build That!' in Context". The Huffington Post. Retrieved August 12, 2012.

Nelson Davis (July 26, 2012). "We Did Build That". The Huffington Post. Retrieved August 13, 2012.

Alan Colmes (August 27, 2012). "I Didn't Write This". The Huffington Post. Retrieved August 28, 2012.

Anthony Gregory (July 24, 2012). "Then, Who DID Build It, Mr. President?". The Huffington Post. Retrieved August 19, 2012.

Jonathan Chait (July 27, 2012). "The Real Reason 'You Didn't Build That' Works". New York (magazine). Retrieved August 13, 2012.

Charles Kenny (July 22, 2012). "Sorry, Mitt: Businesses Aren't Built on Their Own". Bloomberg Businessweek. Retrieved August 17, 2012.

Andy Newbold (August 17, 2012). "Fox Hypes Romney Campaign Attack On Obama Based On Deceptively Edited Comments". Blog. Media Matters for America. Retrieved August 19, 2012.

Justin Berrier (July 25, 2012). "Fox Claims to Offer "Context" For Obama Comments -- Then Airs Another Deceptively Edited Clip". Blog. Media Matters for America. Retrieved August 19, 2012.

Remington Shepard (July 16, 2012). "Fox & Friends Deceptively Edits Obama's Comments On Small Business". Blog. Media Matters for America. Retrieved August 19, 2012.

Mike Burns; Marcus Feldman (July 27, 2012). "Local News Outlets Help Push Bogus "Build That" Attack Against Obama". Research. Media Matters for America. Retrieved August 19, 2012.

"Romney apparently didn't build bogus attack on Obama". MSNBC. July 24, 2012. Retrieved August 28, 2012. "in the annals of controversy political statements, this should not be a particularly controversial one. it's the idea that human beings rely on each other as well as themselves. that they rely on the societies as well in order to succeed."

"WATCH: Jon Stewart Nails Mitt Romney for Basing His Entire Campaign on Obama's Out-Of-Context Quote". Business Insider. July 26, 2012. Retrieved August 13, 2012.

Serena Dai (July 26, 2012). "Jon Stewart Chips Away at 'You Didn't Build That'". The Atlantic Wire. Retrieved August 20, 2012.

Christian Toto (July 26, 2012). "Stewart Rushes to Obama's Defense Over 'You Didn't Build That' Meme". Breitbart.com. Retrieved August 19, 2012.

Carol Hartsell (July 26, 2012). "Jon Stewart Slams You-Didn't-Build-That-Gate in Romney, Fox News' Faces (VIDEO)". The Huffington Post. Retrieved August 19, 2012.

Meredith Blake (July 26, 2012). "Late Night: Jon Stewart rips Romney, Fox on Obama 'misrepresentation'". Los Angeles Times. Retrieved August 20, 2012.

"Colbert's One-Man Show Proves Obama Wrong: Host Does 'The Word' By Himself (VIDEO)". The Huffington Post. July 26, 2012. Retrieved August 21, 2012.

Debra Pangestu (July 26, 2012). "Colbert Jabs Romney for Defending Obama's Business Sentiments". WMAQ-TV. Retrieved August 21, 2012.

Jay Leno (2012). Monologue, Part 1 (7/19/12). NBC. Event occurs at 1:04. Retrieved August 17, 2012. "Jobless claims rose again by 35,000 last week. Not good. But it does show that if you're unsuccessful in this country, you didn't do it on your own. You had help. Thank you, President Obama. Thank you. You're not alone, you didn't do it alone."

Gary Varvel; Michael Ramirez; Steve Kelley (August 11, 2012). "Obama defines success". Political cartoonists index. Cagle Cartoons, Inc. Retrieved August 17, 2012.

Sushannah Walshe (July 25, 2012). "Romney Camp Continues 'You Didn't Build That' Attacks with Swing State Events". ABC News. Retrieved August 13, 2012.

van Sickler, Michael (July 25, 2012). "Two local businessowners tapped by Romney to speak out on Obama have bios that contradict message". Tampa Bay Times. Retrieved August 23, 2012.

"Romney Doubles Down On "You Didn't Build That" With New Website". Talk Radio News Service. July 26, 2012. Retrieved August 13, 2012.

"Built By US". Romney for President, Inc. Retrieved August 19, 2012.

Kevin Bohn; Gregory Wallace (July 28, 2012). "Romney's son plugs 'Built by Us' merchandise jabbing at Obama remark". CNN. Retrieved August 19, 2012.

Wes Barrett (August 21, 2012). "'We Built This'". Fox Nation. Retrieved September 1, 2012.

"Say it in Song". San Francisco Chronicle. Associated Press. August 27, 2012. Retrieved September 1, 2012.

"GOP Announces Convention Theme "We Built This" In Stadium Built With 62% Government Funds". The Daily Dolt. Retrieved August 30, 2012. [self-published source]

Taegan D. Goddard (August 22, 2012). "GOP Convention Held in Stadium Built with Public Funds". Political Wire. CQ Roll Call. Retrieved August 30, 2012.

David Sirota (August 29, 2012). "The four biggest convention stories you won't hear about". Salon. Salon Media Group, Inc. Retrieved August 30, 2012.

Lane Turner (2012). Song At RNC: "I Built It" (480p). Tampa, Florida: TPMTV. Retrieved September 1, 2012.

"Fact check: What President Obama actually said about small businesses". Truth team. Obama for America. July 17, 2012. Retrieved August 13, 2012.

Philip Elliot (July 29, 2012). "SPIN METER: Obama's 'You didn't build that' echoes". North County Times. Retrieved August 13, 2012.

Barack Obama (2012). "Always" - Obama for America TV Ad (360p). BarackObamadotcom. Event occurs at 0:31. Retrieved August 14, 2012.

David Sorasohn (July 28, 2012). "Barack Obama in Portland campaigns right down the middle". The Oregonian. Retrieved August 28, 2012.

"Remarks by the President at a Campaign Event". Office of the Press Secretary. White House. 24 July 2012. Retrieved 27 August 2012.

Byron Tau (August 9, 2012). "Deli owner wants store removed from Obama ad". Politico. Retrieved August 25, 2012.

Mary Bruce (August 15, 2012). "Caterer at Obama Iowa Event Wears Pro-Romney Shirt". ABC News. Retrieved August 19, 2012.

Amy Gardner (August 15, 2012). "Iowa deli co-owner caters for Obama visit, but his T-shirt tells another story". The Washington Post. Retrieved August 25, 2012.

Laura Matthews (August 16, 2012). "Virginia Business Owner Shuns Biden Over Obama's 'You Didn't Build That' Remark". International Business Times. Retrieved August 25, 2012.

Baird, Charles W. "Right to work before and after 14 (b)." Journal of Labor Research 19.3 (1998): 471-493.

"Michigan passes 'right-to-work' legislation". BBC News. December 11, 2012.

Schneider, Mary Beth; Sikich, Chris (February 1, 2012). "Indiana Gov. Daniels signs 'right to work' bill; protest winds through Super Bowl Village". The Indianapolis Star. Retrieved February 1, 2012.

"The South Carolina Governance Project — Interest Groups in South Carolina," Center for Governmental Services, Institute for Public Service and Policy Research, University of South Carolina, Accessed July 6, 2007.

Miller, Berkeley; Canak, William (1991). "From 'Porkchoppers' to 'Lambchoppers': The Passage of Florida's Public Employee Relations Act". Industrial and Labor Relations Review 44 (2): 349–66. doi:10.2307/2524814. JSTOR 2524814.

Partridge, Dane M. (1997). "Virginia's New Ban on Public Employee Bargaining: A Case Study of Unions, Business, and Political Competition". Employee Responsibilities and Rights Journal 10 (2): 127–39. doi:10.1023/A:1025657412651.

Canak, William; Miller, Berkeley (1990). "Gumbo Politics: Unions, Business, and Louisiana Right-to-Work Legislation". Industrial and Labor Relations Review 43 (2): 258–71. doi:10.2307/2523703. JSTOR 2523703.

Roof, Tracy (2011). American Labor, Congress, and the Welfare State, 1935-2010. JHU Press. p. 73. ISBN 9781421400877.

NFL Collective Bargaining Agreement 2006-2012: Art. V, Sec. 1.

Oil, Chemical and Atomic Workers, Int'l Union v. Mobil Oil Corp., 426 U.S. 407, 414 (1976) (Marshall, J.).

Orr v. National Football League Players Ass'n, 145 L.R.R.M. (BNA) 2224, 1993 WL 604063 (Va.Cir.Ct. 1993).

Carter v. Carter Coal Co., 298 U. S. 238, at 311 (1936).

Campbell, Simon. "Right-to-Work vs Forced Unionism". StopTeacherStrikes, Inc. Retrieved November 14, 2012. "Fair share is compulsory dues. A non-union employee is forced to financially support an organization they did not vote for, in order to receive monopoly representation, they have no choice over. It is financial coercion and a violation of freedom of choice. Money is forcibly withheld from non-union employees' paychecks and sent to a private organization. When an agency-shop agreement exists in a school district or county, every employee must pay dues to the union as a condition of their employment. They must pay-up or leave. Should anyone's ability to get or keep a job depend on whether they pay dues to a union? Non-union teachers have struggled in court to try and stop their forced dues from being used for political activity by the union."

Improvement #3: Remove Union Security Clauses Mackinac Center for Public Policy

"Right to Work" Isn't a Civil Right. But Unionizing Should Be| Richard D. Kahlenberg and Moshe Z. Marvit| December 13, 2012

Gould, Elise; Shierholz, Heidi (2011). "The Compensation penalty of "right-to-work" laws"" (PDF). Retrieved 2012-12-11.

Dinan, Elizabeth (January 14, 2011). "N.H. Rep. proposes right to work law". Seacoast Online. Retrieved 2012-12-11.

Greenhouse, Steven (January 3, 2011). "States Seek Laws to Curb Power of Unions". The New York Times.

"Examining the opposition's tangled web — the who's who in the right wing". The Machinist. International Association of Machinists and Aerospace Workers, AFL-CIO/CLC. October 1977. p. 4.

http://www.uawlocal3520.org/right%20to%20workfliner.pdf [dead link] "Questions and Answers about the National Right to Work Committee and the National Right to Work Legal Defense Foundation," United Auto Workers, Accessed February 3, 2008.

"Meet the billionaires behind No Rights at Work". 27 January 2013. Teamster Nation. Retrieved 14 February 2013.

http://reason.com/blog/2012/12/12/when-right-to-work-is-wrong-and-un-liber

Studies mixed on right-to-work's impact| By Susan Samples| 12 December 2012

Holmes, Thomas J. (1998). "The Effect of State Policies on the Location of Manufacturing: Evidence from State Borders". Journal of Political Economy 106 (4): 667–705. doi:10.1086/250026.

Economic evidence mixed on "right to work" laws| By: Gordon Evans| Kalamazoo, Mi| 9 December 2012

Barro, Robert (February 28, 2011). "Opinion: Unions vs. the Right to Work". Wall Street Journal. Retrieved 2012-12-11.

Holmes, Thomas The Location of Industry: Do States' Policies Matter?

Drum, Kevin (2011-2-28) Unions and Growth Mother Jones

Texas v. Ohio, "Texas is prospering while Ohio lags"| The Wall Street Journal| March 3, 2008| Accessed July 18, 2008.

Vernuccio, Vincent; Lehman, Joseph G. (December 14, 2012). "Vernuccio and Lehman: An Inspiration and a Warning from Michigan". The Wall Street Journal. Retrieved December 18, 2012.

http://www.rasmussenreports.com/public_content/business/jobs_employment/january_2012/74_favor_right_to_work_law_eliminating_mandatory_union_dues

http://www.mlive.com/politics/index.ssf/2013/03/poll_michigan_evenly_divided_o.html

"Florida Constitution". The Florida Legislature. Retrieved 2014-07-11.

"South Carolina Code of Laws § 41-7-10".

http://www.statutes.legis.state.tx.us/Docs/LA/htm/LA.101.htm Texas Labor Code, Section 101.052.

Alex Friedmann (15 January 2012). The Societal Impact of the Prison Industrial Complex, or Incarceration for Fun and Profit—Mostly Profit. Prison Legal News. Retrieved 23 July 2014.

Sudbury, Julia. "Celling Black Bodies: Black Women in the Global Prison Industrial Complex". Feminist Review.

Whitehead, John (April 10, 2012). "Jailing Americans for Profit: The Rise of the Prison Industrial Complex". Rutherford Institute. Retrieved June 29, 2013.

Shapiro, David. "Banking on Bondage: Private Prisons and Mass Incarceration". American Civil Liberties Union. Retrieved 29 June 2013.

Schlosser, Eric (December 1998). "The Prison–Industrial Complex". The Atlantic Monthly.

Bennett, Mark W. (October 24, 2012). "How Mandatory Minimums Forced Me to Send More Than 1,000 Nonviolent Drug Offenders to Federal Prison". The Nation. Retrieved 23 May 2013.

Davis, Angela (Fall 1998). "Masked Racism: Reflections on the Prison Industrial Complex". ColorLines.

Gottschalk, Marie (2010). "Cell blocks & red ink: mass incarceration, the great recession & penal reform.". Daedalus 139 (3): 62–73. doi:10.1162/DAED_a_00023.

Goldberg, Evans (2009). Prison Industrial Complex and the Global Economy. Oakland: PM Press. ISBN 1-60486-043-X.

Guilbaud, Fabrice. "Working in Prison: Time as Experienced by Inmate-Workers." Revue française de sociologie 51.5 (2010): 41-68.[1]

Smith, Earl; Angela Hattery (2006). "If We Build It They Will Come: Human Rights Violation and the Prison Industrial Complex". Society Without Borders 2 (2): 273– 288.

Kai, Jonathan (March 23, 2013). "The disgrace of America's prison-industrial complex". National Post. p. A22.

Young, Cynthia (2000). "Punishing Labor: Why Labor Should Oppose the Prison Industrial Complex". New Labor Forum (7).

Pelaez, Vicky (2008). "The prison industry in the United States: big business or a new form of slavery?". Global Research.

"Cost, Performance Studies Look at Prison Privatization". National Institute of Justice: Criminal Justice Research, Development and Evaluation.

Braz, Brown; et al (200). "The History of Critical Resistance". Social Justice 27 (3): 6–10. JSTOR 29767223.

Welch, Micheal (2000). "The Role of Immigration and Naturalization in the Prison Industrial Complex". Social Justice 27 (3): 73. JSTOR 29767232?

Koulish, Robert (January 2007). "Blackwater and the Privatization of Immigration Control". Selected Works: 12–13.

Welch, Micheal (2000). "The Role of Immigration and Naturalization in the Prison Industrial Complex". Social Justice 27 (3): 75. JSTOR 29767232?

Welch, Micheal (2000). "The Role of Immigration and Naturalization in the Prison Industrial Complex". Social Justice 27 (3): 76. JSTOR 29767232?

Welch, Micheal (2000). "The Role of Immigration in the Prison-Industrial Complex". Social Justice 27 (3): 77. JSTOR 29767232?

Golash-Boza, Tanya (2009). "The Immigration Industrial Complex: Why We Enforce Immigration Policies Destined to Fail". Sociology Compass 3 (2): 295. doi:10.1111/j.1751-9020.2008.00193. x.

Boza-Golash, T. (12 February 2009). "The Immigration Industrial Complex, Why We Enforce Policies Destined to Fail". Sociology Compass 3 (2): 302. doi:10.1111/j.1751-9020.2008.00193. x.

Boza-Golash, T. (12 February 2009). "The Immigration Industrial Complex, Why We Enforce Policies Destined to Fail". Sociology Compass 3 (2): 304. doi:10.1111/j.1751-9020.2008.00193. x.

Boza-Golash, T. (12 February 2009). "The Immigration Industrial Complex, Why We Enforce Policies Destined to Fail". Sociology Compass 3 (2): 305. doi:10.1111/j.1751-9020.2008.00193. x.

Chris Kirkham (7 June 2012). Private Prisons Profit from Immigration Crackdown, Federal and Local Law Enforcement Partnerships. The Huffington Post. Retrieved 12 May 2014.

Christina Sterbenz (27 January 2014). The For-Profit Prison Boom in One Worrying Infographic. Business Insider. Retrieved 12 May 2014.

Sullivan, Laura (2010). Prison Economics Help Drive Ariz. Immigration Law. National Public Radio.

Elk, Mike and Sloan, Bob (2011). The Hidden History of ALEC and Prison Labor. The Nation.

Dyer, Joel, "The Perpetual Prisoner Machine—How America Profits from Crime"; 2000 by Westview Press, A Member of the Perseus Books Group, 5500 Central Avenue, Boulder, Colorado 80301-2877; ISBN 0-8133-3507-8 (hc); LC# HV9950.D04 1999

Bartlett, D.L. and Steele, J.B. (1996) The New American Workforce. Kansas City. Andrews and McNeel

Bartlett, D.L. and Steele, J.B. (1992). America: What Went Wrong? Kansas City. Andrews and McNeel.

Danny, M., N.J. loses 7,000 AT&T jobs, 40,500 terminated nationally. (1996, January 5). The Philadelphia Inquirer.

Earle, L. (1996). The myth of the middle-class. Humanist. (56). Ppl.17.

Hoerr, J.P., (1988). And the Wolf Finally Came. Pittsburgh. University of Pittsburgh Press.

Hollreiser, E., Survivors of downsizing need training to adapt. The Philadelphia Business Journal (14), 27.

Jones. D. R., (1995). THE URBAN AGENDA: It's still the Economy, Stupid., New York Amsterdam News, pp. 1G.

Liaison, M. (Producer)., (1996, April 24). Morning Edition. Washington, D.C.: National Public Radio.

Lynch, D. J., (1996, September 20). RICH POOR WORLD: Widening income gap divides America. Dying dreams, dead-end streets., USA Today, ppl. 1B.

Potluck, D. (1996). Strategies for avoiding the rush towards downsizing., Vial Speeches (62), pp.752.

Smith, Adam. (1996). Backlash, Part I., J. Debatable, (Director). A.H. Permitted, (Producer). Adam Smith's Money World. WNET.

Strobes, F. (1995). Corporate surveys can't find a productivity revolution either. (Challenge) (38), pp. 31.

Thurow, L. C., (1996, September 20). Capitalism Drops Efficiency, Uses Fear. Newsday, pp. A29.

Williams, J. B., Corporate downsizing and privatizing have human faces. (1994, December 1). Call and Post (Columbus), pp. PG.

Workers First? Not When the Boss is Asked. (1995, February 15). The Washington Post, pp. 11.

Zarroli, J. (Producer). (1996, April 29). Morning Edition. Washington, D.C.: National Public Radio.

Zeff, J. And Lyons, P. (1996). The Downsizing of America. New York., Random House.

 "History". American Legislative Exchange Council. 2012. Retrieved April 21, 2012.

"Board of Directors". American Legislative Exchange Council.

"Charity Rating". Charity Navigator. Also see "Quickview data". GuideStar. "Total Revenue: $8,425,051; Total Expenses: $8,642,647 [FYE December 2012]"

May, Clifford (1987-08-30). "Transportation Chief Attacks Congress on Safety". The New York Times.

Goodman, Howard (March 23, 2013). "NRA's Behind-the-Scenes Campaign Encouraged 'Stand Your Ground' Adoption". Florida Center for Investigative Reporting.

Griffin, Marshall (January 14, 2014). "'Right-to-work' bill praised and blasted in House committee hearing". KBIA.

"About ALEC". American Legislative Exchange Council.

Greenblatt, Alan (December 2011). "ALEC Enjoys A New Wave of Influence and Criticism". Governing.

Pilkington, Ed (November 20, 2013). "Obamacare faces new threat at state level from corporate interest group Alec". The Guardian.

Hernandez, Sergio (December 1, 2013). "Sex, Lies and HIV: When What You Don't Tell Your Partner Is a Crime". ProPublica.

Greeley, Brendan (May 3, 2012). "ALEC's Secrets Revealed; Corporations Flee". Businessweek. Bloomberg. Retrieved June 2, 2012.

McIntire, Mike (April 21, 2012). "Conservative Nonprofit Acts as a Stealth Business Lobbyist". The New York Times. Retrieved May 15, 2012.

Kraft, Michael E.; Kamieniecki, Sheldon (2007). Business and environmental policy: corporate interests in the American political system. Cambridge, Mass.: MIT Press. p. 276. ISBN 978-0-262-61218-0. "American Legislative Exchange Council (ALEC) provide[s] direct assistance to state legislators and firms eager to minimize any state government engagement in environmental protection. ALEC's membership base includes nearly one-third of all sitting state legislators and most of its resources are derived from corporations and trade associations. It offers regular conferences and training sessions but is perhaps best known for drafting model bills that can easily be adopted by an individual state and introduced into a legislature."

Rizzo, Salvador (April 3, 2012). "Some of Christie's biggest bills match model legislation from D.C. group called ALEC". The Star Ledger.

Greenblatt, Alan (October 2003). "What Makes Alec Smart?". Governing.

Bishop, Bill (2009). The Big Sort: Why the Clustering of Like-Minded American Is Tearing Us Apart. Houghton Mifflin Harcourt. p. 203. ISBN 0547525192.

Rizzo, Salvador (April 1, 2012). "At Arizona gathering, ALEC teaches lawmakers how to turn conservative ideas into law". The Star Ledger.

Schoenwald, Jonathan M. (2002). A Time for Choosing: The Rise of Modern American Conservatism. Oxford University Press. p. 241. ISBN 0195157265.

Lichtman, Allan J. (2009). White Protestant Nation: The Rise of the American Conservative Movement. Grove Press. p. 318. ISBN 0802144209.

Charlie Cray (23 August 2011). The Lewis Powell Memo - Corporate Blueprint to Dominate Democracy. Greenpeace. Retrieved 1 January 2014.

Bill Moyers (2 November 2011). How Wall Street Occupied America. The Nation. Retrieved 1 January 2014.

Barnett, Louis W. [Gov. Jerry Brown's Destruction of the California Judiciary] (2010)

Williams, Juan (April 23, 2012). "Trayvon killing puts American Legislative Exchange Council in the spotlight". The Hill.

ALEC's "Institutional Corruption," From Backing Apartheid to Assault on Clean Energy, Public Sector. Democracy Now! December 11, 2013.

Shadee Ashtari (5 December 2013). Right Wing Group's Extreme Anti-Gay History Revealed in New Document the Huffington Post. Retrieved 13 December 2013

"Duane Parde, president". About NTU: Staff. National Taxpayers Union. 2009. Retrieved May 14, 2012.

Jacobs, Ben (May 4, 2012). "Former Chair Accuses ALEC of Anti-Democrat Bias". The Daily Beast.

Greeley, Brendan; Fitzgerald, Alison (December 1, 2011). "Pssst ... Wanna Buy a Law?". Bloomberg BusinessWeek.

"Meet Our Staff". American Legislative Exchange Council.

Shea, Christopher (28 March 2011). "William Cronon vs. Wisconsin Republicans". Wall Street Journal.

Grafton, Anthony (28 March 2011). "Wisconsin: The Cronon Affair". The New Yorker.

Buhle, Mari Jo; Buhle, Paul (2012). It Started in Wisconsin: Dispatches from the Front Lines of the New Labor Protest. Verso Books. p. 45. ISBN 1844678903.

Eaton, Sabrina (April 3, 2011). "Conservative group denies it masterminded drive to restrict public employee unions". The Plain Dealer.

Schmidt, Peter (25 March 2011). "Wisconsin GOP Seeks E-Mails of a Madison Professor Who Criticized the Governor". The Chronicle of Higher Education.

Krugman, Paul (March 27, 2011). "American Thought Police". The New York Times.

"AHA Today: AHA Deplores Effort to Intimidate William Cronon". American Historical Association. March 27, 2011. Retrieved 2011-08-07.

Bottari, Mary (May 21, 2012). "ALEC in Wisconsin: The Hijacking of a State". PR Watch. Center for Media and Democracy. Retrieved December 14, 2013.

Cole, Michelle (May 26, 2012). "ALEC gains foothold in Oregon, with one-fourth of legislators as members". The Oregonian.

Pilkington, Ed; Goldenberg, Suzanne (December 3, 2013). "ALEC facing funding crisis from donor exodus in wake of Trayvon Martin row". The Guardian.

"Meet Our Staff". American Legislative Exchange Council. 2012. Retrieved April 21, 2012.

"ALEC's 2009 IRS Form 990". Scribd.com. 2012-03-01. Retrieved 2012-08-15.

"Board of Scholars". American Legislative Exchange Council. 2012. Retrieved April 21, 2012.

"Task Forces". American Legislative Exchange Council.

"New Voter Identification Task Force Announced". National Center for Public Policy Research. April 18, 2012. Retrieved April 21, 2012.

Ryan J. Reilly, "Conservative Group with Abramoff Scandal Ties Picks Up Voter ID Issue Where ALEC Left Off" Talking Points Memo

Blumenthal, Paul (14 November 2013). Meet the Little-Known Network Pushing Ideas for Kochs, ALEC the Huffington Post. Retrieved 11 March 2014.

* Frank, John (May 6, 2013). "Private conservative group ALEC carries sway in legislature". The News & Observer.

"Who's Really Writing States' Legislation?". Fresh Air, WHYY. NPR. July 21, 2011. Retrieved April 7, 2012.

Jackman, Molly (December 6, 2013). "ALEC's Influence over Lawmaking in State Legislatures". Brookings Institution.

Fisher, Marc; Eggen, Dan (April 7, 2012). "'Stand Your Ground' laws coincide with jump in justifiable-homicide cases". The Washington Post. "This sharp turn in American law — expanding the right to defend one's home from attack into a more general right to meet force with force in any public place — began in Florida in 2005 and has spread to more than 30 other states as a result of a campaign by the National Rifle Association and a corporate-backed group called the American Legislative Exchange Council (ALEC), which promotes conservative bills."

Amy Goodman; Mike Elk (2012-04-18). "ALEC Drops Push for Voter ID, Stand Your Ground Laws After Public Outcry Sparks Corporate Exodus". Democracy Now! Retrieved 23 April 2012.

Ryan J. Reilly, "ALEC, NRA Pushed 'Stand Your Ground' Legislation at Center of Trayvon Martin Killing" TPMMuckraker

Bedard, Paul (April 4, 2012). "Coke caves in face of Democratic boycott threat". The Washington Examiner. Retrieved April 9, 2012.

McVeigh, Karen (April 6, 2012). "Coca-Cola and PepsiCo sever ties with group behind stand-your-ground laws". The Guardian. Retrieved April 9, 2012.

Kroll, Andy. "The Gates Foundation Is Done Funding ALEC". Mother Jones. Retrieved 10 April 2012.

Kroll, Andy (April 10, 2012). "McDonald's Says It Has Dumped ALEC". Mother Jones.

"Reed Elsevier, Wendy's drop conservative group" Reuters

Peter Overby, Companies Flee Group Behind 'Stand Your Ground' National Public Radio April 13, 2012

Jeremy Duda, "American Traffic Solutions leaving ALEC, joining APS" April 13, 2012 AZ Capitol Times

Julian Pecquet, "Blue Cross Blue Shield quits conservative legislative organization ALEC"

"Statement by ALEC on the Coordinated Intimidation Campaign Against Its Members". Retrieved 2013-08-15.

"Wal-Mart Leaves ALEC, 22nd Company to Exit Conservative Lobbying Group - International Business Times". lbtimes.com. 2012-05-31. Retrieved 2012-08-15.

Sullivan, Laura (October 28, 2010). "Prison Economics Help Drive Ariz. Immigration Law". NPR.

Archibold, Randal C. (April 23, 2010). "Arizona Enacts Stringent Law on Immigration". The New York Times.

Barnes, Robert (June 25, 2012). "Supreme Court upholds key part of Arizona law for now, strikes down other provisions". The Washington Post.

Will Potter, "'Ag Gag' Bills and Supporters Have Close Ties to ALEC", Green is the New Red, April 26, 2012.

Oppel Jr., Richard A. (April 6, 2013). "Taping of Farm Cruelty Is Becoming the Crime". The New York Times. Retrieved April 7, 2013.

Bill Moyers. Ag-Gag Laws Silence Whistleblowers. Moyers & Company, July 10, 2013.

Pat Beall (November 22, 2013). Big business, legislators pushed for stiff sentences. The Palm Beach Post. Retrieved May 21, 2014.

Cheung, Amy (September 2004) "Prison Privatization and the Use of Incarceration". The Sentencing Project.

Elk, Mike and Sloan, Bob (2011). The Hidden History of ALEC and Prison Labor. The Nation.

New Exposé Tracks ALEC-Private Prison Industry Effort to Replace Unionized Workers with Prison Labor. DemocracyNow! Retrieved 29 July 2013.

Verma, Sonia (December 13, 2013). "Republican legislative council pushes for Keystone approval". The Globe and Mail.

Goldenberg, Suzanne and Pilkington, Ed (4 December 2013). ALEC calls for penalties on 'freerider' homeowners in assault on clean energy. The Guardian. Retrieved 17 February 2014.

Kushnik, Bruce (24 July 2012). "ALEC, Tech and the Telecom Wars: Killing America's Telecom Utilities". Huffington Post. Retrieved 22 April 2014.

"Telecommunications & Information Technology Task Force Meeting ALEC States & Nation Policy Summit – Washington, DC". Common Cause. 2010. Retrieved 22 April 2014. [dead link]

Lefler, Dion (1 February 2014). "Proposed bill to outlaw community broadband service in Kansas met with opposition". Wichita Eagle. Retrieved 22 April 2014.

"ALEC's Health Care Freedom Initiative". American Legislative Exchange Council.

Weigel, David (December 17, 2013). "Obamacare Is Over (If You Want It)". Slate.

"How ALEC Serves as A 'Dating Service' For Politicians and Corporations". NPR. December 10, 2013.

Doward, Jamie (July 14, 2012). "US free market group tries to halt sales of cigarettes in plain packets in UK". The Guardian.

Milbank, Dana (December 4, 2013). "ALEC stands its ground". The Washington Post.

Seitz-Wald, Alex (February 2, 2012). "Oops: Florida Republican Forgets to Remove ALEC Mission Statement from Boilerplate Anti-Tax Bill". ThinkProgress. Retrieved April 7, 2012.

Goodman, Howard (April 18, 2012). "ALEC Under Fire in Florida". Florida Center for Investigative Reporting.

Rapoport, Abby (February 3, 2012). "In Case You Were Underestimating ALEC's Role". The American Prospect.

"Full Show: United States of ALEC". Moyers & Company.

http://azcommunitypress.org/2013/05/04/alec-are-corporations-and-legislators-working-against-citizens/

Kumar, Anita (December 27, 2011). "Ghostwriter at work for Virginia's assembly?". The Washington Post.

Graves, Lisa (July 15, 2011). ALEC Exposed: State Legislative Bills Drafted by Secretive Corporate-Lawmaker Coalition. Interview with Amy Goodman. Democracy Now! New York. Retrieved 23 April 2012.

Nichols, John (July 13, 2011). "ALEC Exposed".

"Wisconsin: Groups sue over lawmakers' emails, contact with conservative organization ALEC". Associated Press. October 2, 2012.

Groups sue 5 GOP lawmakers over email records, Milwaukee Journal Sentinel, Patrick Marley, Oct. 1, 2012.

"CMD and Common Cause Prevail in Open Records Lawsuit Against ALEC Legislators in Wisconsin" (Press release). Center for Media and Democracy. October 30, 2012.

Shaw, Hank (June 10, 2002). "ALEC's friends bill taxpayers: Biggest industries come to control lobbying council". The Free Lance-Star. p. A1.

VanEgeren, Jessica (August 10, 2013). "What Madison Rep. Chris Taylor learned at the ALEC conference". The Cap Times.

Friedman, Matt (July 11, 2013). "Alan Rosenthal, politically influential New Jersey academic, dies". The Star-Ledger.

Simpson, Ian (November 5, 2013). "Factbox: Candidates, money in Virginia governor's race". Reuters.

Vekshin, Alison (November 28, 2013). "San Jose Pension Crush Spurs Bid to Ease California Pacts". Bloomberg News.

Baker, Mike (April 23, 2012). "Advocacy group files IRS complaint against ALEC". Associated Press.

"Supplemental Submission IRS Whistleblower complaint on ALEC". July 29, 2013. [dead link]

Salant, Jonathan (April 23, 2012). "Republican Group Subject of IRS Complaint on Lobbying". BusinessWeek. Retrieved May 29, 2012.

"Corporate America's Trojan Horse in the States: The Untold Story Behind the American Legislative Exchange Council (Chapter Four)". ALECWatch.

Sullivan, Laura (October 29, 1010). "Shaping State Laws with Little Scrutiny". NPR.

Koch Industries Climate Denial Front Group American Legislative Exchange Council (ALEC). Greenpeace. Retrieved 14 June 2014.

Abowd, Paul. "Koch brothers pour more cash into think tanks, ALEC". January 31, 2013. The Center for Public Integrity. Retrieved November 21, 2013.

Fitzgerald, Alison (2011-07-21). "Koch, Exxon Mobil Among Corporations Helping Write State Laws". Bloomberg. Retrieved 2012-08-15.

Ed Pilkington and Suzanne Goldenberg (3 December 2013). ALEC facing funding crisis from donor exodus in wake of Trayvon Martin row. The Guardian. Retrieved 11 December 2013.

References

NAFTA Secretariat. Nafta-sec-alena.org (June 9, 2010). Retrieved on July 12, 2013.

Calculated using UNDP data for the member states. If considered as a single entity, NAFTA would rank 23rd among the other countries.

"Clinton Signs NAFTA—December 8, 1993". Miller Center. University of Virginia. Retrieved January 27, 2011.

"NAFTA Timeline". Fina-nafi. Retrieved July 4, 2011.

Signing NaFTA. History Central. Retrieved February 20, 2011

Gantz, DA (1999). "Dispute Settlement Under the NAFTA and the WTO: Choice of Forum Opportunities and Risks for the NAFTA Parties". American University International Law Review 14 (4): 1025–1106

GPO, P.L. 103-182, Section 334

"IngentaConnect NAFTA Commission for Environmental Cooperation: ongoing assessment". Ingentaconnect.com. December 1, 2006. doi:10.3152/147154606781765048. Retrieved July 4, 2011.

Analytic Framework for Assessing the Environmental Effects of the North American Free Trade Agreement. Commission for Environmental Cooperation (1999)

"Trade and Environment in the Americas". Cec.org. Retrieved November 9, 2008.

Lederman, D; Maloney, W; Servén, L (2005). Lessons from NAFTA for Latin America and the Caribbean. Palo Alto, CA, USA: Stanford University Press

Weintraub, S (2004). NAFTA's Impact on North America The First Decade. Washington, DC, USA: CSIS Press

Hufbauer, GC; Schott, JJ (2005). NAFTA Revisited. Washington, DC: Institute for International Economics

Sergie, Mohammed Aly (14 February 2014). "NAFTA's Economic Impact". Council on Foreign Relations think tank. Retrieved 5 August 2014.

"NAFTA – Fast Facts: North American Free Trade Agreement". NAFTANow.org. April 4, 2012. Retrieved October 26, 2013.

Hurtig, Mel (2003). The Vanishing Country: Is it too late to save Canada? (Trade paperback ed. with index ed.). Toronto: McClelland & Stewart. ISBN 978-0-7710-4217-1.

Greening the Americas, Carolyn L. Deere (editor). MIT Press, Cambridge, Massachusetts, USA

"Clark, Georgia Rae. 2006. Analysis of Mexican demand for Meat: A Post-NAFTA Demand Systems Approach. MS Thesis, Texas Tech University" (PDF). Retrieved July 4, 2011.

NAFTA, Corn, and Mexico's Agricultural Trade Liberalization PDF (152 KB) p. 4

U.S.-Mexico Corn Trade During the NAFTA Era: New Twists to an Old Story USDA Economic Research Service

2 Dec 2013"Contentious Nafta pact continues to generate a sparky debate" By James Politi

U.S. Trade Representative - NAFTA Statistics

Newswise: Free Trade Agreement Helped U.S. Farmers Retrieved on June 12, 2008.

"IngentaConnect NAFTA Commission for Environmental Cooperation: ongoing assessment of trade liberalization in North America". Ingentaconnect.com. Retrieved November 9, 2008.

Kenneth A. Reinert and David W. Roland-Holst The Industrial Pollution Impacts of NAFTA: Some Preliminary Results. Commission for Environmental Cooperation (November 2000)

DHS Yearbook 2006. Supplemental Table 1: Nonimmigrant Admissions (I-94 Only) by Class of Admission and Country of Citizenship: Fiscal Year 2006[dead link]

Facts and Figures 2006 Immigration Overview: Temporary Residents (Citizenship and Immigration Canada)

"Facts and Figures 2006 – Immigration Overview: Permanent and Temporary Residents". Cic.gc.ca. June 29, 2007. Archived from the original on August 22, 2008. Retrieved November 9, 2008.

Notice of Arbitration PDF (1.71 MB), 'Ethyl Corporation vs. Government of Canada'

"Agreement on Internal Trade" PDF (118 KB)

"Dispute Settlement". Dfait-maeci.gc.ca. October 15, 2010. Retrieved July 4, 2011.

"MMT: the controversy over this fuel additive continues". canadiandriver.com. Retrieved July 4, 2011.

Statement from USTR Spokesperson Neena Moorjani Regarding the NAFTA Extraordinary Challenge Committee decision in Softwood Lumber [dead link]

'Tembec, Inc vs. United States' PDF (193 KB)

Statement by USTR Spokesman Stephen Norton Regarding CIT Lumber Ruling [dead link]

"NAFTA – Chapter 11 – Investment; Cases Filed Against the Government of Canada; Gottlieb Investors Group v. Government of Canada"

Fiess, Norbert; Daniel Lederman (November 24, 2004). "Mexican Corn: The Effects of NAFTA" (PDF). Trade Note (The World Bank Group) 18. Retrieved March 12, 2007.

Purchase, Graham (1994). Anarchism and Environmental Survival. See Sharp Press. ISBN 0-9613289-8-3.

Subcomandante Marcos, Ziga Voa! 10 Years of the Zapatista Uprising. AK Press 2004

"NAFTA, Chapter 11". Sice.oas.org. Retrieved July 4, 2011.

www.international.gc.ca: "The North American Free Trade Agreement (NAFTA) - Chapter 11 - Investment"

"'North American Free Trade Agreement (NAFTA)', '''Public Citizen'''". Citizen.org. January 1, 1994. Retrieved July 4, 2011.

Red Mexicana de Accion Frente al Libre Comercio. "NAFTA and the Mexican Environment". Archived from the original on May 21, 2006.

"The Council of Canadians". Canadians.org. Retrieved July 4, 2011.

Commission for Environmental Cooperation. "The NAFTA environmental agreement: The Intersection of Trade and the Environment". Cec.org. Retrieved July 4, 2011.

PEJ News. "Judge Rebuffs Challenge to NAFTA'S Chapter 11 Investor Claims Process". Pej.org. Retrieved July 4, 2011.

Arbitration reward between Methanex Corporation and United States of America PDF (1.45 MB)

Arbitration reward between Metalclad Corporation and The United Mexican States PDF (120 KB)

"Eli Lilly and Company v. Government of Canada"

"Canada must learn from NAFTA legal battles " 24 Nov 2013 G+M

"Cases Filed Against the Government of Canada Lone Pine Resources Inc. v. Government of Canada"

"Quebec's St. Lawrence fracking ban challenged under NAFTA" 22 Nov 2013

World Trade Organization: WTO legal texts; General Agreement on Tariffs and Trade 1994

a) The GATT years: from Havana to Marrakesh, World Trade Organization

b) Timeline: World Trade Organization – A chronology of key events, BBC News

c)Brakman-Garretsen-Marrewijk-Witteloostuijn, Nations and Firms in the Global Economy, Chapter 10: Trade and Capital Restriction

Michael Hudson, Super Imperialism: The Origin and Fundamentals of U.S. World Dominance, 2nd ed. (London and Sterling, VA: Pluto Press, 2003), 258.

"The GATT Uruguay Round". ODI briefing paper. Overseas Development Institute. Retrieved 28 June 2011.

"Fiftieth Anniversary GATT". Wto.org. Retrieved 2013-08-16.

"Understanding the WTO - members". WTO. Retrieved 2013-08-16.

"Accession status: Syrian Arab Republic". WTO. Retrieved 2013-08-16.

"2010 News items - Working party established on Syria's membership request". WTO. Retrieved 2013-08-16.

Landon John. (1986). The Development of Social Welfare. New York. Human Sciences Press.

Pyle, Alan. (September 4, 2014). "America's Business Elites Admit They'd Rather Hire Robots Than People. Harvard Business Survey.

January, Nick. (September 11, 2014). "A Wealthy Capitalist on Why Money Doesn't Trickle Down." Yes! Magazine.